Artists on Creative Administration

A Workbook from the National Center for Choreography

Tonya Lockyer, Editor

Contributions by

Nora Alami, Julia Antonick, Christy Bolingbroke, Banning Bouldin, Yanira Castro, Maura Cuffie-Peterson, Katy Dammers, Raja Feather Kelly, Michelle Fletcher, Chelsea Goding-Doty, Miguel Gutierrez, Rosie Herrera, Cherie Hill, Delphine Lai, Tonya Lockyer, Makini, Aaron Mattocks, Jonathan Meyer, Rashaun Mitchell, Hope Mohr, Dominic Moore-Dunson, Cynthia Oliver, Karla Quintero, Antonio Ramos, Silas Riener, amara tabor-smith, Kate Wallich, Marýa Wethers, Pioneer Winter, Miranda Wright

The University of Akron Press
Akron, Ohio

The NCCAkron Series in Dance
   Christy Bolingbroke, Editor

Hope Mohr, *Shifting Cultural Power: Case Studies and Questions in Performance*
Tonya Lockyer, ed., *Artists on Creative Administration: A Workbook from the National Center for Choreography*

Copyright © 2024 by The University of Akron Press
All rights reserved • First Edition 2024 • Manufactured in the United States of America. All inquiries and permission requests should be addressed to the publisher, The University of Akron Press, Akron, Ohio 44325-1703.

ISBN: 978-1-62922-282-0 (paper)
ISBN: 978-1-62922-283-7 (ePDF)
ISBN: 978-1-62922-284-4 (ePub)

A catalog record for this title is available from the Library of Congress.

∞ The paper used in this publication meets the minimum requirements of ANSI/NISO z39.48–1992 (Permanence of Paper).

Cover design by Amy Freels.

Artists on Creative Administration was designed and typeset in Garamond Premier Pro by Amy Freels.

Produced in conjunction with the University of Akron Affordable Learning Initiative. More information is available at www.uakron.edu/affordablelearning/.

Contents

Director's Foreword
Christy Bolingbroke   v
Acknowledgments
Tonya Lockyer   viii
Introduction
Tonya Lockyer   x

Part I: Place

Building an Audience That Cares
Dominic Moore-Dunson   3
Causing a Scene: How I Helped Build the Contemporary Dance Ecosystem in My Hometown
Banning Bouldin   11
8 & 1: The End Becomes the Beginning When Every Body Dances
Pioneer Winter   23
Dance as a Radical Act: An Artist-Led, Community-Centered Approach to Choreographing a Creative Ecology
Tonya Lockyer   33

Part II: Leadership

The Artist Is the Expert: An Interview with Maura Cuffie-Peterson on the Process of Developing and Running a Think Tank for Creatives Rebuild New York
Yanira Castro with Maura Cuffie-Peterson   53
Embodying Equity-Driven Change: A Journey from Hierarchy to Shared Leadership
Cherie Hill, Hope Mohr, and Karla Quintero   70

Crafting Relationships and Modes of Support: Recognizing
the Work of Manager/Producers
*Katy Dammers with Nora Alami, Chelsea Goding-Doty,
Aaron Mattocks, Marýa Wethers, and Miranda Wright*   89

Part III: Capital

Beg, Borrow, Steal (Back): How US Dance Artists Fund Their Work—
Excerpts from the podcast "Are You For Sale?"
*Miguel Gutierrez with amara tabor-smith, Antonio Ramos,
Cynthia Oliver, Rosie Herrera, and Michelle Fletcher*   107

How I Built This: Dance Church®
Kate Wallich   123

The Practice of Questioning and Generating Revenue
Delphine Lai and Christy Bolingbroke   136

Part IV: Pathways

CHOREOGRAPHY, PERFORMANCE, AND THE ABSOLUTE
TRUTH ABOUT BEING AN ARTIST
Raja Feather Kelly   155

Sharing Resource Stories: How Did I End Up Here, and Where
Is Here Telling Me to Go from Here?
Makini   169

The Fruits of Dissatisfaction
Julia Antonick and Jonathan Meyer   181

Administrative Points of View from Creative Living
Rashaun Mitchell and Silas Riener   190

Appendix: NCCAkron's CAR Investigative Retreat Toolkit   201
Notes   205
Contributors   224
Index   233

Director's Foreword

Christy Bolingbroke, NCCAkron Executive/Artistic Director

Established in 2015, the National Center for Choreography-Akron (NCCAkron) was founded to support the research and development of new work in dance by strengthening the national dance ecosystem as an anchor development space for dance; exploring the full potential of the creative process in dance and all its forms; and serving as a catalyst for artistic, cultural, and community advancement and enrichment.

NCCAkron's origin story is wholly unique. The center, initially suggested by Northeast Ohio's premier dance presenter, DANCECleveland, was established through the creation of a special endowment by the Knight Foundation and operates as an auxiliary nonprofit organization in donated space on The University of Akron campus. Neither dance company, funder, nor presenter, NCCAkron may be perceived as any of these ecological players depending on the context and audience. Operating from what I often describe as the cracks in the dance ecosystem, we are more nimble than most conventional institutions. We can improvise as we constantly seek to improve. I recognize that we have a higher threshold for uncertainty, experimentation, and embracing failure than many other arts organizations.

In NCCAkron's work to strengthen the national dance ecosystem, conversations with artists and observations across the country raise questions concerning the creation of work, an audience for the art form, and longevity for the field's workforce. NCCAkron was originally conceived to help new dances get made, but are we complicit in a stressed system if we do not also explore strengthening the operational aspects of the system meant to support and advance creativity?

From 2018 to 2020, Jaamil Olawale Kosoko (Philadelphia), Raja Feather Kelly (Brooklyn, NY), and Brian Brooks (New York City) participated in early prototypes of this thinking as NCCAkron imagined what "an administrative residency" might look like. Learning from these early experiments—where we read aloud to each other from arts administration books; mapped out embodied field research from decades on stage, in the studio, and on tour; and continued dreaming forward—led to the Creative Administration Research (CAR) initiative, generously funded by a major three-year grant from the Mellon Foundation in 2020.

By focusing on how dance is getting made and supported, not just for a single work but for a body of work over time, CAR participants are interrogating the craft of administration the same way artists challenge, excavate, and develop the craft of choreography in the studio. The core premise behind CAR is to develop administrative practices that mirror or complement artistic practices. Since there is more than one way to choreograph a dance, there should be more than one approach to dance administration.

Over three years, nineteen Artist Teams have been identified and accumulated as a think tank to conduct this work. In addition to NCCAkron, Artist Teams include a Lead Artist (a choreographer or choreographic collective), as well as administrative contractors, dancers who double as administrators, board members, and/or longtime stakeholders invited into this experience by the Lead Artist. The Lead Artist also works with NCCAkron to select a Thought Partner whose experience may range from arts education to marketing to cultural and racial equity or fundraising to also join their Artist Team. The core work includes an annual Investigative Retreat with each Team where NCCAkron facilitates discussion looking back at the work and successes of the artist as well as dreamstorming for the future. Then the Lead Artist and Thought Partner meet a minimum of four times throughout the year to expand on the discoveries made in retreat and to experiment administratively. In 2022 and again in 2023, the entire think tank was invited to convene in Akron, Ohio, to connect, share working knowledge, and compare notes.

This book aims to document some of "the how" of the ways others have done things—recognizing artists who have chosen to build their own ecosystems outside twentieth-century definitions of success; choreographing resources behind the scenes and as a by-product of the performance itself; and advocating for themselves as well as for the communities within which they serve or operate.

Director's Foreword

I am enormously grateful to Emily Waters, Emil Kang, and the Mellon Foundation for committing funds and their support for us to do this work. My deepest thanks goes to the CAR Artists and Thought Partners for their trust and for embarking on this journey with us. I often refer to NCCAkron as "the twentieth team" in the CAR think tank since we are learning right alongside the artists, and for that reason, I offer additional gratitude to the NCCAkron team and board members—past and present—for their patience, perseverance, and positive affirmations.

Artists on Creative Administration is the product of extensive, multiyear efforts, and I share in the immense gratitude expressed in the acknowledgments on the following pages to the many people who contributed time and talent to the project. I would like to extend my most heartfelt thanks to Tonya Lockyer, who in addition to being a Thought Partner in the CAR program has also been an instrumental thought partner and creative NCCAkron collaborator as the editor of this book. We hope the experiments documented and shared here create a broader and stronger foundation for the future of dance.

Acknowledgments
Tonya Lockyer

This book began when Executive/Artistic Director Christy Bolingbroke of NCCAkron invited me to develop and edit a book on creative administrative research. I am honored by her initial invitation and eternally grateful for her commitment throughout the process. Thank you to the entire NCCAkron team whose enthusiasm helped get this book to the finish line. Working with Megan Wright as we pulled together the first manuscript was a joy and privilege. It is not an overstatement to say this book would have been impossible without her support and dedication to the project and the contributors. I am thankful beyond measure.

A big thank-you to everyone at The University of Akron Press who brought their care and expertise to this project: Jon Miller, Amy Freels, Nancy Basmajian, Thea Ledendecker, Brittany LaPointe, Emily Price, and Rhye Pirie. Thank you, Jon, for recognizing the need for more US publications around dance, and for being patient with my many questions.

Deep and immeasurable thanks are due to all the contributors who examined and distilled their experiences for this book and who gave their goodwill and encouragement to the venture. Thank you to my NCCAkron Creative Administration Research cohort: Silas Riener, Rashaun Mitchell, and Katy Dammers, for their thought partnership throughout.

Preparing *Artists on Creative Administration* entailed many conversations with artists and administrators around the country, including those who do not have essays or interviews within these pages. Warm thanks to Sydney Skybetter, Melanie Noel, and Mariclare Hulbert, who were irreplaceable readers

Acknowledgments ix

and sounding boards; to Mia Keinenen, Beverly Naidus, April Sellars, and Naomi M. Jackson; to Rosie Herrera and Rosy Simas. For providing space, quiet, and counsel, I thank Byron Au Yong, Kara Gilmore, and Centrum Artist Residencies in Port Townsend, Washington. And gratitude always to my mentor Herbert Blau and the inestimable BC Campbell, who makes everything more possible.

During multiple residencies at Centrum, I participated in the Curator & Arts Worker Residency Think Tank and facilitated a conversation with Centrum's Emerging Artist Residents around some of the questions proposed in this book. These arts workers provided a critical touchstone for my thinking as I began to shape the book's structure and write the introduction. They also affirmed these essays' relevance and cross-disciplinary applications. In this capacity, I gratefully acknowledge Centrum's Michelle Hagewood, as well as David Strand, Berette Macaulay, Hexe Fey, Josephine Lee, Spencer Garland, Allie Hankins, Ari L Mokdad, Christi Krug, and maximiliano.

Informing *Artists on Creative Administration* are those who came before. I want to recognize the fine work in the performance field that has opened pathways for our research. Readers who wish to go further might consult the endnotes which, in many cases, offer a guide to additional material.

Introduction
Tonya Lockyer

Thank you for opening this book. You may be an artist, or an administrator, or some hybrid of both, or studying to be, or you may be interested in how artists carve out lives for themselves. Maybe you're a professional who has already absorbed lots of approaches and information meant to serve you throughout your life and career; yet here you are, choosing to spend your time questioning "best practices" in arts administration, to imagine new futures. If you're longing for different ways of being and working, this book is for you. This book is for anyone looking for paths forward; for anyone who believes we are in an exceptional moment of change—change is happening and needs to happen.

Creative administration is not new. Collectively and independently, artists have long created administrative structures and organizations to benefit themselves and inject creativity into their communities. As artists deal with logistical, financial, and interpersonal challenges in their daily lives, they discover new approaches that work for them. To carve out a life in the arts (especially if you cannot rely on the economic support of family) requires a willingness to ask questions and find new ways; but this labor and expertise has often been undervalued or unacknowledged.

Conversely, inside the offices of institutions, arts workers often have arts backgrounds. Many try, with varying success, to maintain their artistic practices and ways of being within systems that often favor the expectations of donors, funders, and governmental agencies—rather than those of the artists on whose work they rely. Artists are often administrators; administrators are

Introduction

often artists. An important purpose of *Artists on Creative Administration* is to reconsider and reconceive our delineations, language, and practices.

Creative administration research—you might be doing it, but not have had a name for it.

Artists on Creative Administration provides firsthand accounts of creative administration research in action and offers ways to apply it to your own thinking, work, and life. It's a collection of stories, prompts, and provocations; a workbook of case studies, essays, and interviews; a sharing of helpful tools, resources, and survival strategies; a banquet of questions, revelations, and calls to action.

Each chapter is a case study offering a glimpse into the creative administrative mind at work: how artist-administrators think and bring ingenuity to the tasks that get art out into the world, get things done. So this is a book about problem-solving, but in ways that prioritize responding to the conditions and desires of the art and the artists. It's about administrative practices reflecting artistic processes.

The authors were invited to describe specific real-world examples of how they have experimented in their approaches to business and administration, and to share the larger questions and lines of thinking that informed their experiments. What troubled them about the accepted view? What sparked them to question it? What have they learned from their experiments?

These essays and interviews take on big topics: agency, adversity, identity, equity, reparations, family, ethics, care, community, collaboration, transparency, trust. Our stories provide a view of some of the challenges facing the arts and culture sector.

At the end of each chapter are administrative experiments for you to try, adapt to your own situation, add to, toss. Play with them. Devise your own experiments. Come up with workshops and retreats around the material. Share. In the appendix, you'll find NCCAkron's Creative Administration Research Toolkit with three more administrative prompts developed by the NCCAkron team with the Artists and Thought Partners of the Creative Administration Research (CAR) program.

This is not a book to discount the work that has happened up until now. There have been people developing strategies toward more equitable and responsive arts administration for generations. *Artists on Creative Administration* hopes to build on that work—even when we bring it into question—to assess what we have learned so far, to ask where we go from here. For people working in the arts, we hope this workbook furthers connections and conversations. For everyone, we hope it provides tools for your own dream-building and risk-taking.

WHO'S THE ARTIST NOW?

There is an obstacle *Artists on Creative Administration* has to negotiate: the impossibility of generalizing about what an artist is and when, if ever, what we are doing should be defined as *art* or *administration*. The hybridity of the artist/administrator/curator/producer is ubiquitous in the fields of contemporary and experimental performance. Today it's also not surprising to hear artists referred to as "creative entrepreneurs" or "cultural producers"[1]—models some people worry herald the end of the artist entirely. How did we get here?

Artists have always been creative about how they carved out their artistic, social, and financial lives—even as our image of the artist changed radically throughout history. Bach considered himself an artisan, not an artist but a master craftsman. The age of the artisan was the age of the patron, with artists living almost as feudal dependents of the wealthy.[2] In the late eighteenth and early nineteenth centuries, Western values elevated individualism. Romanticism arrived and the image of the "hero artist," the suffering solitary genius, entered the Western imagination. The image of the "solo genius" is such a powerful cultural force that only recently have we begun to talk about the social and economic realities, the networks of intersecting creative relationships buried behind this myth. Artists rarely make it happen alone.

Throughout the last century, the United States built an arts infrastructure to harbor these geniuses: symphonies, opera houses, ballet companies. Master of Fine Arts (MFA) programs sprang up to produce "professionals." Artists competed for secure tenured professorships. In the heat of the Cold War, the National Endowment for the Arts was founded. What better way to spread the word about the United States as a pillar of free expression than to fund radical individualism? A network of state agencies soon followed, and there was a greater incentive to build up administration around fundraising, grant writing, and the financial management and reporting they require.

While the United States was investing in this formal infrastructure, another, independent system also emerged. Artists were creating their own organizations and collectives, often focused on sharing resources, mutual

Introduction

advancement, and community. They were debunking the idea of the artist as solitary and separate from society. A more collective idea of the artist began to take root: the artist as a "cultural producer" mobilizing and altering the direction of organizations and communities.

One might argue this shift started in the early twentieth century, around the time Duchamp fixed a bicycle wheel to a stool to illuminate how the context of an object, its institutional frame, determined if it was art, or not. Duchamp famously said in 1957, "The creative act is not performed by the artist alone."[3] Five years earlier, in 1952, choreographer Merce Cunningham tried taking self-expression out of the equation altogether, rolling dice or tossing coins to determine a dance's content and structure. Artists began increasingly acknowledging and inviting the audience into their creative processes. And increasingly, they wanted to create real social change. By the 1990s, Rick Lowe's social sculpture *Project Row Houses* transformed a long-neglected Houston neighborhood into a visionary public art project and community platform. Lowe's work is seen as poetic yet also practical. *Project Row Houses* is both sculpture and a not-for-profit organization.

Seeing social contexts and not-for-profit organizations like *Project Row Houses* as forms of art can still be challenging for people working both in and outside the arts. Lowe, and other artists like him, blur our distinctions between artist, administrator, activist, and entrepreneur. For some, the entrepreneurial artist-administrator signals the triumph of market-driven values, or a trick to get artists to fix failed social policies. But the entrepreneurial artist-administrator is partially the manifestation of a decades-long movement by artists to integrate the arts more meaningfully into the fabric of life.

Many of the contributors to *Artists on Creative Administration* are cultural producers and creative entrepreneurs. Just as artists in the last century questioned the hierarchy of art above life, many of the voices in this book want to dismantle systems that create a top-down dynamic between organizations and the artists they were created to serve. Many want to dismantle hierarchies that can make the arts seem inaccessible and elitist. Others are seeking alternatives to the values driving the "American capitalist economic model." All the arts workers in this book labor in ways that prioritize solidarity and disrupt paradigms. They inspire us to imagine new futures and build things in new ways, creating a public good in which we all have a stake.

WHO ARE THE CONTRIBUTORS?

One purpose of this workbook is to share some of the learnings of the Creative Administration Research program (CAR) of the National Center for Choreography-Akron (NCCAkron). First prototyped in 2018, CAR is a think tank pairing choreographers with thought leaders in the dance field to "break arts administration out of boxes" that perhaps never fit many artists in the first place.[4] Many of the contributors, but not all, have participated in programs offered by NCCAkron.

When inviting contributors, I also looked beyond the CAR program into the wider field of contemporary and experimental dance to reflect differing approaches to creative administration happening across the United States. Thirty arts workers agreed to share their stories. The authors work in rural and urban communities, within larger institutions, and as independent cultural producers. They are founders of not-for-profits, leaders of multimillion-dollar businesses, and collectives carving paths beyond nonprofit and corporate models. They collaborate with small accessible venues, curated spaces, and Alaska Airlines and Nike. They are new parents and elders. They are immigrants and second-generation activists.

I invited arts workers I knew to be generous and fearless in revealing the nitty-gritty realities of their lives in the arts. People working as artists and administrators are placed in a difficult position when writing on the record about their experiences in the field. I am deeply grateful to the contributors for their candor.

The contributors all work in the field of contemporary or experimental dance. The notion of what is considered contemporary dance is contested and ever-changing. Our work includes staged performances, installations, dance for digital platforms, podcasts, community forums, somatic and social practice. If there is a unifying characteristic of contemporary artists, it might be the dynamic ways we invent our own unique methods and methodologies for research and creation. Our practices challenge traditional boundaries and defy uniform organizing principles. Creative administration extends this way of thinking into all aspects of the long arc of sustaining a life in the arts. Just as there is not a one-size-fits-all approach to contemporary art making, there is not a one-size-fits-all approach to creative administration. You'll see this ethos reflected in the many different ways contributors tell their stories. The chapters are eclectic in their form and approach.

Introduction

WHAT DOES DANCE BRING TO A CONVERSATION ABOUT CREATIVE ADMINISTRATION?

Well, to start, dance artists have an embodied understanding of dynamic systems. The human body is a magnificent example of a dynamic system. Dances are dynamic systems, happening in the exchange between people, ideas, and perceptions, each new creative process and context generating new results. I think you'll find more than a few artists in this book have exceptional systems thinking skills. Many of the contributors bring to creative administration a propensity for investigating underlying ideas and relationships, versus patching up problems without questioning the systems that gave rise to them.

In recent years, in part due to the work of adrienne maree brown,[5] the term *emergent strategies* has become popular in arts and social nonprofit circles. Dancers understand emergence in their bones—how simple actions can activate complex patterns of interconnection. How a small change in a system creates a chain of events with a larger impact down the line. In dance, creative research is often emergent: discovering the way on the way, navigating by trial and error, assessing and adjusting as you go. Creative research is both the practice and the means to develop the process.

Creative administration can be approached in a way similar to choreographing a dance or developing an improvisational movement score: by looking beyond the individual elements to the flows of relationships between them. For example, if a creative arts worker aims to foster a city's dance ecology, they might begin by first noting the elements present (artists, presenters, funding sources, rehearsal spaces, training opportunities, commissioning programs, and so on) and then imagining how dance artists, at different stages in their lives, might *move through* a complex choreography of these elements. Are there ways to optimize nodes of interconnection? What paths will foster artists' career longevity? A linear path toward a single idea of success? Or (as in my essay, "Dance as a Radical Act") a path of intersecting spirals—an iterative system, where artists cycle back, redirect or reinvigorate, building momentum? Dance artists often respond to systems—including communities and cultures—as lived, unfolding experiences, continuously changing, multiple, and malleable.

Many contemporary dancers have developed knowledge and skills from negotiating social and economic precarity influenced, in part, by dance's marginalized status and labor practices. Many dance artists are freelancers, working wherever work takes them, often for low wages and little or no benefits. Today's "freelance revolution" with its gig economy and workers' willingness to give up material security for more immaterial benefits (flexible schedules, the opportunity to travel, working in less hierarchical structures) has been the norm of contemporary dance for decades. The lives of dancers tell us about our society.

COVID-19 AS CONTEXT

Artists on Creative Administration was conceived and written during the time a global pandemic changed the world and so, unexpectedly, this book is also a social document. A decade from now, students of history may find this book offers glimpses into what this tumultuous time was like for some of the arts workers who lived it, through the rare lens of administration. When we began writing this book, we were deep into lockdowns, social distancing, mass testing, and mask wearing. Nearly every theater, school, and arts institution across the United States remained closed. COVID-19 deeply affected the performance field. Tours were canceled, contracts were rescinded without payment; artists, when they could, moved their work outdoors, onto digital platforms, into publications. Every contributor to *Artists on Creative Administration* was affected.

Perhaps no period in the history of the United States has been without tumult, but 2020 to 2022—years of reckoning that arguably began with the 2016 US presidential election of Donald Trump—felt exceptional. The year 2020 saw massive protests following the murder of George Floyd by police officers in Minneapolis's broad daylight. Black Lives Matter activists galvanized more than four thousand protests around the country. The president responded by deploying National Guard troops as the death toll from COVID-19 kept rising. At the start of 2021, the president, freshly impeached (for the second time), refused a peaceful transition of power after he lost the 2020 election, leading to the January 6 US Capitol attack. Meanwhile, the West Coast seemed to be on fire. Many of us had friends and family evacuated from their homes. Red urban skies choked with wildfire smoke—unignorable signs of rapid climate change. We wore masks to protect our lungs from a deadly virus, from tear gas, from smoke.

"The pandemic put a laser focus on the precarity always present in our field," writes Yanira Castro in her essay. It revealed what most arts workers already knew: the field of contemporary dance is a stressed system, rife with inequities and imbalances of power, where even the most "successful" artists struggle to sustain careers of any longevity.

Introduction xvii

Two contributors, Castro and Makini, were founding members of Creating New Futures, a group of artists and arts workers who came together at the start of the pandemic to draft a call to action, shared widely on social media, addressing guaranteed income, mutual aid, and reparations. Castro went on to help codesign a Guaranteed Income program for New York State artists as part of the Creatives Rebuild New York (CRNY) Think Tank. She writes about both in this book.

FROM PLACE TO PATHWAYS

Part I: Place begins this workbook with ecology builders. These arts workers meet administrative challenges with programmatic solutions, successfully mobilizing organizations and communities to transform the field regionally and nationally. Akron-based Dominic Moore-Dunson guides the reader through his seven-year odyssey experimenting with ways to engage audiences "to cocreate the product" of his performances. Moore-Dunson uses Human-Centered Design Thinking, an approach to solving creative problems that starts with the audience and understanding their needs.

Banning Bouldin grew up in Nashville when "southernness was defined by a lack of opportunity." After a dance career in New York City and Europe, Bouldin returned home with the question: "What if it were possible to bring the same opportunities… to Nashville?" Would artists, if given a choice, stay in the South to realize their dreams? It turns out, they would.

Completing Part I are Pioneer Winter's transformative work in Miami; and my own reflections on creating a thriving Seattle dance ecology.

Part II: Leadership brings together twelve arts leaders invested in ways power can be distributed and shared. Yanira Castro cites the Creatives Rebuild New York (CRNY) Think Tank to codesign a Guaranteed Income program as a "significant shift" toward administrative processes of "transformation/liberation." "What was so radical about [CRNY] was that it centered the expertise of the artist: that artists collectively know best what systems will work for them." Castro interviews CRNY's Maura Cuffie-Peterson about developing and running the think tank.

San Francisco's Bridge Live Arts codirectors Cherie Hill, Hope Mohr, and Karla Quintero share their methods and unpack their thinking behind transitioning from a single choreographer-led hierarchy to a multiracial codirectorship.

Katy Dammers, a veteran manager and producer in a field "where the work of a manager/producer is often invisible," provides a brief history of the manager/producer within American independent dance. Dammers draws on the insights of five members of the "newest generation of dance managers and producers" and provides examples of programs around the globe recognizing this important role.

How artists finance their practices is a theme running throughout *Artists on Creative Administration*, but it's a driving focus of Part III: Capital. Miguel Gutierrez's podcast *Are You For Sale?* "looks at the ethical entanglements between money and art making." In the excerpts included here (from the episode "Beg, Borrow, Steal (Back): How US Dance Artists Fund Their Work") Gutierrez, alongside artists Cynthia Oliver, Rosie Herrera, Antonio Ramos, amara tabor-smith, and manager Michelle Fletcher, attempts to demystify the often absurd process of creating a grant application budget, and the impact of charitable foundations on artists seeking their support.

Kate Wallich's "How I Built This: Dance Church®" tells the story of how she transformed a donation-based Sunday-morning dance class in Seattle into a global business that raised a $4.7 million seed round of funding. During the pandemic, Wallich launched the Dance Church® digital platform "with upwards of 10,000 people dancing together online."

Delphine Lai, in an essay coauthored with NCCAkron's Executive/Artistic Director Christy Bolingbroke, advocates for extending the practice of asking questions to the business of fundraising. Lai and Bolingbroke interrogate annual fundraisers, crowdfunding, business structures, and programs like JPMorgan Chase's Community Giving campaign.

Artists seeking alternatives to the "American capitalist economic model" often resist traditional administrative solutions. The essays in Part IV: Pathways vibrate with the tensions between personal integrity and the systems artists often find themselves in: between artistic processes that need time and openness, and administrative practices that prioritize efficiency and hard deadlines; between internal artistic processes that require a dissolution of "self," and administrative processes that require an external branding of "self." Raja Feather Kelly has carried out just about every function of administration there is as the manager of the companies of Kyle Abraham, zoe|juniper, and his own award-winning dance-theatre-media company, the feath3r theory. In "CHOREOGRAPHY, PERFORMANCE, AND THE ABSOLUTE TRUTH

Introduction

ABOUT BEING AN ARTIST," Kelly shifts between stories, lists, letters, and provocations, at one point sharing the evolution of his artist statements—to illustrate how he negotiates administrative pressures.

Philadelphia's Makini was curious about how other artists were making economic decisions and receiving financial support but found artists reluctant to share their "personal resource stories." In response, Makini began to share an economic profile on Makini's website. Makini offers readers prompts for writing their own fiscal biography. Chicago company codirectors Julia Antonick and Jonathan Meyer share their case studies implementing an equal pay policy, experimenting with alternative ticketing structures, and investing in degrowth.

Closing the book, Rashaun Mitchell and Silas Riener's lyric meditations reflect on their choice to move from New York City to a rural home base and their efforts to merge their process-orientated artistic practice Desire Lines with their work, life, and labor. A minor theme in this book is artists leaving academia. As recently as a decade ago, if a dance artist wanted an off-ramp from their freelance career or from trying to sustain a dance company, they often looked to teaching in higher education. Rashaun Mitchell left his professorship in 2021: "A linear career as a dance artist with institutional academic support is ostensibly the dream," but for Mitchell quitting his academic job "was the best decision I could make as an artist."

∽

An effort was made to include contrary views. For example, Kelly and Dammers question whether expanding the administrative capacity of artists is always a good thing. During the pandemic, Kelly was invited to join a group of artists brought together to "imagine a radical future." Frustrated by the limits of their imaginations, Kelly asks, "In a world where the artist is the producer, the HR department, the marketing director, and the lead fundraiser—is dreaming impossible?"

Dammers shares the story of Twyla Tharp sending the National Endowment for the Arts a two-sentence grant application: "I write dances, not applications. Send money. Love, Twyla."[6] Tharp's retort, successful in 1969, "feels impossible in today's world where artists are increasingly expected to do it all—make dances, garner funding, and independently produce their work," writes Dammers. She argues the recent flourishing of programs that "have armed artists with professional development opportunities and classes in accounting, grant writing, marketing, and new work development" is "short-sighted" because they "place emphasis primarily on the artist." Dammers asks: "How might the ecosystem move differently if it saw support structures as teams of intersecting relationships, rather than artists forging through a competitive landscape alone?"

～

Artists on Creative Administration, like all books, is incomplete. Arts workers are everywhere, finding new ways to carve out creative lives. New strategies are emerging all the time. There is much more to creative administration research than is presented here—more for you to discover if you are interested. And one of the purposes of this book is to inspire you to be interested. Another purpose, perhaps the main one, is to provide the tools to understand and deepen your own creative administration practices. We wrote this workbook so that you, the reader, might continue writing it in the world. We hope you will excavate it for ideas, arguments, and methods to adapt to your own situation. Create your own administrative experiments. Write your own book.

PART I
PLACE

Building an Audience That Cares
Dominic Moore-Dunson

My entire dance life, I have lived in northeast Ohio, outside of a few short stints performing for choreographers like Helanius Wilkins in Washington, DC, or attending summer intensives as a young dancer with the likes of Garth Fagan. I love Akron—my small midwestern city that punches above its weight class in lots of ways. For those who don't know, Akron is forty-five minutes south of Cleveland and has a population of around 190,000.[1] We love many things: calling ourselves the Rubber City, as we were once the rubber capital of the world; LeBron James, who still reps the city around the globe; and like most northeast Ohioans, we love those Cleveland Browns. Oh, those lovable losers by the lake who have us all in our highest hopes every year, only to prove once again glory may not be in the cards for people like us.

As strange as it may seem, the Browns are where I want to begin. Sundays in Northeast Ohio are really for two things: church and football. Even so, as a dancer I know something else happens on Sundays as well. The early afternoon Sunday Matinee! Years ago, I was performing as a part of a presenting series at a small performing arts center. We spent weeks rehearsing a concert that was physically demanding. I don't know how other dancers process their audience expectations, but when I am rehearsing I tend to envision what the performance space will look, sound, smell, and feel like. One part of that vision is the number of people in the audience and naturally, the audience is always sold out! However, I quickly learned that visions are different from reality.

When we performed that Sunday afternoon, it seemed like 25 percent of the seats were full. To make it worse, the audience was sprinkled throughout the theater, which really made it feel like 10 percent. I remember talking to a fellow male dancer after the show, "Bro, why do you think folks didn't show up today? I mean the tickets were reasonable, it wasn't a late show, church was over." Then, with the most nonchalant look on his face he said, "Browns are on." I responded, "What do you mean?" "The Browns are playing the Steelers today, man. I mean, I had the game on my phone backstage so I could know the score. I'd rather be watching the game than be at this performance, too!"

This was the moment I remember my curiosity on the relationship between dance and dance audiences awakened. I was so naive. Of course, people in Northeast Ohio are not showing up to a dance performance on a Sunday in September while the Browns are playing. The question was *why*. I spent weeks thinking about *why* while watching SportsCenter. The only conclusion I could come up with was *because no one really cares that much about dance*. Don't get me wrong; I think people enjoy dance when they see it, but Dance—its artists, companies, history, culture—does not hold enough meaning to most people for them to sacrifice their time and money for such an experience.

As I started my own career as a choreographer, I kept this concept in mind. I was determined to find the answer to the question, *How do I get people to care about what I do?* I wasn't interested in creating work no one cared about. I wanted people to be engaged in the process and the product. So, I've been on a six-year journey experimenting with artistic process, marketing, and community engagement in hopes of one day finding an answer.

CREATE SOMETHING THEY CARE ABOUT

I grew up in a working-class Black neighborhood on the Eastside of Akron in the '90s. The '90s were a time when Black gang violence was on the rise, and my neighborhood wasn't any different. My mom had recently retired from the air force when we all came to live with my grandma. Being raised by a woman who had traveled across the entire world from seventeen to twenty-seven years old meant you were raised with a global sense of yourself. My sister and I learned we could be and go wherever we wanted because the world was only a plane ride away. Outside of my house, the neighborhood taught you differently. You didn't leave the Eastside because there is nothing out there for you.

In sixth grade, I was sitting at a lunch table with the six other Black boys in my grade. We were talking about what we wanted to be when we grew up. Everyone there wanted to play in the National Basketball Association (NBA), or the National Football League (NFL). When it was my turn to speak I said, "I want to dance in Paris or play professional soccer in England." The table went dead silent. One boy chirped, "Bruh, that ain't Black!" The table erupted with laughter while I looked confused by this notion that my skin color had something to do with what my passions were allowed to be.

Fast forward: I am touring with a professional company in 2015, the year after Tamir Rice was killed in Cleveland and the country was met with a barrage of news about the murders of unarmed Black men and women. At home, a similar narrative was happening in Akron regarding boys I went to school with dying or ending up in prison. I felt compelled to create something to pour something back into the community—a work that would potentially help us amid the harm we were dealing with daily while challenging the way we saw ourselves as Black people.

I created *The Black Card Project*,[2] a live-action dance theater cartoon about Artie Alvin Beatty III. Artie's mother is concerned about his lack of understanding of his cultural identity, so she sends him to Booker T. Malcolm Luther Park's Academy of Absolute Blackness. In a single school day, Artie must pass various classes to earn his *black card*.[3]

As this would be my first foray into creating works that address social issues, I saw this as my opportunity to create something people would care about. However, I knew I couldn't expect an audience to materialize out of nowhere. So, I tried a creative process based on Human-Centered Design Thinking, HCDT.

Design thinking is a "process for creative problem solving that starts with people and their needs."[4] To me, this sounded like an interesting way to build an audience by centering their thoughts, needs, and feelings from the very onset of the design process, giving them choreographic input on the work. In this way, I would be able to understand my end user, or rather, my audience member, better. I would also be able to examine my own assumptions. Through this process, I could define the obstacles of my end user, then design and redesign as necessary the product for the user.

I partnered with Miller South School for the Visual and Performing Arts, Akron School for the Arts, and the Goodyear Black Network of Goodyear Tire & Rubber Company. One important note to make here is that each group of community partners consisted entirely of Black participants, as my intended dance work was specifically intended for Black audiences. In each of these partnerships, I led the participating individuals, who ranged from dance students to account managers, in movement exercises to explore the concepts of identity. The results of these workshops were conversations that informed the work I was doing in the studio. Once I created in-studio, I brought my work in progress to each group and gave them an opportunity to make corrections, talk about the alignment of our conversation with the movement they saw, and anything else that drew their attention. This process took nine months, and the result was an incredible amount of engagement but also an overwhelming number of opinions. After collecting all our conversations with community partnerships, I went into the studio and created a ninety-minute narrative-based dance theater work that was sculpted by those exchanges.

As the premiere of the work approached, we gained a lot of media attention, with ticket sales skyrocketing. Full transparency—the tickets were free to attendees, thanks to foundational support from the Knight Foundation to remove any barriers to entry. We only expected to sell one-third of the theater. However, due to overwhelming demand, well over four hundred people attended! It felt great! After the performance, when I walked over to the spaces where we had set aside tickets for the various groups I worked with, I noticed a majority of them didn't come to the performance. When I looked out at the audience, the majority of the attendees were white. The people who engaged most deeply and whom I wanted most to impact didn't follow all the way through the performance. Somewhere along the process, I lost them. My experiment of using a human-centered design process didn't show the response I was hoping for because the people who helped design it didn't become end users. *The Black Card Project* was a success on so many levels. However, I now had a different question to answer: *How do I get the people I am creating the work for to care about what I do?*

BUILDING A BLACK AUDIENCE OF STORYTELLERS

In the summer of 2020, the world was on COVID-19 lockdown and all eyes were on the brutal murder of George Floyd. That summer my wife and I were pregnant with our son. For the first time in my life I realized, *I am going to have to teach my Black son about the police... and I have no idea what to tell him.* As an artist, I process my world through my art. I needed to have hard conversations, with myself, my family, and everyone around me. So, I started the process of interviewing Black students, teachers, community leaders, Black police officers, elected officials, and anyone who could help me make sense of my questions: *How is it that safety for some guarantees danger for others? What is it like to participate in society as a Black person on the other side of the blue line? And ultimately, how do I tell my son about the police?*

In creating a dance piece that delved into these questions, I wanted to put my community members in the position of becoming storytellers. I also wanted to put my potential audience in the middle of the creative research/process of the work. However, I questioned if there was a way to give them access to that process—an inside look—without handing them the power to overwhelm with their opinions regarding the work. Whatever I did, I knew I couldn't center myself as a creator; I had to find a way to center the people I was connecting with in the parade of interviews. I landed on the idea of creating a podcast. *InCOPnegro: Black and Blue*[5] features interviews conducted during my creative research and is the companion piece to *inCOPnegro: Aftermath*, a dance theater piece exploring the impact of police violence in Black communities. As of this writing, I have launched the first season of the podcast and it is available on all major platforms. Over two seasons (Spring 2022, and Spring 2023), the podcast will put more than fifty community members in the position of becoming the storytellers. Unlike *The Black Card Project*, instead of stopping at creating a piece I think Black audiences will respond to, I am putting potential audience members in the middle of the creative research and centering them in the live performance, creating both early and late buy-in, with the hope that podcast participants and listeners will eventually become ticket buyers.

At its core, the podcast is about creating an entry point into the work before a person engages with it on stage. The method isn't new. If you are a sports fan, you know this kind of outreach well. Sports leagues like the National Basketball Association have created multiple access points into their product, which are the games. We have access to online content about players, television talk shows about the league, and hourlong pregame shows about the behind-the-scenes drama of the game you are about to watch. I am simply creating my own content ecosystem for the project.

inCOPnegro, and its content ecosystem, is targeted toward Black audiences. Both the podcast and the stage work look at our relationship to police from different angles. My hope is that, by meeting my target audience in a place that is familiar, podcasts, I will encourage them to meet me in a place that they may find unfamiliar, the theater. By hearing voices on the podcast who may be their student, their teacher, their pastor, their parents, they will be willing to engage in a relationship with the project past the audio experience.

Though this idea has potential in theory, there are obstacles. Each adjacent piece of content created for *inCOPnegro* requires additional funding, more collaborators to coordinate, and more administrative work that often replaces the artistic work on a weekly basis. The weight of creating these extra pieces, which are often outside my expertise as a dancemaker, can take a toll on in-studio practices as I find myself with less time to spare.

Though small, the podcast has extended beyond the region to garner a national and international following. One lesson I have learned is that people are more willing to engage in this topic immediately after a tragedy occurs than as a part of their regular consumption of media. I want to be sensitive regarding what I am about to write, but I feel it is important to illustrate my point. As I write this, my city is reeling from our own police-involved shooting of twenty-seven-year-old Jayland Walker.[6] In the five days following the tragedy, the podcast had an increase of ninety-seven downloads, the most ever within that same time period. The topic of this podcast will continue to be evergreen for the foreseeable future, unfortunately, but I hope that it gives my community a feeling of agency over their own experiences in a time when we may be feeling hopeless.

As viewership of the podcast continues, I do not know how it will impact the premiere of *inCOPnegro: Aftermath* in Spring 2023. However, this opportunity has transformed my understanding of what it means to build a project. Now it's no longer about a single dance theater project. It's about the ecosystem I built around the work as breadcrumbs for new audiences to my work.

BUILDING AN AUDIENCE VS. CULTIVATING A COMMUNITY

As I'm creating these projects and experimenting with new methods of audience development, I've come to realize there is a much deeper question I am asking now: *How do you move from building an audience to cultivating a community?*

Like most millennials, I enjoy spending hours a week watching social media. My favorite creators are comedians because they remind me of choreographers in the way their careers are structured. They are often independent, go on tour with others, and are gig-based. What I admire most about comedians is how they've adapted to the digital age and used it to cultivate community around themselves and their work. Comedians have taken their art form and transformed it to fit a small screen, using their short videos to build a following. Once they have a following, they convert those loyal followers into subscribers on a subscription-based platform like Patreon, and give them a collective name, which gives the followers an identity as it relates to the artist.

I do a big eye roll when I hear the word *followers*, but I think it's important to understand how this group of supporters exercises its power. In these private platforms, the comedians create exclusive work for their community, they have transparent conversations with their community, and they ask for their communities' opinions about works in progress. They also offer prerelease tickets and merchandise to their community. The reciprocal relationship kicks in when it's time for the comedian to go back on tour. Guess who sells out the performances? Their community.

As an artist, the ability to guarantee ticket sales to a presenter puts you in a different category. The pain point of many presenters is the difficulty of selling tickets for dance. If you, because of your community you've built online, can solve that problem, you can become a valuable asset in the industry. And not to mention, be able to negotiate the rates of your contracts more favorably.

During *The Black Card Project* and currently with *inCOPnegro*, I have focused on the concept of building an audience. However, I've come to understand what I have been craving since my initial question: *How do I get people to care about what I do?* What I've really wanted is a community who cares about me as much as my work. An audience is a group of individuals who voyeuristically connect with the products you produce for them. A community is a group of people who want to engage in-process, be a part of process, experience the product, and interconnect with one another to build a stronger foundation with the artist.

At the end of the day, I want my connection to people who experience my work to reflect my creative process. People connecting across common themes to have conversations and experiences that bring them closer together. Six years into this process, I think the way I market my art is slowly being revealed as an organic process that fulfills me and my eventual community.

Administrative Experiment

Grab a journal, your memo app on your phone, or a friend. Ask yourself the following questions and make a list for each answer:

- What do I do? How many ways can I name it? (Example: choreographer, dancemaker, movement artist, et cetera.)
- How would I share what I do with someone in a way that lives outside of that practice?
- How do I get people to care about what I do?

Make a list of experiments you could try next week. Choose one. Begin!

Causing a Scene
How I Helped Build the Contemporary Dance Ecosystem in My Hometown
Banning Bouldin

"I didn't know people from Tennessee wore shoes," my new resident adviser joked. I laughed, trying to hide my shock and embarrassment. I could feel the heat in my face turning my cheeks bright red.

"Yeah, don't you sit on tree stumps at school instead of chairs?" The young dancer next to me laughed, air-quoting "school" with their fingers.

It was the summer of 1996. I had just turned fifteen and was thrilled to be one of forty young dancers attending Juilliard's first-ever Summer Dance Intensive.[1] It was my first time in New York City, and the first of many times navigating being stereotyped as a southerner. That summer, the assumptions other dancers made about me on hearing my accent or learning where I was from were clear: *How could someone talented enough to get into Juilliard come from a place like Nashville, Tennessee?* A small city known primarily as the home of country music,[2] Nashville was hardly considered a metropolis at that time. And everyone made sure to let me know.

Eager to blend in and excel in my dance studies, I spent the next month working to eradicate my southern drawl and adopt new ways of behaving that seemed more neutral to me. Just as my mind and body were learning new ways of moving through modern and contemporary choreography, I was trying on new pronunciations and body language outside the studio. By the end of that summer, I had gained new friends and a new vision for my future: I wanted to become a professional contemporary dancer and there was nowhere else—I thought—where I could receive the kind of excellent, diverse training and networking opportunities I had begun to taste in New York City. Grudgingly, I went home to Nashville and begged my mother to help me strategize a way to leave Tennessee.

Back home, the issue of my southernness was defined by a lack of opportunity. In Nashville, I had access to good ballet training at Nashville Ballet, but there was nowhere in all of Tennessee where I could continue the kind of modern and contemporary training I had experienced at Juilliard. I already knew: I would have to leave Nashville to get the education I needed and to have the career in contemporary dance I wanted. Two years later, I was accepted to Juilliard on scholarship and early admission. I left Nashville with no intention of returning. Why would I? There was nowhere for me to dance.

Here I am twenty years later—telling the story of how I came home and helped build the contemporary dance scene in Nashville.

Benjamin Harkarvy[3] and the faculty he assembled as director of Juilliard's Dance Division shaped many of the values and philosophies that still drive my work today—gifting me with a lifelong appreciation for collaboration, creative process, and approaching movement like a researcher.[4] Ben saw dancers not as men or women but as *artists*—before terminology like "gender nonconforming" and "nonbinary" were available to discuss the nuances of gender identity. He believed contemporary dancers were limitless in our capacity to embody and express, and this invigorated me. As a ballet dancer, my gender had predetermined every step I danced and role I played. Now as a contemporary dancer, I felt seen and at home in my body. To prepare us for contemporary repertoires, Ben continued Juilliard's legacy of stressing both modern dance and ballet technique, while also doubling down on opportunities to be in creative process with choreographers inventing new dance languages.[5] I emerged from four years of rigorous study as a dance polyglot—able to speak multiple movement languages with my body, thanks to choreographers like Ohad Naharin, Margie Gillis, and Robert Battle, and the numerous methods I studied.

Over the next eight years, I lived the dream I had conditioned myself to pursue. I worked with major choreographers and companies, lived in New York

City, Stockholm, and Paris, and toured internationally; I was almost always in rehearsal, performing, or on the road. Approaching my thirties, I was fatigued and disillusioned by the realities of a life that *sounded* like what I had always wanted. But instead of feeling successful I felt used up—with so many of my best ideas exploited by a system that viewed women as muses, not makers. Choreographers took advantage of my collaborative nature and composition skills by crediting themselves fully for material I made without publicly acknowledging my creative contributions to their (really our) work. No matter how avant-garde the works were aesthetically, the infrastructures driving many of their creative processes were patriarchal, and at times, abusive. In stunning contrast to my experience at Juilliard, I was often sexualized by directors. These realities of my professional experience left me questioning whether I wanted to dance anymore. Feeling unmoored, I left the security of a full-time company job in Stockholm and retreated into project-based work with trusted friends and colleagues—Aszure Barton and Artists, and a collective led by fellow Juilliard graduates Stephan Laks and Rachel Tess called Rumpus Room Dance.[6] After two years of jumping from project to project, I sought a safe space far from the dance meccas I knew, where I could process all that was troubling me. I left Paris and returned to Nashville.

In 2010, I found a small apartment not far from where I had grown up and began sifting through what I believed was the wreckage of my dance career. To make ends meet, I taught weekly contemporary technique and improvisation classes for Vanderbilt University and at Nashville Ballet. My approach to these classes was light at first. I felt no ambition; I was sharing what I knew with people who were dancing for fun. Not one person in my classes had heard of the famous choreographers I had worked with. I was surprised by how refreshing this anonymity felt. The names I had worn like badges on a letterman jacket meant nothing in Nashville, and it was totally liberating.

With this new freedom, I began to question the relationship between access and success, geography, and opportunity. In my classes, I met and worked with talented dancers who, like me years before, lacked access to networks, information, and experience. They danced for fun because it was all anyone in Nashville *could* do. Almost every talented dancer I had met in New York City was from somewhere else: Texas, Florida, Georgia, Maryland.... What if it were possible to bring the same opportunities for contemporary training, creative residencies, and performances that existed in San Francisco, Chicago, and New York to Nashville? Could artists be given a choice in whether they stayed or left to realize their goals?

Still troubled by the disparity between the way the field talked about collaboration and how it actually played out, I needed to know dance environments could value the voices and mental health of everyone in the room—including mine. This process of questioning and embracing the needs around me allowed me to let go of unhelpful influences in the past, and I dived deeper into my own interests. Over the next three years, I devoted myself to growing a following for my dance classes in Nashville and getting to know the fragmented local dance community—all the while uncovering my own choreographic voice and passion for pioneering a new contemporary dance scene in the South.

By 2013, there were ten dancers regularly taking class with me two times a week. They came from different corners of the Nashville dance community—some were young students who aspired to dance professionally; others were former ballet dancers; some were teachers; there was even a contemplative psychotherapist in our ranks. Though different in many regards, we all shared a love for research and longed for more opportunities to move and create together. My relationship with these dancers, and our collective awareness of the challenges we faced as artists craving access to what had never been available to us in Nashville, are what catalyzed New Dialect into existence.

That April, inspired by our solidarity, I outlined what became New Dialect's Mission and Founding Vision Statement, and penned a business model diagram on a napkin.

I saw three major challenges facing the state of dance in Nashville:

- There was no infrastructure in place for advanced artists in the modern and contemporary dance communities to train daily.
- There was no professional modern or contemporary dance company or project capable of financially supporting part-time or full-time artistic and administrative staff.
- There were few opportunities for audiences to experience professional contemporary performances in Nashville, and ticket prices were often high ($40–$120 per seat)—prohibiting lower-income folks from experiencing professional-level productions.[7]

Moved to meet the needs of the growing dance community and to raise the level of contemporary dance training and performances available in my hometown, I set out to build an organization that would address these challenges by

- Creating and facilitating Nashville's first-ever year-round, open-to-the-public, daily class series for contemporary dancers, choreographers, and instructors to train and research together on a regular basis.
- Becoming a 501(c)(3) nonprofit arts organization capable of remunerating dancers, choreographers, instructors, and administrators on a part-time and full-time basis.
- Facilitating a healthy working environment to build a confident collective of professional artists who positively impact their communities.
- Producing inspiring, professional contemporary dance performances at affordable prices and in unique spaces, believing that high-quality art experiences can happen anywhere and can be made available to everyone.

Could what was once considered by many a "dance desert" become an ecosystem where contemporary artists thrived?

Yes, I hoped.

~

On April 29, 2013, we officially began Nashville's first daily training program for contemporary dancers: New Dialect's Contemporary Cross-Training Series. These low-cost classes were open to anyone in the community and met every weekday morning from 9:30 to 11:00 a.m. Finding studio space five mornings a week was our first big hurdle. Thanks to my teaching at Vanderbilt, we had access to the university's dance studios on Tuesdays and Thursdays; as for the rest of the week, I had a long road of research ahead. There were a number of dance schools in Nashville, but their doors were closed and locked until children's after-school dance classes began in the afternoons. I abandoned the quest for a conventional dance studio, and reached out to friends at abrasiveMedia, a local interdisciplinary artists' collective that ran a mixed-use warehouse space in Wedgewood Houston.[8] They agreed to let us use their space—

which at the time was under construction and often covered in sawdust—three days a week, with the understanding that other people would be there working on their own projects. Not ideal, but a start.

Bolstered by a new partnership and informed by the values that had defined my Juilliard training, I devised the programmatic philosophy and logistics of Contemporary Cross-Training. Each morning we studied a different method. On Mondays and Wednesdays, we trained in floor work or ballet for contemporary dancers; on Tuesdays and Thursdays, we investigated improvisation methodologies and contemporary technique(s); on Fridays, we studied a somatic practice like Alexander Technique or Feldenkrais. These sessions were led by various teachers in the community. We treated the time and space we shared as a research laboratory for both students and facilitators to experiment. Every five weeks the teachers and methods would shift. This format gave dancers the opportunity to dive into certain methods, while also allowing them to gain fluency in a number of different approaches over time. Rotating facilitators in five-week cycles also allowed us to include several artists from across the city in our teaching lineup, which in time, I hypothesized, would help unite the different factions of the dance community.

Successfully establishing our daily classes was a collective financial investment. We had no start-up capital, which meant that to cover our costs, no one could attend for free. I researched the prices of community classes in other cities, as compared to tuition prices for adult ballet programs and fitness classes in Nashville, and laid these findings against our projected overhead to build the tuition scale for Contemporary Cross-Training. Dancers paid $12 to "drop in" to a single class. Five- and ten-class passes were discounted at $10 per class. For those of us who wanted to train every day, we paid $7.50 per class, which came to $150 per five-week series. We used these earnings to pay teachers $50 per session—a total cost of $1,000 per month in artist fees. Another 10 percent of our tuition income went toward rent to our friends at abrasiveMedia. The rest of the money we set aside to save up for legal and filing fees associated with applying for nonprofit status through the IRS.

One month after the launch of our Contemporary Cross-Training Series, on the recommendation of a friend, I contacted the Arts and Business Council in Nashville (ABC), who directed me to their Volunteer Lawyers and Professionals for the Arts (VLPA) department—a small rotating team of lawyers who provide pro bono legal and business services to artists.[9] I emailed their general information address, "How do I apply for nonprofit status for an arts organization?" and attached New Dialect's Mission and Founding Vision Statement. Their response was a 200-page packet called "Starting a Nonprofit Arts Organization: Incorporation & the Tax Exempt Application Process."[10] As promised in the title, the workbook walked me through every step of incorporating in the state of Tennessee, assembling a board of directors, writing bylaws and activities statements, drafting a conflict of interest policy, creating a three-year projected annual operating budget, annual reporting, and so much more. In two months' time, the activities in the workbook led me all over the city to meet a dozen business leaders and creative directors—giving me a broad sense of the skill sets I and others would need to grow New Dialect from a series of morning classes to the multifaceted ecosystem-builder I envisioned. I returned my homework to the VLPA, where they converted my answers to their questions into legal documents and an application to the IRS for federal tax-exempt status. Using the money we had saved from the first two months of Contemporary Cross-Training, I paid the $850 filing fee for the form 1023 and a meager $30 membership fee to the Arts and Business Council for accessing their services. Five months later, I received notification from the IRS that our application had been approved and New Dialect was officially a 501(c)(3).

Equipped with nonprofit status, we began to strategize New Dialect's next steps. In the fall of 2013, a small group of dancers and I volunteered four hours a week to research choreography after morning class. We used this material to make our first film, *Shelby* (named after the park where it was filmed), and screened the movie at our first fundraising event—a silent auction at the home of our board president, where we raised $6,075. That winter, we were able to apply for our first grants as a nonprofit, expanding our financial capacity to include project support from our state and local arts commissions. At the same time, two very important new partnerships came into view, Metro Parks Dance Division and Nashville's brand-new contemporary performing arts center, OZ Arts Nashville[11]—partners whose support would help us take the next big steps in our evolution from learning environment to professional dance company.

Metro Parks Dance Division donated the use of a long-shuttered, well-kept dance studio, thanks to the efforts of Kathryn Wilkening, a New York University graduate and fellow Nashville native. Kathryn had spent the better part of a decade working with the famed choreographic residency program, Harkness Dance Center at 92nd St. Y, before relocating to Nashville to take up her new post as the director of dance for Metro Parks. Her vision for Metro Dance would draw on her experience at 92nd St. Y with hopes of creating numerous new opportunities for Nashville-based choreographers and dancers to be in residence, just like they were at the Harkness Center.[12] That spring, we met for the first of many coffees, where I told her about the scope of my vision for New Dialect and invited her to watch a class. In June 2014, New Dialect became a dance company in residence at Metro Parks' Centennial Performing Arts Studios. The arrangement: New Dialect would receive free studio space, Monday to Friday from 12:00–3:30 p.m. for a new, daily rehearsal practice, year-round, in exchange for helping develop curricula and providing teachers for a new contemporary dance program at the Studios. This tremendous in-kind donation allowed us to put the money we earned from classes, grants, and donations directly into artist fees for rehearsals and what was to be our first performance at OZ Arts Nashville.

Lauren Snelling's arrival in Nashville, and tenure as the founding artistic director of programming at OZ Arts from 2013 to 2019, was another boon to New Dialect's transition from research lab to professional company. Having worked with organizations like Park Avenue Armory and Melbourne International Arts Festival, Lauren was eager to introduce Nashville audiences to cutting-edge, international performances, and to elevate local artists by providing us with a platform to create new works. Thanks to our ongoing residency at Centennial Performing Arts Studios, we had the space and time to create and refine new works in a daily studio practice. When Lauren invited New Dialect to perform during OZ's inaugural season in August 2014, we were ready. I had just choreographed my first two theatrical works for New Dialect in collaboration with ten local dancers and two dear friends, choreographer/dancer Ana Lucaciu, and composer/musician Lev LJOVA Zhurbin. Our double-bill debut, *Multilingual*, was my first performance in Nashville as a professional dancer, and my first as a director and producer.

OZ's marketing arm promoted our show lightly as a local act through their social media channels. New Dialect had no marketing department. The dancers and I enthusiastically posted rehearsal photos to our small Instagram followings and invited all our friends and family. We hung posters in coffee shops and bookstores. At five dollars per person, ticket prices were in line with our values about accessibility, and we thought that would encourage folks skeptical about watching an avant-garde dance performance to attend. Together with

Causing a Scene

OZ, based on their attendance records and our joint promotional efforts, we anticipated an audience of 150 people. The venue's casual, flexible seating was set up to accommodate precisely that number—with risers, chairs, and cushions on the floor. The night of the performance, feeling a mix of nerves, I watched from the wings as people poured into the warehouse in throngs. Lauren rushed backstage to tell me there were seven hundred people in the audience, and my jaw dropped. OZ had to turn people away at the doors, or risk breaking fire codes.

The buzz generated by the record-breaking crowd and enthusiastic standing ovation that night catapulted New Dialect into the local limelight.[13] Over the next five years, we received invitation after invitation to perform, facilitate professional development sessions, and share community creative process workshops with diverse organizations across Nashville: the Frist Art Museum, Tennessee Performing Arts Center, Cheekwood Botanical Gardens, Zeitgeist Gallery, Tinney Contemporary, Belmont University, O'More School of Design, Symphony Center, Intersection, Intermission, Vanderbilt University, Vanderbilt Children's Hospital, Hispanic Family Foundation, and many others. Our partnerships with Metro Parks Dance and OZ Arts Nashville also continued to thrive, with the expansion of New Dialect's education activities in Metro Parks' community centers, including their Dance with Parkinson's Disease program, and four more sold-out engagements at OZ Arts in 2015, 2016, 2019, and 2020. We said yes to *every* opportunity to collaborate that came our way; and the growing number of productions we were involved in each season meant we were in rehearsal thirty-five weeks a year.

To support this dramatic increase in our activities and hours, we had to expand our company's revenue streams. Annual grant awards from Tennessee and Metro Nashville Arts Commissions and the National Endowment for the Arts, foundation gifts, donations, and earned income from presentations paid for artists' fees. Over the course of three years, we were able to increase the hourly rehearsal rate for dancers to twenty-five dollars per hour. Funding support also enabled us to commission and host choreographers, composers, and instructors from outside the Nashville community. Artists like Roy Assaf, Sidra Bell, Rosie Herrera, and dozens of others traveled to the South on our invitation to share their methods in open-to-the-public community classes and create new works with our company dancers—shaping the ethos and approaches driving the new contemporary dance scene we were building in Nashville. To help manage our growing administrative workload, my husband, Kevin Bouldin, with his background in grant writing and nonprofit development, joined New Dialect as administrative director.[14] When funding allowed, we contracted members of the company on an hourly basis at an additional twenty dollars an hour, to assist with administrative tasks like registration and payroll.

By 2018, New Dialect's programs had grown to include daily classes and rehearsals, multiweek Summer and Winter Intensives for teens and preprofessional dancers, community workshops for people with no dance experience, Choreographers' LABs for midcareer choreographers, and our annual Third Voice residency for young composers, choreographers, and visual artists to collaborate in the creation of experimental new works. Excited by new opportunities to train in the South and New Dialect's community-centered approach, dancers were traveling from across North and Latin America to participate in our Intensives. Seeing an opportunity to contribute to our growing dance community, freelancers and dancers just graduating from BFA programs like Boston Conservatory and SUNY Purchase began moving to Nashville to join in New Dialect's ongoing classes, even to start their own projects.[15] As news of our work in the South spread by word of mouth and through articles in *Dance Magazine*[16] and *Dance Teacher*,[17] New Dialect was selected for a new touring initiative through South Arts supported by the Mellon Foundation. Opportunities to perform outside Nashville at Jacob's Pillow and Perry-Mansfield's 20th Annual New Works Festival arrived, with more invitations on the horizon. We had gained national recognition for our efforts to increase the visibility and accessibility of contemporary dance in Nashville. I could sense it was the end of a chapter, and that another steep learning curve was ahead.

∼

When the pandemic hit in March 2020, New Dialect was already at a crossroads. I was fatigued from founder burnout. Many artists who had danced with the company for years now wanted the flexibility to create their own work and participate in other projects. Theaters were being shuttered and performances canceled, just as our company was preparing to tour throughout the Southeast.[18] Faced with these challenges, and with support from NCCAkron's Creative Administration Research program,[19] I opted to experiment with an adaptable structure for New Dialect that would allow us to respond to pandemic-related hardships and the Nashville dance community's evolving needs with sensitivity and agility. New Dialect left the traditional dance company model behind for something unknown.

Two years later, we refer to ourselves as a practice, not a company; we work in a decentralized, team-based structure and on a project basis—building the artistic and administrative teams for productions, residencies, and intensives as they happen, and prioritizing space for our collective reflection and assessment. We left the scarcity mindset that drove our visibility in the beginning behind and instead adopted a philosophy of injecting more of our passion and resources into fewer activities—to do less *better*. To this end, New Dialect has shed certain programs, such as our Third Voice residency, and reduced the overall number of classes we offer each year. If any program no longer seems relevant to our mission, we let it go.

Since New Dialect first began our work in 2013, the contemporary dance scene in Nashville has grown tremendously. Today, there are several projects, small companies, new multidisciplinary collaborations, and even new festivals that are led by artists who have worked with New Dialect or relocated to join us in blazing a trail. Where ten years ago, I and a small group of dancers longed for access to the opportunities we saw in other cities, now many more of us are facing a whole new challenge together: *sustainability*. Increased access and opportunities are only part of the picture. While the number of contemporary dancers, choreographers, classes, and productions in Nashville has multiplied, the resources available to support our work are relatively unchanged.

To date, New Dialect's vision for fostering a thriving contemporary dance ecosystem in Nashville remains aspirational. The shift in our emphasis from access to sustainability is bringing to light new questions about partnership, combining resources, the value of competition, and the role we hope to play in our art form's evolution. As I look to the future and consider the many lessons I have learned, I trust my passion for research and collaboration to guide me across the unknown terrain that lies ahead.

Administrative Experiment

Step One: What needs do you perceive in your local arts community? Identify three to five critical needs.

Step Two: Devise an arts program to address one, or more, of those needs. Include whom the program intends to serve, where and how often it happens, and what earned and contributed income will support program activities. (Bonus points for drawing the business model on a napkin like I did.)

Step Three: What kinds of partnerships will ensure the success of your arts program?

Draw a partnership model for your program that includes potential stakeholder individuals/organizations, shared activities, proposed responsibilities, and goals.

8 & 1
The End Becomes the Beginning When Every Body Dances
Pioneer Winter

I founded Pioneer Winter Collective (PWC) because I felt limited and unfulfilled as a dancer; the way I communicate best is through choreography. As a choreographer, I collaborate with other artists whose voices are intrinsic to our work, our relationship rooted in the understanding that our sole objective is sharing our human experience, as completely as possible, with audiences. Company dramaturg Jeremy Stoller describes our process: "We engage deeply with power and consent, with leading and following. Performers share the role of leadership, and we endeavor to make those handoffs intentional and fluid."[1]

My earliest memory of this flow: I am five years old, standing on the tops of my mom's feet as she dances in the living room. I remember the feeling of shifting from one foot to the other, the continuity of her movements, and my role as her abiding partner, neither controlling nor directing the dance but a part of it nonetheless. A collaboration. I especially remember the Shim Sham, a tap routine that begins not on the usual starting count of 1, but at the end of the previous count set (8 &), creating an easy fluidity as you repeat, reverse, and vary the routine, continuously flowing into the next set of counts. It could go on and on. It reminds me that endings are also beginnings, that there is a connection among all things in dance, from ideation to administration to performance; that everything we do is a cycle of repeated becoming.

A moment of regaining footing in *Forced Entry and Other Love Stories* (2017). Photo credit: Mitchell Zachs

All bodies are in a cycle of becoming.

It was this realization that led to Pioneer Winter Collective being formed as an intergenerational and physically integrated dance-theater company that creates performance on stages and in public spaces, museums, galleries, and schools around the Greater Miami area where we are based, and on film so that anyone can view our work.

Every body dances, and every body carries validity and virtuosity.

I began choreographing in 2010, at age twenty-two, while I was in graduate school for epidemiology and public health. Through an internship program, I matched with a small nonprofit that focused on HIV/STD testing and prevention. Doing this work, I was reflecting on the devastation that HIV/AIDS brought across communities to which I belong—the queer community, the dance community—and how we carry that in our bodies. The dancer's body is imagined as strong and powerful, which is not the image we are presented with of someone living with HIV.

Stigma and discrimination cause us to fear, rather than to seek understanding.[2] An individual living life as an HIV+ person *can* dance, and their body *can* be strong. Disease doesn't need to define them. I sought a conversation within my communities around the stigma of the disease, to explore my own relationship to it and for mutual healing. Acknowledging the power of the arts to delve into transgressive topics, I sought to do this through the language in which I feel most fluent: movement.

I applied for a community grant to present *Reaching the Surface*, in partnership with the clinic where I was completing my internship. I put out a call for dancers affected by HIV/AIDS willing to participate in a project that aimed to confront and dismantle stigma around the disease. The project took on new meaning during the rehearsals when one of the performers got tested at the partnering clinic and their test came back positive. As they confronted their internalized trauma and fears—and I strove to create a safe, vulnerable, and creative rehearsal space—dance provided a way to communicate when nothing else did. When individuals confront their internalized trauma and fears, traditional forms of communication may sometimes fall short. However, dance can offer a unique and profound way to express emotions, experiences, and thoughts that are difficult to articulate through words alone.

∼

The heart of this work resides in dissolving barriers that exist in both the professional dance world and the broader culture, bringing real bodies and lived experience to the forefront. We are responsible for making work that truly accounts for our shared truths and is crafted in a meaningful, sustainable process. In both the culture at large and the dance field that exists inside it, certain bodies are upheld as the ideal, and those that do not conform are *othered*. Within our Collective, we embrace otherness.

I have found that by willingly sharing our vulnerability through dance, we move out of the crosshairs of judgment, toward empowerment. We take control of ourselves, and we model the embrace of *every* body. Our collaboratively devised work aims to expand the definition of dance so all bodies survive, thrive, and are witnessed. We never lose sight of how, why, and for whom this work exists.

This bringing together of queer/queered collaborators from a variety of backgrounds and experiences requires a balancing of individual and group impulses and desires. Stoller reflects: "We are growing into our collectivity, our ability to match each other's movements. We are doing this by building a shared vocabulary, for gaining a better understanding of our individual needs, physicalities, and of the histories that imbue them."[3]

In an effort to provide local LGBTQ/allied youth with mentorship and performance opportunities, PWC launched the Leaders of Equality through Arts and Performance (LEAP) program in 2012. Over its six years, LEAP continually evolved to meet the needs of the youth—offering dance, spoken word, and new media classes; and later focusing on leadership and creative intervention techniques through performance. LEAP served over 150 youth, and in its final year, a cohort of elders. In 2017–18, we partnered with Lambda Living and the Love the Everglades Movement for our first intergenerational day trip to the Everglades, where over twenty folx between the ages of sixteen and sixty-one spent a day talking, reflecting, and sharing a sense of community. As proud as I was of the program, I came to the realization that with its evolution away from a dance focus, combined with the increase in other service organizations in Miami that were devoted to working with LGBTQ youth and were doing it with greater reach and funding, it was time to reassess PWC's education and engagement initiatives.

From that reevaluation process, several new initiatives were born:

- **Werqshop Join** offers free weekly movement classes open to the dance, drag, and queer performance community. Classes include group improvisation exercises (such as those in the Administrative Experiment below), improvisations, and learning a movement combination from PWC's repertory. From 2018 to 2019, we offered over forty free workshops, and were poised for expansion prior to the COVID-19 pandemic. In addition to serving as a professional development opportunity for dancers, Werqshop Join provides a way for me to get to know local dancers from a variety of performance backgrounds, and for them to get to know me, in a relaxed environment, and without the pressure or constraint of an audition.
- **Werqshop Coin** exists to incentivize rehearsal, skill-building, and peer-to-peer resource sharing among queer Miami-based

After a Werqshop. Photo credit: Lisa Nalven

drag artists. These are performers who don't typically have access to rehearsal spaces—meaning they rehearse either in cramped quarters or not at all. PWC provides free rehearsal space, with staggered arrival times so performers always overlap in the studio, giving time both to work on their own projects and to be in community. We also offer stipends matching the performers' gig fees, with the ultimate goal of investing in the craft and technique of queer performers, and elevating performance art in South Florida.

- **Grass Stains** fosters site-specific and site-adaptive work from emerging local artists, providing them with rehearsal space, financial support, and mentorship. With Grass Stains, I acted on the opportunity I saw to support local choreographers and develop quality site-specific work in Miami. Traditional performance spaces in Miami are limited and cost-prohibitive for early-career choreographers, which leads them to often premiere their early works outdoors in nontraditional public spaces, like parks and beaches, without much consideration for the site's own history and context.

My experience as an audience member at these performances is that they rarely showed off the artists to their best advantage—a triple pirouette that looked so stunning in the rehearsal studio is far less polished in the sand between mangroves. Nor would they engage with the history or geography of the space in a meaningful way. Dance cannot ignore context; nor is it merely decorative. I found myself wondering: *Why* a pirouette? Aren't there myriad ways to revolve, spin, and twist *within* an environment that doesn't work in opposition to it?

I feel this is the way a lot of so-called engagement practices operate too: "Let's take what barely works in a boardroom and transplant it into a neighborhood." Merely importing strategies that work in different contexts may overlook unique circumstances and fail to establish meaningful connections.

Grass Stains has provided over eighty thousand dollars to nearly fifty artists, as well as mentorship from renowned choreographers including Stephan Koplowitz (New York City), Ana Sanchez-Colberg (San Juan, Puerto Rico), and in 2024, Gabri Christa (New York City). Based on artist-participant feedback, the program has evolved to emphasize a more cohort-driven, group-devised process facilitated by the mentor.

In 2020 and 2022, Grass Stains emphasized process rather than performance by inviting over twenty South Florida–based artists (choreographers, performance artists, filmmakers, musicians / sound artists, poets) to work with the visiting artist mentor in a lab setting over the course of a week. Each artist received an honorarium for committing to the week, which included exploration, process, and a culminating public performance. This model of Grass Stains has proved to be a successful intervention into dance ecologies that normally constrain the flourishing of the emerging generative artist, and we'll continue this model for its 2024 iteration.

By embracing the unique qualities of a space and exploring diverse movement possibilities, site performance work can become more authentic, engaging, and relevant to both the artists and the audience. Similarly, community engagement practices should prioritize understanding and responding to the specific needs and dynamics of the communities they aim to serve.

Artist reflection following Grass Stains 2020. Photo credit: Mitchell Zachs

I continue to look for ways to better serve my art, and my community, and to stay present in the becoming of my body, my craft, and the Collective as a whole. Our latest endeavor, Creative Connections, which launched in 2022, a few months prior to my submitting this essay for publication, is a resident artist structure. I wanted to make a different sort of commitment to my collaborators, both for their benefit and for the Collective as a whole, because our larger mission is not project-based or commodity-driven, but about long-term commitment and support.

I believe that when people feel supported and respected—and confident that their basic financial needs are being met—this releases them to be fully present as artists in a collaborative space. During a residency period, resident artists receive a monthly retainer both to cover their time in rehearsal and to acknowledge the overall contribution of each artist's energy and creativity to the Collective's work. This approach recognizes that artistic exploration and development extend beyond specific project timelines and encourages a more holistic engagement with the creative process.

All resident artists are additionally provided a stipend to enact a project aligning with our current research. These projects could be a series of workshops, panel discussions, or other growth opportunities of their choosing. For example, Creative Connections artists Frank Campisano and Aeon De La Cruz offered two unique sets of free movement workshops; Barbara Meulener developed a film-based collage focused on joy in Black and Brown bodies; and Niurca Marquez organized a panel series on motherhood, queerness, and art making.

Our inaugural 2022 slate of four resident artists completed a nine-month residency. We learned a lot in that time. Still, I hesitated to make significant changes to Creative Connections' structure without another cycle. Now in its second iteration with a cohort of six artists, I've come to realize that my assumption that all Collective members would want to develop their own projects is not correct. Some just want to dance. So Creative Connections opened up to artists who worked with PWC previously, but may not be currently active—a *bridge* back to one another.

Ultimately, the success of this resident artist structure lies in finding a balance between supporting individual artistic growth and fostering identity. By respecting the desires of those who simply want to dance while still offering avenues for growth and development to those who seek it, we can create an environment where artists feel valued and can contribute uniquely.

Open and ongoing communication has been key to understanding their aspirations, goals, and comfort levels. I hope this new model will radically reshape the choreographer-dancer relationship, and foster stronger bonds and more consistent experimentation. I look forward to sharing what we learn and how we further develop Creative Connections after its third cycle.

∼

As ever, I aim to remain in this process of becoming, alongside a growing community that will change with me, challenge and support my growth as I do theirs.

An abiding partner, neither controlling nor directing the dance, but a part of it nonetheless.

Administrative Experiments

KINETIC COLANDER

1. Organize into pairs, and have each pair designate an A and a B partner. Play music for 30–45 seconds, having every A improvise movement while B observes (witnesses).
2. Pause the music, and instruct B to recreate (paraphrase) and build on the movements they recall from A's improvisation. Play the music for another 30–45 seconds.
   Note: Music is not required, but it's important each partner has the same amount of time per turn.
3. Repeat this cycle five to six more times, having each pair continue to recreate and build on each other's movements.

As the exercise continues, there is more movement to incorporate, but still the same amount of time allotted in which to move through the material, which compels the mover in the moment to make choices: What is important enough to keep? What do you let go of? Maybe certain movements don't feel comfortable in one person's body. Maybe entire sections of choreography are forgotten. This is not meant to be a memory game, but an exercise in decision-making by necessity; not holding things precious for the sake of preservation or iteration, but out of function.

TAKING TURNS

1. People stand in a line on one side of the room. Designate one person to start as the movement leader. That person steps forward and improvises movement that the others follow, until someone else decides they want to be the leader, and steps in front of the first leader. This continues until the movers reach the opposite side of the room. Note: Alternatively, this can be done in a circle—with one person stepping into the center to take the lead—so it can continue without being limited in duration by the width of the rehearsal space.
2. Try the exercise again, with the exchange of leadership requiring a person to step forward *and* to call out, "ME." How does that change it?

3. Discuss the exercise. What made for a strong leader? What was challenging? How did it feel to assert control, physically—and then verbally? When was communication clear or unclear? In what ways was the group accountable to each other? What happened when the movement was easy to follow or execute, versus more difficult?

RECOMMENDED READING

Free Play: Improvisation in Life and Art by Stephen Nachmanovitch reconsiders existing notions of creativity and intuition, tapping into (and reviving) that space with "play" and joyful improvisation.

Wonderbook: The Illustrated Guide to Creating Imaginative Fiction by my uncle Jeff VanderMeer, while centered on writing, replaces instructional text with images contributed by over thirty artists in order to break down the complex into simple parts.

Both books seek to revise old ways of thinking to reimagine how one may create with greater ease and intuition.

Dance as a Radical Act
An Artist-Led, Community-Centered Approach to Choreographing a Creative Ecology
Tonya Lockyer

Our student was crying in the hallway, "I don't want to leave Seattle, but there's nothing here for me." Her friend, a recent Cornish graduate,[1] had tried to have a dance career in Seattle, but months after moving to Manhattan, he had been found dead from a diabetic seizure. I wanted my students to no longer need to head east after graduating. A few weeks later, a friend said offhand that trying to have a dance career in Seattle was "enough to make you want to jump off a bridge." I asked, "Have you seriously thought about jumping?" She, too, felt there was nothing here for her. Our contemporary dance community was in a crisis. It was 2007. There are many stories of that time—what led to the crisis, and the remarkable decade of collective ecology building that followed. This story is mine.

In 1998, when I arrived in Seattle as a performer and choreographer from the East Coast, I joined a community of dancers creating a network of companies, festivals, programs, and alternative spaces—to develop the resources they lacked. They often worked collectively; almost all of them were women, many of whom were queer.

There was d9 Dance Collective—nine dancers and coadministrators performing works they commissioned from leading American choreographers; SFADI—the international Seattle Festival of Alternative Dance and Improvisation, organized by Dance Art Group and curated through a community process; and Velocity—a not-for-profit contemporary dance hub with daily classes taught by some of Seattle's best-known dancers, guest artist workshops, affordable rehearsal space, and in-studio performances. Velocity, cofounded by Michele Miller and KT Niehoff, inspired such intense community co-ownership that dancers took class standing on the floorboards where they had personally hammered in the nails. Artists served on Velocity's board and ran the administrative office.

All this activity coexisted in and around Oddfellows Hall, a "cultural nucleus and point of convergence for community and arts organizations"[2] with a baroque ballroom, four theaters, eight large rehearsal studios, and dozens of offices and storefronts. Amazon hadn't yet eaten Seattle. An unheated loft was mine for $400 a month because I cleaned up the drug-fueled destruction of the previous tenants. In 2001, I watched a riot unfurl beneath my windows. The next day there was a magnitude 6.8 earthquake. The loft upstairs vacated. Because it now had a crack running down its wall, I was able to convince the landlord to give me, and a quickly organized group of six artists, the lease for a new studio collective, RED.

They weren't "the good old days," but Seattle's arts community was, at that time, powerfully collective and capable of moving group thinking and processes into action. I immigrated to the United States with one suitcase, but in Seattle, in community, I was able to create, curate, and produce dance, theater, and multidisciplinary events; become a teacher and scholar in live art; and sustain an international performance career that took me across three continents. I also became an administrative activist.

CULTIVATING A COLLABORATIVE, CONNECTED COMMUNITY

In 2004, I learned the new directors of On the Boards (OtB), Seattle's inter/national contemporary performance presenter,[3] planned to host New York choreographers to give "feedback" to Seattle dancemakers. I reached out to them and offered that it might be a disaster: Seattle choreographers were doing their own work, on their own terms—by design. It might be a greater benefit to us, and OtB, if they got to know our community first. OtB's directors invited me to help organize an alternative. We cocreated the Seattle Dance Forum.[4]

The forum brought together nearly a hundred dance artists of all ages and stages to take stock of the state of local dance and to spark ideas for our future. "Even before the three-hour forum officially began, the lobby was abuzz with input and ideas."⁵ In the welcoming introduction I offered four questions, the last being: "What would help create the kind of community you want to be a part of?"

The crowd self-divided into four discussion groups: students and recent graduates; midcareer artists and companies; established artists and companies; and dance advocates (supporters, department chairs, presenters, critics). When we reconvened to share summaries of our conversations the students were most interested in how to find work after graduation without having to move to New York. The midcareer artists focused on the possibilities of sharing resources. The established artists focused on touring and grant acquisition. The advocates were concerned with raising Seattle Dance's profile.

Each group also shared an idea for the future. Then I asked, "Who here wants to facilitate moving this idea forward?" Participants formed subcommittees and scheduled their next meetings. One group linked arms to develop the Seattle International Dance Festival.⁶ Another committee revived DanceNet as a listserv. Another group formed around establishing ongoing mentoring and feedback systems. The collective ethos of Seattle dancers and the change-making power of a community-centered approach triumphed that day. And I was becoming a socially-engaged artist. OtB supported this development by commissioning my next research and performance project *Consumed (on making art in a capitalist society with little or no capital)*.

Then in 2007, the year I found our student crying in the hallway, a developer purchased Oddfellows, raising rents 300 percent. Artists and community organizations were pushed out. Velocity was forced out of its home and into an emergency capital campaign. Its three-year "transition was long, costly, and draining."⁷ In 2010, Velocity's leader resigned, leaving it "with a substantial debt."⁸ "Things were frazzled to the point of unraveling."⁹ The contemporary dance community contracted. Artists urged me to apply for the job of Velocity's new director.

At first I was reluctant, but the idea of art as a social practice awakened in me a determination to not leave my choreographic thinking at the office door. Some of my past performances were works of institutional critique. Now I was invited to perform institutional critique from the inside.

～

On my first day as Velocity's artistic executive director, I faced a dusty office of unpacked boxes. Sliding an official-looking paper from a teetering pile, I discovered Velocity had failed building inspections. We had "one week to vacate." I was the only full-time employee. I reduced my salary and hired two part-time positions: Operations Manager Stefanie Karlin and Development Manager Rosa Vissers—both dance artists in our community. The public story was—"Velocity landed on its feet!"—but it was a perilous touch-and-go. Maxed-out credit cards kept appearing in desk drawers. Class attendance was meager. Ticket sales were a third of capacity. Velocity had a debilitating deficit as our country slogged through recovering from the Great Recession.[10] A consultant asked, "Do you want Velocity to die quickly or slowly?" That's the moment I started saying to our staff and board: "Velocity isn't a building. Velocity is the people who activate it."

Seattle's dance community was abundant with untapped, collaborative, innovative leaders. We reached out to artists of all life stages who were willing to show up, pitch in, or provide guidance and direction to specific programming. We asked anyone willing to share: "How can Velocity help you create the kind of community you want to be a part of?" We listened. Younger artists sometimes said they didn't "feel a part of the dance community." So I asked: "What if community is an active verb—something you *do* and participate in, rather than passively feel a part of?" Many of these young artist-partners went on to spearhead some of Velocity's most impactful new programming. The *Seattle Times* celebrated:

> Velocity started a late-night Monday open mic called Sh*t Gold where new and experienced performers try out their weirdest new material.... And it incubated the now-wildly-popular Dance Church[11] which started as a small free-for-all dance experience led by choreographer Kate Wallich and now sometimes draws 150 people.[12]

Over those first months, our collaborative visioning process included one-on-one brainstorms, forums, and surveys culminating in the community's final approval of a new mission, vision, and strategic plan. I became committed to facilitating programs that were community cocreated or cocurated.

Looking back, I see one critical advantage: We had already built trust. Many of these artists were my current or former students, colleagues, mentors, collaborators—or advocates who knew my creative work and history in the community. Later, as newcomers came to our city, I sometimes took this need to build trust for granted, assuming my record spoke for itself.

A year and a half later, Velocity's debt was gone, "earned income was up 123 percent and donations were up 145 percent."[13] The number of people participating in Velocity activities "skyrocketed 398 percent" as we "launched dance beyond (Velocity's) walls and across the city like a confetti bomb."[14] Velocity became a national nexus for dance. Dancers moved to the city from across the country. Dancers coming out of local colleges stayed. We raised millions in direct and in-kind support for artists, and transformed Velocity "into both a dance venue of national import and as an incubator for Seattle talent."[15]

Velocity's artistic and financial revitalization required strategy, nimble action, and collective determination. (And for a few years, a severe lack of sleep.) Revitalization doesn't have to look like tons of money (unless you want it to), but in 2011 it was critical that Velocity become financially stable to survive. It was also critical that Velocity reimagine itself. My vision of Velocity was that it was more than a physical space or a dance studio. It was a dynamic system with entry points and networks—animated by people and their relationships. Velocity was not just a building, it had the potential to live way outside the architecture of that space, including in the virtual world.

How could we foster a system that was more accessible, fair, and thriving? I experimented with a range of curatorial approaches including lottery, self-nominating proposals, community surveys, artist curatorial panels, guest-curated events based on themes, and cocurating with partner organizations. I developed more accessible opportunities to experience, develop, and discuss new work; and more varied sites for interactive experiences and performances. Velocity began producing events around the city, including in St. Mark's Cathedral, the Waterfront, the old Greyhound Station, Freeway Park, the Moore Theater, Seattle Art Fair, and annually in New York City. I wanted to help expand Velocity's impact—to foster a broader range of risk-taking artists and emerging ideas, and to connect them with a wider public.

What follows are a few of the approaches that worked for me, in a particular time and place, within a specific history and community. These experiments don't provide tidy administrative rules, but they demonstrate how programming, artist development, marketing, audience development, fundraising, and community building can be integral to one another. I believe we wouldn't have sustained the effort necessary for Velocity's transformation if I'd thought of administrative and creative processes as discrete. I still don't silo them.

EXPERIMENT ONE—SO YOU THINK IT'S DANCE?

Seattle Dance had an image problem. The press coverage could be demoralizing. Dancers responded with angry missives to critics. KT Niehoff's letter made it into the alternative newspaper *The Stranger*: "I don't want to call you out on what rotten, ignorant critiquing your paper is giving to dance. I want you to be better critics."[16] *The Stranger* responded to Niehoff's blast by calling it "a bristling letter of the 'you are snarky/sarcastic/unappreciative of our hard work/dead of soul/incapable of appreciating our wonderful wonder' variety."[17] They ran Niehoff's letter in the Theater section; a Dance section didn't exist. *The Stranger*'s annual Genius Arts Awards also didn't have a Dance category.[18]

Within Seattle arts, contemporary dance was marginalized. Regardless of how choreographers self-defined their work, it was often recategorized at others' convenience. A local presenter of French artist Christian Rizzo asked me to give a preshow talk: "Rizzo calls himself a choreographer, but I'd love you to tell our audience he's really a performance artist." He thought audiences would be more receptive if they didn't think Rizzo's work was dance. On funding panels, choreographers' boundary-pushing work could be dismissed with a breezy: *But is it dance?*

Dancers want to be respected, but so do journalists, and in 2011 our local arts writers had their own pressures. Seattle media companies were contracting in the face of economic pressures and social media. Arts journalists told me it was increasingly challenging to make a case for more dance coverage. So I started a conversation for local dancers and journalists to begin thinking through these challenges together.

So You Think It's Dance?[19] took a playful approach to a performative conversation billed as a free Show and Tell. The theme: *What qualifies as dance? Does it matter?* We found a strategic community partner in Seattle's *City Arts* magazine.[20] They collaborated on the concept and promoted the event as part of their City Arts Festival. They also convinced four major arts editors to participate as a panel.

The afternoon began with performances by well-known choreographers who experienced difficulty being viewed, reviewed, and funded as "Dance": Jessica Jobaris, The Cherdonna and Lou Show with Maile Martinez, and Douglas Riding. Between sets I told one-minute stories:

> A man brought a civil case against International Dance Festival Ireland for false advertising. Raymond Whitehead alleged he was "shocked, traumatized

and deeply embarrassed" by the work of Jérôme Bel because "not a single step of dance had taken place"[21] during the performance. Asked by the court to define dance Mr. Whitehead said, "people moving rhythmically, jumping up and down, usually to music, but not always."[22] The festival brochure read: "Everything you think dance is, Jérôme Bel is not."[23] The case was found in favor of the festival.

The performers then joined the arts writers and editors for a conversation facilitated by boylesque pioneer Waxie Moon and choreographer/filmmaker Dayna Hanson: *What had everyone just seen? Was it dance? Did it matter?*

The editors and writers first argued for arts categorization: *Audiences want to know what they're getting into; funders can only allot so much money per art discipline.* They opened up about diminishing arts coverage[24] and how it was easier to get a thumbs-up from editors if they framed a show as theater. *The Stranger*'s Brendan Kiley folded his arms; he found the whole subject "about as interesting as watching a car spin its wheels in the sand."[25] The audience of dancers pressed back: *So then why not just call it dance? Especially if dance is what these artists say is at stake in their work?*

It was clear that within the structures of power at play, what artists wanted was the least of the journalists' priorities. But then I saw a metaphoric lightbulb go off over *The Stranger* critic's head. Choreographer Amy O'Neal had just returned from Berlin, where an artist choreographed construction cranes over that city's skyline. The conversation shifted to how choreographic thinking is alive in the world: "minds were prodded, motivations questioned."[26] I was thrilled. As Velocity's new artistic executive director, I had begun the curatorial conversation at the most basic level at which the dance world exists: the question, *Is it Dance?* What I hoped to communicate: *What if dance is everywhere? Definitions are expanding.*

After the event, *The Stranger*'s Genius Awards added a dance category, and local dance coverage expanded. Dancers began gracing *City Arts* covers. Brendan Kiley moved on to the *Seattle Times*—calling me regularly requesting historical or theoretical context to inform his journalism. The quantity of sarcastic, dismissive, or hostile dance coverage diminished. I began hosting "press rehearsals" for Velocity productions where artists were encouraged to try out ideas—both artists and writers asking each other questions. This inspired artist profiles, previews, and think-pieces about dance and culture. The resulting ongoing positive visibility of dance in the press also helped grow audiences, class attendance, and contributed income. I got a glimpse of how deep the change was when a local critic wrote of a conceptual dance work we presented: "Dance is decentralized here—or, looked at another way, made so diffuse it permeates everything."[27]

EXPERIMENT TWO—SPEAKEASY SERIES

So You Think It's Dance? launched Velocity's first humanities program, the Speakeasy Series and our companion online journal *Stance*.[28] These community-led events included show and tells, performance lectures, community conversations, and weeklong forums. They were free or by suggested donation and open to the public; and people were invited to propose their own project. Velocity's Speakeasy Series fulfilled multiple aims:

It provided *a programmatic framework for regular community gatherings and exchanges*, interdisciplinary symposia, and even book clubs *about the intersections of dance and society*.

And offered a nimble format for *community feedback* and *resource sharing*.

It created opportunities to *encourage and support research, inquiry, and dialogue* as parts of artists' labor.

And as artists shared their interdisciplinary research, audiences expanded their *dance literacy*.

Speakeasy events helped audiences *consider the social, political, and philosophical implications of what dancers are doing*. We hosted forums on race, gentrification, art in prisons, among other subjects.

This attracted *new audiences*—people who wanted to engage more deeply with dance, without having to take a dance class.

And it activated *cross-disciplinary dialogue around timely issues*. The focus wasn't always dance, but it helped dance become a part of Seattle's civic conversations, *enhancing dance's public visibility*.

Anyone could propose and host a Speakeasy. To avoid lectures from lecterns I asked that every event include audience interaction. Hosts were invited to consider a question they wanted to think through with others, and were encouraged to bring their choreographic thinking to consider how everyone in attendance might move through an experience.

Speakeasies engendered ownership. After Trump was elected president, artists organized a Post-Election Community Response Forum that drew nearly a thousand attendees. In partnership with CD Forum,[29] we hosted the city's first symposium on Seattle Black Dance History.

Powerful institutional learning came from Speakeasies cocurated with guest artists. San Francisco artist Keith Hennessey's *Turbulence (a dance about the economy)* is an affirmation of the global movement for economic justice and an experiment in alternative modes of producing performance. In that spirit, Hennessey and I cooked up Velocity's first Open For(u)m, *FAILURE: Conversations Around Art + the Economy*—a week of multidisciplinary art, happy hour book clubs, workshops, roundtables, and family-style dinners. Midweek, award-winning author Mattilda Bernstein Sycamore[30] participated in a roundtable on queer histories, drawing a new audience who returned for the performances. A free family-style dinner, donated by a local restaurant, provided meals for performers and attendees, including neighbors living in a queer youth shelter. The Open For(u)m connected dance with new communities, sold out our theater, and expanded *Turbulence*'s impact.[31]

Velocity gained a reputation for humanities programs that roused adventurous audiences. Larger presenters began to partner with us when they brought challenging dance experimentalists to town. For example, OtB invited me to guest-curate Tere O'Connor's *BLEED*. Having studied with O'Connor, I knew of his rare ability to speak about the politics and poetics of dance. To create *BLEED*, O'Connor choreographed three other dances and then "collapsed"[32] them into a fourth "labyrinthine dance"[33] with all eleven of the other works' performers. OtB's Lane Czaplinski and I decided to combine our resources and bring all four original performances of the *BLEED Project* to Seattle, and to provide Seattleites with the opportunity to engage directly with this "mentor of New York's avant-garde"[34] throughout the week. O'Connor loved the idea.

Tere and I cocurated Open For(u)m: *Irreconcilability* as a nine-day immersion in the *BLEED Project*—an opportunity to come together to engage with his work and the thinking driving his process—through a choreographic workshop, a book club focused on Tere's writing, a book reading, performances, press interviews, and a culminating community forum. Our audiences were primed to participate; many attended every event. Over the nine days, ticket sales went from sluggish to oversold. In *Artforum*, Claudia La Rocco captured the power of the collaboration:

> This mini-survey came courtesy of On the Boards theater and Velocity Dance Center, making Seattle the only place other than the American Dance Festival to showcase this particular moment in O'Connor's extensive body of

work; lucky them, and unlucky the rest of the country. I had seen all of these dances before.... But the cumulative weight of experiencing them all together like this—I wasn't expecting it to feel so important.[35]

EXPERIMENT THREE—BIG BANG! REMIX PARTY

In those first tenuous months, Velocity needed to excite artists, audiences, donors, and funders to invest in Velocity again. We struggled with low earned revenue. Income from theater rentals and ticket sales were dismal. Individual donors were exhausted from the emergency capital campaign. Funders were skeptical.

Our first attempt to get funding for the Speakeasy Series failed. The foundation director said: "There is no way the Seattle dance community can pull this off. They are too inward looking." At the time, it was a fair assessment. I also understood why no one wanted to rent Velocity's small, ill-equipped theater. We had to cultivate, and show, the benefits of producing in our venue: *What if we brought artists of many disciplines and backgrounds together, and no corner of Velocity's building was off limits for experimentation? The artists might show us, and each other, what was possible.*

The first opportunity to try this experiment was Velocity's annual fundraiser—The Fall Kick-Off, traditionally a three-day showcase of ten-minute pieces with artists donating their time and work. The net income was tiny. To revamp the Kick-Off, I launched the Big Bang! Remix: a performance party of thirty-two performances and interactive installations happening simultaneously in every nook and cranny of Velocity—closets, loading docks, heating vents—overflowing onto surrounding rooftops and into parked sedans, with audiences streaming through, drink in hand, 7 p.m. to midnight. My invitation to artists: *Choose a zone anywhere in or adjacent to the building; perform a five-hour durational action of your creation. Audience interaction, optional.*

Dance critic Mariko Nagashima wrote of the "marathon performance": "Dance was happening everywhere you turned.... Not only was art being displayed, but it was being created on the spot as audiences joined in."[36] Looking back on the focused cacophony, it's notable how many creative seeds were planted by then-emerging artists: Filmmaker Wes Hurley projected the beginnings of what would become *Potato Dreams of America*—his SXSW Jury Prize and HBO Outfest Audience Award–winning film. Dani Tirrell danced while sharing an oral history of the voguing movement.[37] In a closet suffused with

Dance as a Radical Act

flashing lights, Kate Wallich + The YC set up a synthesizer and a live-feed camera, inviting attendees to create their own dance party. I invited the transgender performance project GenderTender to enact a Kiss-In, a tactic of ACT UP.[38] Alice Gosti, who two years later founded Yellow Fish // Epic Durational Performance Festival,[39] wrapped herself head to toe in white tissue for five hours. The Big Bang! was also intergenerational: Coriolis contemporary ballet collective pressed up against Butoh legend Joan Laage, while at their backs Deborah Hay collaborator Amelia Reeber lolled in a polar bear costume, and a mosh pit body-slammed in the background under strobe lights. Big Bang! was a sometimes-hallucinatory palimpsest, reflecting, in a few glances, the diversity of contemporary dance practices in our city.

Part of my Big Bang! curatorial strategy[40] was to replace the notion of performance as a product with the notion of dance as an experience, in this case a social experience—with meaning cocreated with the audience. At the time, performance installations were rare in Seattle. Those of us creating them were considered the fringe. Big Bang! brought interdisciplinary ideas from the edges of experimental performance into Velocity's more mainstream modern dance community. Trepidatious artists were offered dramaturgical and technical guidance. We embraced DIY production values to take the pressure off any expectations of perfection. We brought extension cords, lamps, projectors, and strobe lights from home. Velocity became a hive of activity and cross-pollination.

As audiences flowed through and around the building, they drew passersby on their way to restaurants, clubs, and theaters. Neighbors who had walked past the building for years finally ventured inside. At midnight, the entire space became a dance party with upcoming Seattle bands curated by Thunderpussy frontwoman Molly Sides (Molly soon went on to curate a similar quarterly event: *Trigger. New Dance Happenings*.) A local reviewer wrote: "Was it overwhelming? Absolutely, but what a wondrous thing to be overwhelmed by! The beauty of the Big Bang! is how it showcases the multiplicity of ways dance can be performed, viewed, and experienced."[41]

The Big Bang! far exceeded fundraising goals and inspired larger donations. Smaller community contributions are important, but when your organization is in desperate need of revenue, large donations make an immediate impact. In one weekend, a major donor experienced the breadth, innovation, and quality of Seattle Dance and Velocity's vision and became a multiyear season sponsor.

Artists and influencers were reignited to invest in our organization. Earned revenue from rentals dramatically increased. Self-producing artists were drawn to our freewheeling, supportive venue. The cash bar of the Big Bang! became a frequent feature. So did the social spirit of a performance party. Soon out-of-town artists reached out, hearing Velocity was a welcoming venue to try out new material. Lines of audiences began regularly snaking down the block.

Key to Velocity's growth was the variety and unexpectedness of our curated programming. Big Bang! embodied Velocity's new curatorial vision, as a space for adventurous artists—bringing together a multiplicity of communities and practices. Over the next few years, working with diverse cocurators, I also transformed Velocity's summer education programs to better reflect the bricolage of techniques and approaches informing contemporary dance. Diverse faculty "queer, trans, abled and disabled" shared influences from "pop culture, political activism, indigenous ritual, mixed abilities, gender exploration" and more.[42] We continued looking outward, to public spaces and presenting partners, activating cathedrals, waterfronts, public parks, and train stations. After its third year, *The Stranger* wrote of the Big Bang!: "It'll be cool to see what these dancers...accomplish in the coming year under the guidance and protection of Velocity, an organization that is less a dance company and more like a hotbed of creativity that nurtures and supports dancers as they explore performing art to sometimes extraordinary limits."[43]

EXPERIMENT FOUR—MADE IN SEATTLE

> "Velocity and Made in Seattle saved my creative life."
> —Amy O'Neal

I developed Made in Seattle, now Velocity's "cornerstone program,"[44] in 2012 to work one-on-one with artists to help them realize their artistic and organizational goals. Our work brought deeply realized projects, national visibility, new funding, and touring to Seattle choreographers. Artists catalyzed Made in Seattle—asking for partnership in pushing their practices; their aims more wide-ranging than choreographing their next dance. With each collaboration the program evolved—into an unorthodox residency, a holistic artist incubator, and a creative producing program.

Through Made in Seattle, artists were able to work on ambitious, multidimensional projects. I told artists their residencies could "take as long as it takes"—usually eighteen to twenty-four months—with Velocity providing responsive support throughout the projects' conception, research and development, workshopping, presentation, and dissemination.

One of my aims was to help artists become more aware of the interdependent contexts in which they operate. We considered the potential for cultural participation as they devised their projects. Artists were invited to consider an expansive approach to creative research, including community dialogue, humanities programs, and other dance activations. Along the way, we focused on their driving questions, their aims, and their place in the wider field of dance and society. In its first seven years of existence, fourteen choreographers participated.

Made in Seattle had a remarkable record of developing seminal projects that propelled artists onto the national stage. Just three years into the program, when *Dance Magazine* named the "25 Dance Artists to Watch," three were recent Made in Seattle alumni.[45] Made in Seattle artists including Alice Gosti, Cherdonna Shinatra / Jody Kuehner, Ezra Dickinson, and Amy O'Neal (all of whom became National Dance Project awardees, with Kuehner and O'Neal also winning *Stranger* Genius Awards) as well as Kate Wallich, Andrew Bartee, Mark Haim, Babette DeLafayette Pendleton, Mary Sheldon Scott, and Danielle Agami—made a mark on Seattle and beyond.

In 2012, as part of her Made in Seattle residency, Agami founded her company Ate9 (named one of the country's "hottest cultural commodities" by *Dance Magazine*)[46] and premiered Ate9's first work; in 2015, Gosti transformed St. Mark's Cathedral into her first immersive, durational performance installation. Through Made in Seattle Kuehner transitioned from a performance duo to create her first solo as Cherdonna Shinatra, touring to American Dance Festival; and Wallich expanded Dance Church® while creating her first evening-length performances, including *Industrial Ballet*, which sold out Seattle's 1,800-seat Moore Theater before touring to Jacob's Pillow. Made in Seattle productions were consistently sold out and critically lauded.

No specific outcome was required. Velocity's support responded as artists learned more about their project as it developed. Offerings might include studio space, commissioning fees, production residencies; advocacy with donors, press, funders, and presenters; producing events; and providing thought partners ready to assist with everything from dramaturgy to career strategy. A unique aspect of Made in Seattle was the option to engage with a visiting artist, an inter/national leader in the field selected by the Made in Seattle artist to work with them on a collaborative project.

I met with artists regularly, but the rhythm and scope of our meetings varied. A few artists dropped by whenever inspiration struck to bounce off ideas. One artist asked to meet every Monday, arriving with a list of questions covering everything from taxes and financial planning, to the history of feminist performance art. A few appeared in the weeks before grant deadlines, spending hours at my desk as we strategized and wrote their applications.

Most Made in Seattle artists wanted a thought partner to help them navigate an important turning point in their career. I often found myself in the role of an arts strategist: asking questions, listening, building bridges between the creative and business aspects of projects—sharing my understanding of the relationship between artists and audiences, place and power.

It can take a moment for it to sink in that you have time to take a more holistic long view of your life and work. You have time to experiment. You can try things out—with a curator you trust, or friends in a room, or in front of an audience—or you can just take a nap. To help artists access this feeling of spaciousness, I often asked: "What if this project began the moment you started thinking about it, and it ends the moment the last person stops thinking about it?" I framed it choreographically: "Along this journey, where are there opportunities for activating meaning-making and connection?" We considered their community of collaborators—their creative team, but also producing partners and advocates, audiences and the media—anyone who helps create a project's meanings, myths, and memories. We connected with venues and communities beyond Velocity's walls, and as a result contemporary dance became "a lot more integrated in the city...on a lot more stages."[47]

Made in Seattle became about helping artists carve out space—literally and figuratively—to create the change they wanted to see in their work, life, and communities.

EZRA DICKINSON, *MOTHER FOR YOU I MADE THIS* (MADE IN SEATTLE, 2013)

Part performance and part activism, *Mother for you I made this* activated conversations about America's failed mental health care system by sharing Ezra Dickinson's childhood memories living with, and unknowingly caring for, his schizophrenic mother. Ezra's Made in Seattle project began when he asked me to join him for coffee. He revealed he had made a series of solos as gifts for his mother over a seven-year period. He was now ready to share them with audiences. Might I help?

"Perhaps you haven't shared them because the proscenium stage doesn't feel right. If you could perform these solos anywhere, where would you perform them?"

"At a courthouse," he said.

I introduced Ezra to the audio walks of Janet Cardiff and George Bures Miller.[48] Ezra returned a few days later having mapped out a path for audiences through forgotten city blocks of downtown Seattle where his mother, for a brief time, lived unhoused. Sound artist Paurl Walsh was ready to collaborate. I made a call to a donor and the necessary headphones arrived in Velocity's office.

I asked Ezra, "What are your aims with this project, if anything is possible?"

"For people to feel love for my mother. And to find my mother." They had lost touch.

Building on the relationships with journalists I developed with *So You Think It's Dance?* I asked an editor if he was interested in following Ezra as he made this new work but also, as an investigative journalist, to help Ezra find his mother. He said, "Yes." But our National Public Radio arts reporter said, "My editor doesn't do dance."

"It's not about dance. It's a story about a young man raised by his single mother with schizophrenia. He just happens to be a choreographer. The difference is, after your show your listeners can experience his performance." Her editor agreed. Soon Ezra's story was picked up by every local television station and newspaper.

As Ezra and I prepared for his first radio interview I asked another question: "Who do you *really* want to be in conversation with?"

"People impacted by mental illness."

Ezra hoped to bring people together to overcome the shame and stigma of mental illness, so we held community story-circles where people shared personal stories about mental health care and how it impacts our families and society. Many participants became docents for the performances, guiding audiences through busy streets and providing information about mental health resources. There were fourteen sold-out performances. At the end of one performance a woman experiencing homelessness approached Ezra. She had been a dancer. She asked how he might help her find a pathway back to being in her body again—not in the guarded, anxious way brought about by living on the street, but in the way she remembered as a young dancer.

After another performance an elderly couple handed Ezra a photo album with the title *Ezra for you we made this*. It contained photos of Ezra as an infant.

He was meeting his grandparents. In a TEDx Talk we gave about our process, Ezra shared the project's impact:

> When I began making these gifts for my mother I felt isolated and alone when dealing with her schizophrenia. This project has been about finding place and the resource that lies in community. I have made connections with organizations that provide support to the mentally ill, and offer counseling to those who care for them. I've made connections with artists who, through their art, are processing their own mental illness or the mental illness of a loved one. Through this project I've come to the realization that I'm not alone in this subject.[49]

Applying with *Mother for you I made this*, Ezra received National Dance Project support for his next work, which was presented by OtB.

CODA

When I left Velocity in 2018, Velocity's landlord assured me, "The arts are the soul of a city." Velocity had "nothing to worry about." But two years later, a global pandemic engulfed our planet. Velocity lost its lease. But this time the organization didn't throw itself into an emergency capital campaign. It used its new network of partnerships and recent history of off-site performances to keep activating dance around Seattle and online—its resilience a testament to the artist-led, community-centered approach.

I remain more interested in what dance can be, than in what it is not. Dancing can be a spiritual practice, a medicine, a ritual of belonging, a collaborative social practice, an organizing principle, an embodied experience of thought, a way of seeing movement in the world. Creative administration can be approached in ways similar to choreographing a dance or developing an improvisational movement score: by attending to the individual elements (for example: individuals, venues, funding sources, producing opportunities, and so on) but with an emphasis on the flows of relationships between them. (How might the system move differently if we focused on intersecting relationships?) Ecosystems—including communities and arts organizations—are lived, unfolding experiences, continuously changing, multiple, and malleable.

In my first months at Velocity, I commissioned T-shirts with bold red letters: *TO DANCE IS A RADICAL ACT*. It was a signal and a sign of a sea change. Velocity was no longer defined by its building. Velocity was the people and movements who activated it. Everyone a dancer. Dance in the widest sense of the word.[50]

Administrative Experiment

Journal about one or more of the following questions, or discuss them with a trusted thought partner:

- What if you can bring everything you are to this creative moment? Is there a part of you that has felt left behind—a part you want to welcome?
- What if research and dialogue are equal parts of your creative labor? What are your questions? Who do you want to be in conversation with?
- What are your true aims for this project, if anything is possible?
- What is in your way?
- Who might help?

Thought Experiment: What if you think about your project as a durational art experience cocreated with your audience and collaborators? It exists from the first moment a person thinks about it, until the last moment they think about it. How might you choreograph moments for meaning-making and connection along the way?

PART II
LEADERSHIP

The Artist Is the Expert
An Interview with Maura Cuffie-Peterson on the Process of Developing and Running a Think Tank for Creatives Rebuild New York

Yanira Castro with Maura Cuffie-Peterson

DREAMING TOGETHER: AN INTRODUCTION

> We must lead together to work and act towards equity and shared risk in our field. This is and must be a mutual effort to radically reimagine our ecosystems.
> —*Creating New Futures: Phase 1 Working Guidelines for Ethics & Equity in Presenting Dance & Performance*[1]

In Fall 2021, I was invited to participate in the Creatives Rebuild New York (CRNY) Think Tank to advise, codesign, and advocate for a Guaranteed Income program for artists.[2] I imagine I was invited because of my work as a founding member of Creating New Futures, a group of artists, presenters, and arts workers who came together in Spring 2020 at the start of the pandemic to address the precarity of individual artists within the performance field. In our drafted call-to-action, we addressed guaranteed income, mutual aid, reparations, and other forms of reimagining just and thriving livelihoods as part of a call to transform performance systems.[3] The pandemic put a laser focus on the precarity always present in our field. Many art workers have since left the field and more are reassessing their ability to stay in a field that struggles with the will and capacity for radical change.

While I know that no singular process is a revolution and that weaving transformation/liberation is a lifelong embrace, I do hold CRNY's Think Tank process as one of those nodes of experience that personally felt like a significant shift. If replicated and expanded by other funders, programmers, festivals, and presenters, it has the potential for change. At the heart of this process, and what was so radical about it, was that it centered the expertise of the artist: that artists collectively know best what systems will work for them.

∼

The Think Tank was responsible at CRNY for codesigning its programs, actively working alongside the team and advising on real, immediate, and actionable outcomes. We were not rubber-stamping a program already imagined by CRNY or making shifts at the margins. CRNY came to the Think Tank acknowledging the power and complexities of bringing people to the table to develop programs collectively and developed methodologies for being in working conversation.

I've participated in advisory roles where there was little accountability from the organization to the advice, ideas, feedback requested from artists. Working inside late capitalism, we are all exhausted. Expediency is deemed a virtue. But the process of CRNY was distinctly different, and so this interview is an advocacy piece and an offering. I advocate for moving together, building slower, and most importantly doing the work of communing.

> *We must gather and engage in difficult, uncomfortable conversations and dig into mutual work in order to radically change our field in community with one another. We must face together the scope of the harm within our communities. This work requires deep listening, and is ongoing, slow and needs to reverberate across spaces, disciplines, communities, geographies. And so, we emphasize that this document is not the work, the work is what we do together driven not only by the desire for change but by love.*
> —Creating New Futures: Phase 2 Notes for Equitable Funding from Arts Workers[4]

I invited Maura Cuffie-Peterson, director of strategic initiatives, guaranteed income at CRNY, into a conversation to share with the field—a process, a way of working together collectively that centers the expertise of the artist as

The Artist Is the Expert

essential. It is my hope that it serves as inspiration, as a place for deeper thinking, and more importantly, transformative, communal action.

Before the interview, I am providing the following language from CRNY's website for context on how they describe their programs:[5]

> **Creatives Rebuild New York** is an extension of Mellon Foundation President Elizabeth Alexander's work on the Governor's Reimagine New York Commission in 2021. The initiative was further developed in collaboration with Emil J. Kang, Program Director for Arts and Culture at The Andrew W. Mellon Foundation, and CRNY's Executive Director Sarah Calderon, who was previously managing director of ArtPlace America.
>
> CRNY officially launched in Spring 2021 amid a national movement of broad-based employment programs that put artists back to work. These vital relief programs have helped thousands of artists maintain their livelihoods and mitigate financial disaster amid an ongoing global pandemic. Now, rooted in a belief that improving the lives of artists is paramount to the vitality of New York State's collective social and economic wellbeing, CRNY's programs build upon COVID-19 relief to envision longer-term, sustainable opportunities for artists across New York State.
>
> **CRNY's Artist Employment Program** (AEP) funds employment for up to three hundred artists, culture bearers, and culture makers (artists) in collaboration with dozens of community-based organizations across New York State for two years. Participating artists will receive a salary of $65,000 per year, plus benefits, with dedicated time to focus on their practice. Participating organizations will receive funds that range between $25,000 and $100,000 per year to support artists' employment.
>
> By supporting artists working in collaboration with community-based organizations, AEP will offer a pathway to transforming relationships between artists and organizations. Equitable relationships encourage creative solutions, expansive thinking, and new methods of engagement while building capacity and stability for all involved. CRNY believes such partnerships can also support and enrich communities, demonstrating the power of artists as agents of social change and the importance of their labor to New York State's social and economic vitality.
>
> Building off vital relief programs that put artists back to work amid the ongoing global COVID-19 pandemic, AEP seeks to support artists and orga-

nizations within historically marginalized communities—as well as artists who face systemic barriers to employment.

CRNY's Guaranteed Income for Artists program will provide regular, no-strings-attached cash payments for 2,400 artists who have financial need. Each artist will receive $1,000 per month for eighteen consecutive months.

Guaranteed income programs build safety nets to ensure that no individual falls below a defined income floor over time. They enable people to weather crises and plan for the future. CRNY's Guaranteed Income for Artists program takes inspiration from economic and racial justice movements of the past, government actors, reparations-focused philanthropists, and recent pilots and programs across the world.[6]

This interview has been edited and condensed for clarity.

YANIRA

The National Center for Choreography-Akron has given me an opportunity to try to say something about how our field is changing: artists as the bridge between twentieth-century working knowledge and twenty-first-century ecology building. And when I was thinking about what I wanted to write about, the CRNY Think Tank process kept coming back to me as one thing I've done recently that I felt had an impact.

MAURA

I'm honestly really excited that you thought of me for this and our process together. I care about process a lot. I worked before on this massive thing at ArtPlace that I loved.[7] And it was all about process and all about shifting control. Somehow I keep finding myself in these big, messy, huge, emotionally taxing, ultimately rewarding, projects.

YANIRA

I want to start with your history in trust-based philanthropy. And to dig into that a little bit because it feels to me like the work that you did in ArtPlace was a stepping-stone to the work you're doing now at CRNY. Can you give me a little of your thinking around what trust-based philanthropy is, and how that's connected to giving direct control to artists?

There's money everywhere. It needs to move.

MAURA

I think from all the things I've been a part of, it's becoming more apparent to me that the thing I care about and want to contribute my effort and time toward is moving money, because there's so much of it. There's so much of it, and it's tightly held in the wrong places.

So, just to name redistribution as a principle: it's been important to me, to center artists and the people who are impacted. In its final years, ArtPlace brought me on to answer this question: If you want the communities to have some say in how the money is spent, what would you do?

What an opportunity! I was given a lot of agency in designing that process. And it was clear to me that there should be nothing, or very little, of ArtPlace in the center of what we were doing, that it really should be about gathering and convening, creating the space for the right questions to emerge, and then providing people with the actual dollars to develop answers to them on their own terms. That work is care work. It's not straightforward. It's not easy. But it's important and it's worthwhile. And I think with the CRNY Think Tank, my hope was that we could showcase to the funders that this is worthwhile: It is worthwhile to involve people in the outcome. That in all good processes the stakes have to be shared. Otherwise, we can vision ourselves away into not doing anything.

Money doesn't solve everything, but it sure helps. And we don't actually live in scarcity. Money is tied up in endowments, in infrastructure, in investments. There's money everywhere. It needs to move. Money doesn't belong to philanthropies in the first place.

When I joined ArtPlace, it was my first time working in philanthropy, which was a beautiful and strange experience. I think most people who were on that side of the aisle, so to speak, care profoundly. They wouldn't be there if they didn't. But the longer you're there, the more jaded you see people become, the more control there is. Philanthropy exists to protect itself, and to shore up its resources, to ensure that there are more resources in the future, toward unknown problems. And that just feels like such a weird logic. So, it's not everything, but for me, what I can contribute is: How to start moving more resources in the hands of the people who are impacted by the things we're trying to shift.

Small experiments with radical intent.

YANIRA

It often feels to me inside those philanthropic systems, when I'm invited into conversations with funders, that it is about control. But my experience is that the funding programmers I'm speaking to are struggling with control. Meaning that there is a hierarchical system—the board, the bylaws, the lawyers—that makes it so that actual systemic change *seems* impossible. How do you think change happens?

MAURA

I do think we have, myself included, a short span of understanding of how change happens. So even the three years at CRNY, although it is exciting, three years isn't enough if we're going to do a great thing.

People will get money that they need right now and that's really important. But change takes twenty years or more, and focused attention and discipline. We [the philanthropic sector] haven't, myself included, haven't had discipline toward that change. We keep trying new things, new mapping projects, new this, new that. Intentional closing [of a program] can be a good thing. Decomposition, as a principle, is embedded into CRNY. We have three years to do something amazing and then something else will follow. That's in contradiction with the reality that change can take decades. There's a balance that I don't know how to strike.

What is the thing an organization must do toward collective shifting? You can't know unless you try a little bit. That's where I think experimentation is actually one key. That's something I learned through EmcArts: "small experiments with radical intent."[8] And, even so, as I'm being contradictory with this three-year CRNY initiative: it is important to try something big and splashy and see what happens. And be okay for it to fail.

YANIRA

I'm struck with what you said about the Think Tank being an opportunity to showcase to funders that a process that involves people in the outcome is worthwhile. How did it emerge that CRNY was going to do a Think Tank? What was the impetus?

MAURA

I wish I could take credit, but I actually think it's Sarah Calderon [executive director of CRNY]. Sarah's work has always been grounded in place-based neighborhood, community work—to try not to sort community without context. So, relational. I think she already had a mindset that if we're going to do this, we have to include artists in the mix. If this is about artists in New York State, we have to include them. And I think that she looked to the Local Control, Local Fields work at ArtPlace as one iteration of how to convene people and brought me on.[9] I think she did the hard work of convincing the funders that, yes, we are going to do this. It's going to take some time. I was the one who came in and said, okay, at a minimum, that's three months and this many meetings. Ideally, it'd be more. It all happened really fast. I joined in August (2021) to shape and steer the overall design of the Think Tank process as well as to lead the Guaranteed Income for Artists program.

YANIRA

There was an investment in the Think Tank process that I have rarely felt. I've been invited into other situations—feedback requests, artist advisory councils—and I've given my two cents, and I don't know that it goes anywhere, and I rarely hear back. There is little accountability. By accountability, I don't mean a particular outcome, but transparency. I have a desire for more organizations to do this kind of work with artists and pay them well to do it.[10] You made us care at CRNY by holding us accountable to one another. The caring got deep.

MAURA

The Think Tank was a really special group; finding cohesiveness like the cohesion of that group—and over Zoom—is hard. I think we're aware that people will tune in to what they're able to, and that will have to be enough. And I think that's an important aspect of any kind of gathering of folks. That's why I see it as process work and care work because you can't force people to be in the space that you want them. That's why we're shifting control, right? And I think a lot of these processes, where they go wrong, is literally your example: We just want your high-level thinking on what you think we, as an organization, should do. What should our mission be? Which is quite a controlled aspect! All right, we only want your opinion if it's not actionable.

It's risky work. Convening people makes it more complicated. So, I get why lots of folks would rather not. I've certainly been burned by the process too.

But, in the end, if I really believe in shifting power and control, then it's worthwhile. Because who am I to believe that I have the answers to how these things should happen? I think it behooves us to try to make our egos a little smaller.

What's the biggest thing we can do?

YANIRA

So how did you develop the Think Tank?

MAURA

I was trained to think about processing containers, like: What's the pot? Looking at the actual time we have and what is the container? What's the vehicle that we need? Which means we first had to do a lot of thinking: What is it that this Think Tank is doing together? Are they having some dialogue? Are they designing? Are they codesigning? What does codesign mean? If it's codesign, is it consensus-based? What are the decisions that need to be made? What are the decisions that can be made? Where are our hands bound because of legal things? Where don't we have the authority to invite someone into this decision? Where's the authority and agency? And then what's the biggest version within those constraints? What's the biggest thing we can do that still honors people's time, respects their energy and compensates them?

It was clear to me that we needed committees, subcommittees. We couldn't do everything all together, all thirty people [the size of the entire Think Tank for both GI and AEP], because that's how we would have easily spun out into not being specific enough for what we needed to do. So it was clear to me, we need to have different groups for the two programs [GI and AEP].

I knew we needed to have the groups continue to connect for transparency and accountability. I knew we had to meet more than once a month because it wouldn't get done, and it would have been shallow. It would have been impossible to move at the speed of once a week. Even the speed of twice a month [with each subcommittee] was really challenging on us as a team because we had to make sense of everything that happened, figure out what's the next move, coordinate with our facilitation team, The Federation, and do that tender dance of what we think we need versus what our facilitators think we need.[11] And then also coordinate with Tides [CRNY's fiscal sponsor] about what's possible.[12] And then do the performance that is facilitation: having presence and showing up for people and putting part of yourself in a corner so you can show up well. We couldn't facilitate it ourselves. We had to be listening. And we had to participate.

The risk of it.

YANIRA
What about the CRNY Think Tank would you replicate in future processes? And what would you not replicate?

MAURA
I would totally do it again. It's important to have the community involved in the mix. I would absolutely have facilitation teams [The Federation] that are not part of the organization. I think it was also right to have a facilitation team that was not based in New York but adjacent, Philly, not too far.

Some things I would change: I wish I had some of the authorizing people in the room. If we had Tide's legal team for a few of those [Think Tank] meetings, I think it would have made our process as a team more seamless. Some of the big work we did on the run-up to launch was tightening, addressing, figuring out, and having to prove things to the legal team.

With the Artist Employment Program—I think this happens in most processes—there was a table-flip moment. Maybe a third of the way through, the Think Tank [AEP Subcommittee] was clear, "We don't like the way y'all are doing this. And I'm not sure if we can move forward." So we really had to scrap everything and, I wouldn't say start over, but, as far as designing the process, we had to start over.

YANIRA
What wasn't working for them? And what was the shift that needed to be made so that you could go forward?

MAURA

Some of the role of the host is to do the work that no one else can or has the time to. And some of that is about accountability. Some of that is about power. But it gets tricky. Because people want to be involved. And I'm someone who—I want to prepare everything. That's my love language: I'll take care of it. I'll do it. I'll figure it out. But, if I have not even asked what people are willing to do.... If I haven't given them the opportunity to either consent or name their boundary.... Maybe they want to be involved! I seem to keep needing to learn this.

So where that shows up for that flip-the-table moment in the AEP subcommittee is: I felt that the way to move through AEP was to figure out the model. And so we had a moment where we presented three or four models. And by models, I mean:

> Organization and artists come together and work on a community project.

> All the artists join a worker-owned cooperative, and it's up to them to connect with organizations.

> Create a marketplace where we do a regional approach where there are five hubs across ten regions of New York State. In each of those hubs, we fund an anchor organization that serves as...

That's what I mean by models. So we presented those, and I think a couple of things happened. We didn't present well. We took a little too long. Our slides weren't super tight. I think we basically showed up as if it was already baked. And I think people resented that, and fairly. So, the Think Tank [AEP Subcommittee] revolted.

As a process, we [CRNY team] thought that what we were doing was shared learning. "We're going to come back to you with some models, and then we'll work on the models until we create one that makes the most sense. And then we'll figure out the details." And I think what the Think Tank said was, "We know what the model should be. If you give us the chance, give us a piece of paper, we can think about what the model should be."

And that's what we did. We basically developed the architecture: "Any employment program needs to have these kinds of things." And we pulled it apart and put it back together in different ways. Small groups on one topic, small groups about the entirety, putting it all together. At every little step

The Artist Is the Expert

CRNY tried to figure out: "We think this is what you're saying, is this, right? We think we hear this…. Is this close?" That's the finish line.

YANIRA

Can you tell me about the facilitating team, The Federation? It was miraculous to me that as much information as you were giving us, my eyes were not glazing over. And that had to do with your facilitation team, and their energy. They kept us present.

MAURA

The idea of insider/outsider is really interesting to me, in facilitation. I think the old thinking used to be: to be a good facilitator, you have to be neutral. I've just always not agreed with that, because I don't know how that's possible. And it feels really numbing, to numb yourself from being affected by the work. Whereas I feel you must be complicit. It makes the work better.

Zoom facilitation is a whole different game. And I think this team of facilitators [The Federation] are very diligent in considering: What is the decision? Or, what is the "object of movement" in this situation? Is it a task? Is it a dialogue? Is it understanding, creating? Is it making relationships?

Moving people through an activity to then say, "Oh, what I wanted you to think is this, and see by this activity, you agree!" Versus: creating a vehicle that's going to deepen our relationships so that we can have hard conversations or know in the future that we have to make decisions. That's how I think about it. What is the thing we're trying to achieve? It takes a lot of effort and doesn't always go as planned. But I think that intentionality and agenda design are deeply important.

YANIRA

The Think Tank really shaped CRNY's process. But even if you had ended up with a system that you think you would have created anyway—I wouldn't say it would have been wasted time because you still would have had artists who were invested and behind you.

MAURA

I agree with you. I think even if we ended up with the programs we thought we were going to build, I still think it's worthwhile. It would have been affirming. It would have meant that it was the right people on the team, right now, who are actually in tune with the way the ecosystem is thinking and shifting and working together. But, our programs did change. The Think Tank, I think, helped narrow what was possible. Even now, whenever we're in a moment of, "Oh, we haven't thought about this? What's the right next step?" As a team, we always say, "Well, I think that what I understood from the Think Tank: this is what they would have wanted, and, therefore, this is the decision to make." That's how our team meetings go. It really set a compass for us. Of course, the Think Tank was not a full consensus-based process. Some of the direction we take has our own interpretation and bias added, but I think that's the risk of working together and being a human. And I think that's okay.

If you can't provide the care, name it.

YANIRA

Bias is going to be in the room. It's going to be there. Awareness is critical.

MAURA

Yes, I couldn't agree more. So, for the Artists Employment Program, the [initial] idea of a three/two model—three days a week working and two days a week doing your [artistic] practice—was abolished fairly early in the Think Tank process. And what's interesting is that was one of the harder things in our [AEP] application process to try to make clear to applicants: how you negotiate working time in the employer/employee relationship.[13] I think we're going to continue to learn about what that means. There's just going to be so many kinds of collaborations, and it's our job to capture the stories. And, I don't think we have to make sense of it so that there's one best practice. Who cares? I don't know about best practices. I think it's always changing, right? But I do think it's good learning to see what's in the realm of possibility.

I also think about the language of reciprocity in the Artists Employment Program: the fact that the program is about the relationship between people. That is quite different from a workforce development lens: creating an employment program, jobs for artists, a pipeline. I'm not sure we would have come to that [the language of reciprocity].[14] I think we shared those principles, but I'm not sure we would have come to that as so central in the program, had we not gone through the Think Tank process.

We could have done a whole program that was about pipeline work: How do you get artists ready to be employed by different kinds of employers? That could have been the program.

I don't know what we would have done on our own. But the program is absolutely not a pipeline. I think in the Guaranteed Income program the real deep concern the Think Tank [GI Subcommittee] held about the details just encouraged me and gave me guidance on the little decisions that I had to make that I didn't know how to make, and to try to be as caring as possible. And sometimes that caring means a boundary: If I can't provide the care, to name it. That's actually been a huge principle for me. Hard learning, with over 22,000 applications [for GI]. I can't call everyone to tell them, "This is what happened…" I can't. There's no version of doing that. I also don't think it's right to spend hundreds of thousands of dollars to hire people to call all those people. I have to learn how to face disappointment and try to act with abundance when I can.

YANIRA

I love the lesson of the boundary. If you can't provide care, then you have to be clear about that. Rather than obfuscate. It is "care" to be honest about your limitations. The model that the Think Tank advised for AEP has a radical sense of agency: the artists develop/build with partners their own working relations. But I know for some applicants, it was confusing: they wanted to know what was "wanted" from those partnerships, so that they could shape their proposal.

MAURA

Well, it is systems change. And you can see how we've all been socialized to behave a certain way when it comes to getting money. People have been programmed to fit into what the grant wants of us.

The same was true for Guaranteed Income. I don't know how many times I've said, "It's a randomized selection process." And I'm getting Facebook messages from people that I haven't spoken to in years: "How come I didn't get it? What was the criteria? I should be in it." I'm trying to find the words to articulate that it was anonymized and randomized. No one looked at who you were to determine whether or not you were selected. We had data analysts put all these things together. And they're also over 20,000 people who applied and there are only 2,400 slots.

YANIRA

I just went through this process with the NYC public high schools, and the way a randomized process can cause anxiety because people feel that they don't have control. When I asked, "What are you upset about?" what comes out is ideas about the merit/worth of their child. They are not considering the merit/worth of the entire student body. Ultimately, they are looking for how to feel safe and control the outcome for their kid. A randomized system can trigger fear.

MAURA

Yes. We all have so little control in our lives. And I think sinking into that reality can feel dark. And maybe part of the work is finding the reverse of that.

So, the one big tension I have is the intention of being trust based, and yet, the need for verification. So, we're going through that process, and not just with our legal team, but it's all the comments on Instagram. Not all, but quite a few comments, are trying to sort of catch other people in a lie. There's a lot on the feeds about: "Did you get it? Who got it? Are they worthy?"

I think the future is also about dismantling or readdressing the idea of worthiness and "deserving" in ourselves. Our intention was for this [GI] not to be competitive. But we're really hard wired to think about money in this way. So I think there's some mindset shifts that I'd like to be paving the way for if we [CRNY] can have any role to play in that.

YANIRA

In these last couple of minutes, what are you taking with you to the future?

MAURA

I think that some of the future is: What do we know about employment versus guaranteed income? What does economic stability and flexibility look like across those two? I think the future is also, actually, for me in this work: How do we continue to align arts workers with other workers, rather than continue to separate artists as special? I think the future is building systems of support where artists are included, rather than something completely separate.

Dismantling the idea of worthiness, and that, in fact, we are all worthy, and we are all deserving. This wasn't a system to control or game. No one failed. There's no failure. If there's no competition, then there's also no failure, right?

It's one thing for me to say that and it's another thing for someone who's facing immense debt, who's learned someone is sick, who, you know, has been dreaming of this day of getting the funds. So, yeah, I think it's important for anyone who holds processes like these to not skirt over the hurt. To hold it and be present with it. I think we owe it to honor all the people who tried and who needed it.

Some of the lessons for all of us from this CRNY process: If there are 22,000 artists who have financial need, what are the systems we have in place to support them? Yeah, that's not just a three-year practice. I wonder if there's a way to talk about the magnitude and weight of that.

YANIRA

Yes. Let's put a pause here and repeat that, sit with that. If there are 22,000 New York artists who have financial need, are under the poverty line, what are the systems we have in place (as a community) to support them?

The artist is the expert.

YANIRA

The theme of this interview is that the artist is the expert that needs to be in the room. Do you see the Think Tank as a model for partnership between artists and other kinds of organizations—funders, museums, festival creators, theaters?

MAURA

I do. And beyond the arts, honestly. Other guaranteed income programs, as an example, don't do this [construct Think Tanks with the people for whom a program is intended] and should.

I see it as wide ranging. We have a lot of ails in our society. And we keep giving little startups big chunks of money, and people thinking: "I know how to fix this. I'm going to do XYZ." But what would it look like if we actually pooled the resources of the people who know, who live it. Really honor the intellect, the creativity. There's creativity to just having to live life.

I think it applies in the social service sector. I think it applies in the arts ecosystem. I think it applies in place-based work. Yeah, I really think… toward shifting, innovating administrative practices.

What if we just started to meet artists' basic needs, period. But you can't do that unless you know what artists need. And you can't know what artists need without asking them.

YANIRA

I was coming to this talk thinking about the artist as expert and how critical and transformative to the entire art ecosystem it would be to have artists deeply involved in forming all programs. But I am also walking away from this conversation considering the humanity of redefining worth in relation to community. Thank you, Maura, immensely.

Administrative Experiment

QUESTIONS FOR COMMUNING: A SCORE FOR UNFILTERED, DEEPER CONNECTION.

This is a score for two people that can be done within a group setting by pairing people.

Agree on a theme: a project you are working on, a problem you have encountered, the reason you have gathered.

This is a score for unfiltered/nonpredetermined questions. It is one that needs to take place with consent and with care. Before engaging the score, define consent and care together. Unfiltered questions might be risky.

The questions emerge when you enact the score: spontaneously, improvised, in the moment, unconscious. You may be surprised about what emerges. The questions may not immediately make "sense." They may not be on topic. None of this matters. Once you begin with questions, let them move through you. Don't try to remember them. Let them pass through.

∼

Face one another. Take time to shift your bodies, without verbalizing, so that you feel that you are on an even plane together, that you are sharing a space.

This will depend entirely on the bodies and the space that you are in. Take time for micro-shifts, for larger shifts.

You have come to an understanding of shared space when you find stillness. Let this take at least five generous minutes. If you have found stillness before a felt five minutes, be in silent equilibrium together.

In the presence of each other, in this stillness, (take time): one of you (without pre-deciding) begins to pour out questions on your agreed theme. The pace of this pouring is entirely dependent on the person: a rush, a dribble, a singular drop. But it lasts for at least five minutes. And if there are no more questions, be in silence.

The person receiving the questions can shift in any way they need to. This pouring is done when a felt five minutes has passed and there is silence.

Without verbalizing, you switch roles, shifting your bodies together as may be needed/desired (you might shift to another space, to another relationship to the ground, to yourselves). The second person pours questions, and the other receives. When the second pouring is done, be in stillness and let the questions resonate between you. Let that take longer than might feel comfortable.

Then together, give time to name the questions between you. If there was harm, name it. If there was surprise, pleasure, bafflement, revel in it. There is no one way of doing this. Do it together.

Embodying Equity-Driven Change
A Journey from Hierarchy to Shared Leadership
Cherie Hill, Hope Mohr and Karla Quintero

HOW DO WE IMPLEMENT EQUITABLE MODELS OF LEADERSHIP IN DANCE?

A commitment to equity in arts administration requires more than the transient opportunities and progressive optics that come with diversity. Diversity alone does not change power relationships. A commitment to equity in arts administration requires a long-term, activist commitment to change power structures. This is a story of how we have put that commitment into practice.

We are Hope Mohr, Karla Quintero, and Cherie Hill, the first codirectors of Bridge Live Arts (formerly HMD/The Bridge Project), an arts organization based in unceded Ohlone Territory, colonially known as the San Francisco Bay Area. Our mission is to create and present equity-driven live art that centers artists as agents of change.

Starting in 2020, Bridge Live Arts made the transition from a hierarchical, founder-led, choreographer-led organization, to a codirectorship and model of distributed leadership. Our model continues to evolve as we explore opportunities for shared decision-making over programs, money, and vision among staff, board members, and artist partners.

Distributed leadership is an umbrella term for what consultant Mike Courville refers to as a participatory approach, an "intentional effort to include people in decision making from many different levels within organizations."[1] Distributed leadership models are dynamic, emergent, and unique to each organization. Over the past two years, we have seen interest in distributed leadership rise in the arts as organizations grapple with white supremacy in their internal structures. This interest has put us in conversation with new allies in the field who are also looking to transform their ways of working. There are many stories; this is ours.

STRUCTURAL MOVES

Distributed leadership implicates both public-facing programs and internal organizational structures. Often there is a disconnect between the two. This disconnect can show up in many ways: program staff may be ahead of board members in terms of their commitment to cultural equity; demographics of the staff or a board may not reflect the artists that an organization serves; an artistic director may employ a collaborative ethos in the studio, while organizational decisions remain top-down. All these schisms suggest that the organization has work to do to value-align its internal structures with a commitment to equity.

Faced with these disconnects, we had work to do. Our decision to move to a model of distributed leadership was a moral imperative bound up in our commitment to cultural and racial equity. In the words of our public announcement about our shift to distributed leadership:

> There is no such thing as a race-neutral arts organization; every arts organization is producing either racial inequity or equity. A commitment to institutional restructuring is an essential step in becoming an inclusive, anti-racist, multicultural organization. As our programs became increasingly driven by a commitment to cultural and racial equity, it became clear that there was a pressing need for the organization to evolve toward distributed leadership and increase artist ownership over programs. Only in this way could we align our internal structures with the values that drive our programs.

When it is value-driven, distributed leadership must be more than moving items from the founder or director's "to-do" list onto someone else's. It must be more than cosmetic or perfunctory title changes.

We've found many benefits to distributed leadership, including:

- Maximizing creativity by opening up space for everyone's ideas and initiatives;
- Increasing staff ownership over their work;

- Creating a more sustainable organization by preventing founder burnout and locating energy in multiple people;
- Building trust and relationships with a wider community; and
- Creating opportunities for learning and change within the organization.

WHAT DOES IT LOOK LIKE TO DISTRIBUTE POWER?

For Bridge Live Arts, the shift to distributed leadership has involved the following structural shifts:

- Working with an equity-driven consultant (Safi Jiroh of LeaderSpring) to help us navigate the power shift mindfully and show us our blind spots;
- Announcing our plan to move to a model of distributed leadership to the community;
- Convening a series of community meetings about what our distributed leadership model could look like (with all participants paid);
- Founder moving off selection panels for artist partners to disentangle founder from programs and aesthetics;
- Founder moving off the board; changing founder seat to rotating staff seat;
- Transitioning to a board of 100 percent working artists;
- Moving to a cocuratorial model for all public programs;
- Launching a paid curatorial Artist Council with authority over 30 percent of our production budget;
- Implementing pay equality across the organization so that dancers and codirectors are all paid the same hourly starting wage (with conversations ongoing about measures to ensure equitable pay, including cost of living increases and how to reflect seniority in wages);
- Revising our values, operating principles, and mission statement;
- Meeting with funders as a team to shift those crucial relationships out of the founder's exclusive control;
- Renaming the organization from "Hope Mohr Dance" to "Bridge Live Arts."

Embodying Equity-Driven Change 73

Bridge Live Arts
Timeline of Structural Moves

2020 FEB
- Hired Leaderspring
- Board transitions to 100% working artists
- Announced move to distributed leadership

JUN
- Community meetings
- Implement pay equality across the org, dancers and administrators are now paid the same rate

JUL
- White founder steps off of artist selection panels

AUG
- Unpacking & redistributing staff power
- Meetings w/ funders

SEP
- Board & staff retreat

DEC 2021
- New Mission, Values & Operating Principles

FEB
- More unpacking & redistributing staff & organizational power

JUL
- More meetings w/ funders

OCT
- Paid Artist Council with power over 30% of program budget

JAN 2022
- Founder steps off the board
- Transition founder board seat to rotating staff seat.

MAY
- Organizational name change and rebranding to *Bridge Live Arts*
- Artistic Director transitions to a resident choreographer

ORGANIZATIONAL CULTURE CHANGE

Beyond structural changes, distributed leadership must be a parallel shift in organizational culture—a change in how work gets done on a daily basis. Some of the ways an organization's internal culture must shift in order for distributed leadership to be meaningful include

- Certainty → Uncertainty
- Culture of efficiency → Culture of democracy
- Action-oriented → Process-oriented
- Founder/Director time → Multiple approaches to time
- Cult(ure) of personality → Culture of community
- Culture of control → Culture of trust
- Fixed roles → Fluid roles
- Diversity mindset → Equity mindset
- "People of color are who we serve" → "How can we give power to people of color?"
- Regranting/Gatekeeping resources → Facilitating direct artist access to resources

Shifting to a model of distributed leadership is time-consuming, slow, and expensive. It floods the organization with uncertainty: What's my role in this meeting? Will the organization lose its funding? Whom do we serve now? Often, especially in times of crisis, arts leaders hunker down and prioritize organizational survival above all else. But a logic of scarcity works against the acceptance of uncertainty that shifting leadership models requires.

THREE PERSPECTIVES ON MOVING TO DISTRIBUTED LEADERSHIP

HOPE MOHR

I founded Hope Mohr Dance in 2008 with the intent of creating an organizational platform for my choreographic work. When we began the shift to a model of distributed leadership, I had been running the organization for twelve years. The work of transitioning a hierarchical organization to an equity-driven model of shared power is emotionally challenging—and worth it. I want to talk about the challenges inherent in this work in the hopes that others will decide to commit to similar journeys of organizational transformation.

Because the art world has historically been white-dominated, changing power structures in the arts means that white people need to reposition themselves. Repositioning, unlike diversity, asks white people to give up power. As a white person in the arts, repositioning myself means that I must redefine what leadership means—through an equity lens. Arts leadership needs to look different depending on position, perspective, and privilege.

Below are some ways I am questioning and redefining my leadership as a white person in dance.

CHANGING MY RELATIONSHIP TO TIME

Transitioning to a model of distributed leadership has asked me to shift my relationship to time. For over ten years, I ran HMD prioritizing efficiency, perfection, and quick response. In some ways, this approach served the organization well: we have a strong record of securing grants and opportunities. But as cultural and racial equity became a priority, this approach no longer reflected our values. Now, instead of responding immediately to an email, I need to wait. I need to let someone else respond or I need to bring other people into the decision. Democratic process takes more time than fiat.

Moving to pay equality has had a big impact on my relationship, as a founder, to time. For years, I worked constantly with no idea how many hours I put into the organization. Now, I track my time. For so long, the organization was my "baby"—inextricably wrapped up in my personality. When the organization experienced success or setbacks, I took it personally. The concrete step of tracking my time helped me build a boundary between my personal life and work. Tracking my time also translated the work into discrete, tangible tasks, which in turn made it easier to delegate the work to others.

CHANGING THE ORGANIZATIONAL NARRATIVE

I have had to learn how to make space for those stepping into power to shape, share, and own the organization's story. It's important to tell the story of distributed leadership to the community. And it's important to distribute who controls that narrative. Power is both felt and perceived. Although staff may make a shift to sharing power, it may take a long time for funders to stop assuming that they should call the founder first. If the organization carries the founder or artistic director's name, this is an obstacle to the community believing that the organization operates on a model of distributed leadership.

One mistake I made early on came from my desire to control the organizational narrative: I did not give my codirectors of color space and time to vision the future of the organization. As people of color move into leadership, it's crucial that their voices are heard. Do staff have the time, interest, and bandwidth to assume positions of expanded power? How do new leaders of color feel and think about the organizational shift and their new roles? Do they have the tools they need?

Another narrative shift related to equity-driven distributed leadership is recognizing the assumption that often exists within arts organizational narratives that people of color are people whom the organization "serves." This assumption, common in language that white-led and regranting organizations use in funding applications, positions people of color in the passive, subservient role of receiving help. This assumption denies agency to people of color and ignores that many people of color are cultural leaders.

CHALLENGES TO THE WORK
MOVING BACK: IT'S PERSONAL

Shifting power is hard because it's personal. Inability or unwillingness to share power are not mere business decisions. These are emotionally charged habits of moving through the world. These habits can take the form of complacency, habit, self-interest, fear, ego, inertia, lack of imagination, and a sense of being underappreciated and even victimized. When faced with challenges to their power, white people often assume defensive postures such as denial, defensiveness, perfectionism, retreat into intellectualism, self-absorption, silence, criticism, numbness, and urgency.[2] These defensive postures prevent white people from engaging fully in the work of changing power dynamics.

After years of struggling to build their careers, white artists may feel wronged if they forgo opportunity. As a feminist, I have sometimes felt a tension between my commitments to cultural equity and feminism: moving back sometimes feels contrary to feminist teachings that tell me, as a woman, that it's important to take up space to counter how patriarchy undervalues women.

Knowing when and how to move back can be confusing and difficult for many white artists and curators. Trans performance theorist Julian Carter asks, "What is the line between stepping back and retreating into white silence?"[3]

Not taking things personally is a prerequisite to sharing power. Faced with criticism, white people must check their reactions and make "a commitment not to panic, overread, or catastrophize."[4] This is counterintuitive for white people and takes work.[5] Some questions that may prevent white curators, founders, and directors from relinquishing organizational power include: What about my career? Didn't I start the organization and build it from the ground up? The company has my name in it! Yes. And now it's time for change.

We need to situate arts leadership within the context of social movements for racial justice, as opposed to organizational bottom line or career. This work is larger than any one person or institution. Often, despite myself and my politics, I perpetuate structures I want to disavow. In the course of trying to hand over power, I catch myself focusing on my own interests; conversations about decentering whiteness often end up centering whiteness. These patterns are insidious even in the context of virtuous work. Prison abolitionist Ruth Wilson Gilmore says that "our focus should not be on organizational (or career) preservation, but on furthering the movement of which an organization is a part."[6]

When a white cultural leader steps back from socially engaged work, it threatens to reify the assumption that socially engaged art is not white people's work, but the domain of people of color. How can white people redistribute power without avoiding the structural work of antiracism? In moving back, how can white people not withdraw our resources, networks, and position, but connect people of color directly with these existing assets?

Inside, moving back, there is always a choice. I can step back and withdraw emotionally. Or I can step back and stay accountable and engaged. Choosing the latter requires that I resist ancient habits of avoiding emotional exposure. At times, a more accurate image for the work might be "moving to the side": making space for other voices while staying in relationship. How can I move back without disappearing? How can I show up in the world in a different way?

THE LINE AT THE STUDIO DOOR

Distributed leadership challenges the cult of personality common in the arts. The single choreographer vision has been the dominant model for making and promoting Western concert dance since the late eighteenth century. In the twentieth and early twenty-first centuries, many dance companies, like those of Alvin Ailey, Mark Morris, Martha Graham, and Alonzo King, began anchored in the work of a singular choreographer, but then expanded into additional programs associated with a school, residency, or community outreach.

As a white artist who has created an organization first to serve my own work and then later branched out into social justice-driven public programming, I have many questions. In the studio environment, control over authorship has different stakes than in the curatorial decisions of a theater or the pedagogical decisions of a school. How might distributed leadership manifest differently in these different realms? What are the implications of distributed leadership for choreographic practice? Is it necessary to disentangle public programs from the founding choreographer's artistic work for the organization to evolve? Does committing to distributed leadership as a curator mean that I need to resign from my position as a choreographer?

These questions have been the trickiest for me in the work of distributing leadership. They touch on my identity as an artist. They implicate financial viability (does the organization's financial future rest in my choreographic voice or in work that serves a broader community or social movements?). These shifts can also be confusing for donors and patrons. In response to a survey we sent out to our entire mailing list (donors, audience members, artists, funders) regarding our shift to distributed leadership, a major donor asked: "I always thought HMD's purpose was to be a place for Hope to express her artistic vision. Does Hope have to give up her vision in order to repair inequities?" For me, this question misses the point. What if repairing inequities is part of my vision as an artist?

I've spoken with several established white choreographers who support the sharing of power in some aspects of their organization but draw the line at the studio door. "It's what I do," said one, explaining why she will not give up her role as a single-author choreographer. "It's who I am," echoed another. Sharing power challenges us to let go of the stories we tell about ourselves. For white arts leaders, implementing new models means breaking habits of self-interest and the logics of scarcity. In the studio, as artists we must ask, "What does the work need?" and "Who is the work for?" As administrators, curators, and organizational leaders, the questions are the same. How can we respond with listening, observation, and imagination?

WHITE FOUNDER LEARNINGS

Lessons I continue to learn in the work of distributed leadership:

- Start with values. When you're trying to change a system, if the root values haven't changed, the new system will grow to look like the old one.

- Do your own cultural competency work. Don't expect other people to educate you about racial justice issues.
- Cultivate a sense of identity separate from the organization.
- Hire an equity-driven consultant to hold safe space for difficult conversations and call people on their blind spots.
- Stay in relationship. Moving back need not mean disengagement or emotional withdrawal.
- Ask people moving into leadership what they want and need. As you shift position, don't just dump labor into BIPOC laps.
- Transform structures. Don't just recast who holds power in a toxic system.
- Frame the work as an affirming, exciting aspect of your creative practice. Don't succumb to a victim or martyr narrative of renunciation.
- Stop trying to control the public-facing story of the organization's change.
- Actually give up power, don't just wiggle around in your current operating context. Without a real shift in power, institutions will shapeshift, and racial inequities will retrench.
- Translate distributed leadership models in the arts into language that donors can understand and get excited about.
- Put organizational change in the context of social movement, not the organization's financial bottom line.
- Bring the wisdom of our moving bodies to the work. Organizations tend to calcify. Like skilled dancers, we must constantly reawaken ourselves and our organizations to respond to a changing world. We can build authentic community by constantly aligning our intentions and our structures with collective liberation.

KARLA QUINTERO

Bridge Live Arts' approach to distributed leadership evolved in three strands:

Strand 1: HMD / The Bridge Project's three staff members (Cherie Hill, Hope Mohr, and I) transition to codirecting The Bridge Project.

Strand 2: Staff and board, in conversation, reimagine the function of the board.

Strand 3: Staff engage artist partners in decision-making and power-sharing, through initiatives like our paid curatorial Artist Council.

Each of these strands is ongoing, and we have by no means arrived at our deepest expression of distributed leadership. Nonetheless, they represent concrete steps toward a more people-centric, equity-driven organizational model.

STRAND 1: FORMING A CODIRECTORSHIP

When Hope Mohr, founder of Hope Mohr Dance and The Bridge Project, and someone I worked for as a dancer and administrator, approached me about codirecting The Bridge Project, my first reaction was one of skepticism. Though I know Hope to be a generous, dependable, and aware person, my mind and heart instantly felt dread as I replayed past work traumas and considered what this role would mean for me within the field.

I identify as a Latin American woman. The daughter of Nicaraguan and Colombian immigrants, I grew up in a mostly Spanish-speaking neighborhood in New York City, in a community that has fallen to gentrification. I began my "professional" career as a dancer at the age of thirty. I currently divide my time between my work as a performing artist and as codirector of Bridge Live Arts.

Prior to my life in dance, I worked for an advocacy group coleading pedestrian safety campaigns for New York City's seniors and within low-income, immigrant communities. At twenty-one, I was one of only a handful of women of color publicly active on pedestrian safety issues in New York City. I enjoyed my work, our mission, and my colleagues. As the only Spanish speaker on staff, I was given a lot of responsibility right off the bat that I didn't feel prepared for and leadership opportunities that often lacked structural support. The questions that circled persistently in the recesses of my mind were: Why was I being entrusted with so much responsibility? Was it out of necessity, or was it symbolic?

When Hope approached me and Cherie about stepping into codirectorship, similar concerns resurfaced. In addition, I had new concerns about whether stepping into codirectorship would obscure, and in turn limit, my work as a performing artist. In our first meeting with consultant Safi Jiroh, I was able to voice and discuss these concerns directly with Hope and Cherie well in advance of making any decisions about how our working relationships would shift.

For any team stepping into codirectorship, but particularly for a team that is multiethnic and multiracial like ours, conversations unpacking tokenism and the unique costs and benefits for those involved are as vital to the success of the endeavor as are conversations about roles and responsibilities. Since concluding our work with Safi, we continue to have monthly codirector team meetings where we break down how distributed leadership is manifesting and track the impact of our efforts to distribute organizational power. These meetings also serve as a space to continue to practice open communication around our needs and challenges so we can move in this direction together.

STRAND 2: BOARD TRANSFORMATION

According to *Nonprofit Quarterly*, "the principal roles of the board of directors are to represent the public interests in [an] organization and to represent the organization as its legal voice."[7] A nonprofit board leads organizational governance, a term which covers oversight for organizations, large-scale planning, and overall direction of the nonprofit. It is also common practice in the arts sector for board members to play a central role in helping money flow to an organization—from businesses and corporations, their personal networks, and even themselves.

Bridge Live Arts' (then known as HMD/The Bridge Project) 2018 board prospectus reflects this default model by outlining primary expectations for future members: fundraising; networking with presenters, donors, and cultural influencers; and expertise in nonprofit management, special events, and fundraising. Early in our move to distributed leadership, we began to question how board priorities might shift in alignment with our organizational values.

Data from the 2021 Leading with Intent,[8] BoardSource's index of best nonprofit board practices, revealed that regardless of organizational commitments to diversity, equity, and inclusion, nonprofit boards, by and large, do not represent the communities they serve. In 2018, before our move to distributed leadership, Bridge Live Art's board was no exception. Our board was majority white, whereas our programs primarily served artists of color.

Our 2018 board members were extremely dedicated. As administrative manager, I witnessed them support Hope Mohr and The Bridge Project in countless ways—through facilitating in-kind donations, making personal donations, sharing marketing and branding wisdom, and attending performances. They rallied around fundraising campaigns and decisions in favor of higher artists' pay. They unanimously supported our transition to codirectorship. Nevertheless, we saw a need to shift the board to a model more inclusive and reflective of the community of artists we are in partnership with. A board that had a personal understanding of the dynamics within communities of color.

We began this transition, as we do most of our work, in dialogue—with existing board members and potential board members. As the organization shifted to distributed leadership, two of the five members transitioned off the board of directors, but they continue to serve via our advisory council and as donors. Our 2022 board is now more racially diverse (80 percent of members identify as BIPOC) and it is 100 percent composed of practicing artists.

In September 2020, Jiroh helped organize a board visioning retreat, among the redwoods, where staff and board discussed their visions for the board within the organization's new structure. During this retreat, we learned of aspects of the current board culture that members wanted to retain. Pre-pandemic, board meetings always began with a sharing of food and socializing. Board members wanted to preserve this social vibe and soft entry into meeting agendas. They also appreciated HMD's tradition of staff attendance and participation in board meetings. We learned that a barrier to deeper participation from board members was confusion around how to support the organization outside of traditional functions, such as fundraising, in particular when their expertise rested in other areas.

A lot has shifted since this first conversation. Our board prospectus, reimagined with the leadership of current board member Tristan Ching Hartmann, now states: "Expectations for the *Bridge Live Arts* board differ from those of conventional boards. Board members are not required to have prior board experience, nor are they expected to make a financial donation. However, board members are asked to make a contribution of their time or resources that feels personally significant and meaningful." "Passion for the arts, as well as a commitment to anti-racism and equity" are now priorities, as is a "willingness to question and step away from traditional organizational structures and traditional ways of thinking."

Since this initial meeting, board members are now active on the organization's equity committee, a space for engaging in deeper conversations around how we are furthering equity; former board member Suzette Sagisi took leadership over a staff and board brainstorming process to develop our new organizational mission; and current board members Tristan Ching Hartmann, Sophia Wang, and Megan Wright have also been instrumental in dreaming up our inaugural community party, an annual celebration by and for Bridge Live Arts' artistic community.

STRAND 3: DEEPER ARTIST PARTNERSHIPS

As part of Bridge Live Arts' move toward distributed leadership, we hosted three community meetings inviting past and present artist partners (HMD dancers, current and former Bridge Project artists) to be in dialogue around this transition. Staff shared a desire to be in relationship with artist partners more long term, whereas artists expressed interest in curating.

Bridge Live Arts had engaged guest curators to nominate artist rosters since 2016. However, program visioning, decision-making, and implementation were by and large led by staff. This way of staff-led curating was bolstered by the arts funding infrastructure, which before 2020 required artists and organizations to provide granular details up front about future productions in funding requests. This requirement limited the time we had to cocurate and vision our programming in cooperation with artist partners. To arrive at a deeper expression of distributed leadership, one that shifted organizational resources and curatorial power into the hands of artist partners (and more specifically artists historically underrepresented by arts institutions), we needed to internally prioritize process over production, even if in conflict with funder processes. Our 2021 Anti-Racism in Dance Series seemed like a great place to start this transition.

I reached out to David Herrera (artistic director/choreographer with David Herrera Performance Company, cultural bearer, and former Community Engagement Residency artist) and Mario Ismael Espinoza (social worker and former professional dancer), whom I had been in conversation with throughout the pandemic around equity issues specific to Latinx artists. Without a specific vision in mind, I asked if they would like to cocurate an event for the series. Cocuration felt organic, an extension of dialogues we had been having around decolonization, anti-oppression work, and uplifting artists. We coalesced around a vision for an online exhibit featuring recorded, bilingual interviews that would explore liberation, anti-oppression, and concepts of decolonization from the lens of the personal—a platform for Latinx, Indigenous, and Hispanic artists to tell their own stories, in all their multidimensional glory, free of the reductive framing of North American media. *Danzac-*

uentos: Voz, Cuerpo, Y Raíces was rooted in the question: *What can we learn when we listen to the lived experiences of Latinx, Indigenous, and Hispanic artists?* It spotlighted four dance artists: Snowflake Calvert, sisters Dulce and Marianna Escobedo, Cinthia Pérez Navarro, and Lyvan Verdecia.[9]

Conversations around values, purpose, and shared interests served as our bedrock, which in turn made decisions around program structure, implementation, artist curation, and event format flow with ease. I credit their voices and our cocuration with opening up this new, intimate pathway to social justice in the arts.

CHALLENGES TO THE WORK
FUNDING PATTERNS AND CLASS DYNAMICS

If the arts are to become more inclusive and equitable, the entire ecosystem must rethink funding models and grapple with class. In an essay published in Community-Centric Fundraising's blog, Sidra Morgan-Montoya speaks to the current impasse many folks working to challenge power imbalances and funding models in the nonprofit sector are experiencing:

> It's a little like setting off to explore the wilderness of radical change, only to realize you're in a man-made hedge maze leading in one direction. Each bend of the maze is erected by a network of public and private entities—including the state, businesses, individuals, and nonprofits themselves—who make decisions that uphold the power each of them has in society. The result is a labyrinth that restricts how we can move within nonprofits, funneling our work in certain directions and walling off others. It turns radical possibilities into dead ends, ensures that the path of least resistance is one that does not challenge those in power, and amplifies corporate and state interests over the voices of those most impacted by inequity.[10]

Radical change doesn't happen in a vacuum. Funders in the arts committed to inclusion and equity need to be in dialogue with artists, collectives, and organizations to ensure that they are including support for the inward-facing, longer-term work that undergirds radical change, and not erecting new structures to uphold inequity. For example, multiyear operating support is crucial to both organizational sustainability and change, yet this kind of support remains scarce. A recent study by the Center for Effective Philanthropy confirmed that this vital support makes up only 12.4% of all grants in the United States.[11]

To add, access to institutional funding for POC-led nonprofits remains walled off. Insight Center executives Annie Price and Jhumpa Bhattacharya expand on why this is a systemic issue and not an individual experience:

The lack of accessibility in the philanthropy space echoed by multiple leaders of color shows that this is not an individual experience, but rather a collective one. The results of this lack of investment mean that impact is kept at the margins—POC-led nonprofits cannot maximize their impact if they are constantly chasing after a tiny grant for a few dollars here and there to cobble together the next year's budget.[12]

Radical change requires multiyear investment in artists, collectives, and organizations by and for people of color. For organizations that have shifted from white founder-led to shared leadership, like Bridge Live Arts, funders need to be open to building relationships with the full, more diverse leadership team.

In the case of boards, many in the arts function as fundraising engines, and as a result tend to be populated by wealthy individuals.[13] Making boards more inclusive means rethinking this model. Traditionally, upper-class folks have subsidized arts nonprofits. As we democratize organizations, is it also possible to democratize our funding sources?

CHERIE HILL

Equity and inclusion are two values that I hold dear, and movements I strive toward. To be equitable means I am thinking about the needs of those who are marginalized, and to practice inclusion means there is space available for others to join. At the center of our work are artists, and the inclusion of artists has been integral to our building of distributed leadership from the start. I was thankful for this because as our world shifted in 2020, the importance of equity and inclusion became even more apparent.

With the help of our consultant group, LeaderSpring, we held three vision meetings with multiple artists involved in The Bridge Project. With facilitation, many artists boldly and passionately expressed opinions around the organization dismantling whiteness and decentering Hope's work as the white founder. They asked questions about ways Karla and my experiences and ideas would be included, and how collective leadership could emerge. Hearing these voices as a codirector newer to the organization was greatly impactful, and when I curate and participate in decision-making, I often think back to what was stated in these 2020 community meetings. I know that building this distributed leadership (DL) model is not all about me and that it is growing in conjunction with the opinions and concerns voiced in these early DL meetings. How can we as codirectors make decisions, and hold the wisdom of the artists we work with?

One of my favorite parts about our DL process is that the programs we curate are also our training. The wisdom of the body is a shared value of Bridge Live Arts artists and staff, and our leadership is supported by embodied knowledge. All staff are encouraged to participate in the workshops we hold, and participating in the workshops we curate provides professional development. One workshop I was deeply impacted by is "The Keystone of the Arch: Embodied 100 Years Vision," taught by Tammy Johnson and Yalini Dream. This workshop is one of the first that we cocurated for *Power Shift: Improvisation, Activism, and Community*. Tammy and Yalini opened the portal for us to envision, move, and think about what a just world could look like fifty and one hundred years from now, along with the steps to arrive there.

For me, leading is largely based on faith and vision. Growing up as a Black person in America, I learned that the dominant society has been programmed to show me that achieving in life is hard and that people like me struggle more than others due to in my case race, gender, class, religion, and spirituality. When you are constantly working to survive, dreaming and visioning become luxuries rather than part of the work, at least this is largely taught. Remembering these society-prescribed norms is important, especially when working with leaders of color, and making space for shared leaders to dream and vision together is essential to creating an inclusive environment. I consciously hold onto the visioning I participated in at the Keystone of the Arch workshop while I work with staff and board members on evolving the organization; similar to how I think back to the artists' voices I heard early in our DL process. Bringing these aspects into the "room" and decision-making process helps ensure that my work continues to be in a type of partnership with community input.

In addition to cocurating The Bridge Project, codirectors have worked together to reenvision and structure the Community Engagement Residency (CER) program to be more equitable and revolve around artists' needs. This is a program I took the lead on when I joined HMD. Some of the advances we have made include:

- Moving the CER application from an invite-only process to an open application.
- Hope as the founder stepped off the application committee; applicant decisions shifted to being made by myself, Karla, and past CER artists.

Embodying Equity-Driven Change

- CER projects do not require performance or public showing; artists are supported for work that significantly engages with the community.
- Professional development workshops and resources are based on the cohort's needs.

CHALLENGES TO THE WORK

What attracted me to the invitation to join Hope and Karla in DL was that it felt creative and open. As a woman of color and a newer leader in the arts, I have found working with founders can be challenging for different reasons. One is that when you join founders in executive leadership, the playing field is never even. There is no way that in six months, or even years, one could have the same knowledge, commitment, and connections that a founding executive leading an organization for over a decade has. Second, many employers expect leaders to fit into a position and its status quo, leaving little opportunity for creativity. Luckily, this invitation did not come with a specific job title or contract; instead joining leadership was more of an invitation to collaborate and experiment, which was something I found an interest in, so I said, "Yes."

As a Black woman working in the nonprofit sector, I found knowledge of white supremacy cultural norms essential to understanding the dynamics often embedded within arts organizations. Before having language such as *a sense of urgency, worship of the written word, perfectionism, either-or thinking,* and so on,[14] I did not know how to explain the awful feelings I experienced. Knowing these terms has helped me name decisions, language, and practices that can be harmful and oppressive within myself, my colleagues, and our organization.

Everyone involved in a distributed leadership process needs to take accountability for their actions. Relying on Black or POCs to keep equity in check is unsustainable. Sharing leadership requires all on board to commit to doing their best to change harmful habits and adopt healthy practices. POCs taking time and space for extra love and care for themselves is essential.

As codirectors of different identities, we named some white supremacy cultural norms that we saw interpersonally and within the organization early in our distributed leadership process. We participate in antiracism and microaggression trainings, and we continue to work on strategies to build an antiracist and inclusive culture.

Distributed leadership requires others to take on more responsibility so the person who was once the sole decision-maker can step back. This labor can go unrecognized and needs to be explicitly acknowledged. Hope realized she was not fully acknowledging how the coleaders of color were now cobuilding the organization's future. As coleaders, we are adding to Hope's legacy as a white founder. We have found there is a tendency in the eyes of those close to the organization's older model, and the press, to fail to recognize and value the labor of the new coleaders. A question that needs to be explored is, "How can we prioritize recognizing the labor of leaders of color moving into shared leadership?"[15]

Administrative Experiment

CALL TO ACTION: POWER MAPPING IN YOUR ORGANIZATION

Organizational change can happen regardless of your budget size, staff size, and operating context. In conclusion, we offer the following call to action. Unpack where power sits in your organization on a granular level. Who has powers of implementation? Who holds the big picture of the organization's financial capacity? Who has access to budgets? Who has the authority to sign contracts with artists? Who writes the checks? Who holds funder and donor relationships? Who has control over the art? Survey your staff to learn each person's answers. Set up a spacious meeting in a neutral location, perhaps outdoors, to compare perspectives, share answers, and discuss how you want to shift who has power over what. Get specific about what these shifts will look like. For example, you might identify that the white founder has historically single-handedly held relationships with funders and that you as a team want to redistribute these powerful relationships by having a series of team meetings with key funders. These are just some examples of action moves that can begin to implement your vision of shared leadership.

ACKNOWLEDGMENTS

We want to thank Safi Jiroh and LeaderSpring for their invaluable support and teachings in our work of distributing leadership.

Crafting Relationships and Modes of Support
Recognizing the Work of Manager/Producers

Katy Dammers
with Nora Alami, Chelsea Goding-Doty, Aaron Mattocks,
Marýa Wethers, and Miranda Wright

Barbara Bryan opened our meeting by telling a story. She recalled being at the culmination of a decade-long process of experimental dance research that included a week-long run of performances and a companion video installation of documentation. One day a box office manager, seeing Barbara loitering in the lobby, recommended she go into the theater and see the screening. Barbara remarked that she was intimately familiar with the material—as the project director she had been an integral part of its creation and development, traveling with the piece over the past several years. The box office manager looked at Barbara with surprise, noting that there was no mention of her name in the film's credits or special thanks section. If Barbara was so involved throughout the duration of the project, why wasn't she acknowledged?

As Barbara spoke, many of us sitting around the table nodded in agreement, recognizing ourselves and our experiences in Barbara's story. Lili Chopra, then-director of the Lower Manhattan Cultural Council (LMCC), had brought us together to talk about our experiences as part of the newest generation of dance managers and producers. Over the last several years, we had met regularly to discuss our work with choreographers. This forum served as a critical space to articulate the diversity of our practices, provide peer-to-peer support, and advocate for the importance of the manager/producer role in the dance field. While I have worked independently with dance artists over the past decade, this group was the first time I spoke intentionally with others about how I have learned to work with artists, what my practice is, and why I do it. In a field where the work of a manager/producer is often invisible and where that work is often done independently, it was liberating to gather and share our experiences. In these conversations I had moments of revelation, compassion, and sadness as we shared our ways of working together, our challenges, and our hopes for a changing field.

We found that our practices were different—individually crafted specifically for each context, in relationship with each artist's needs, and in dialogue with our own desires. There is little standardization in this field, and working methods and pay rates vary widely. Much of this diversity comes from the reality that each manager/producer crafts their role in relationship with an artist as a complex, intimate duet. This essay includes both my own work and that of my peers to demonstrate the breadth of methods and means, while grounding this writing in the personal and complicated realities from where my own practice develops. I have worked with dance artists as an independent manager/producer for the last ten years, and the bulk of my time has been spent with choreographers Rashaun Mitchell + Silas Riener, in addition to Jennifer Monson, Donna Uchizono, and Tere O'Connor. As much as my practice is my own, it is a product of the unique qualities of the artists I work with, the places we present work, and the realities of the times. It is my hope that this writing will help illuminate what manager/producers do, how they do it, and why. While this work is crucial, it is poorly recognized, in large part because it is underfunded and little understood. I hope additional insight might start to change that reality.

~

When Rashaun + Silas and I first began working together in the fall of 2013 I used the title project manager, which felt fitting since my work was focused on the development of their piece *Way In* at Danspace Project. After that premiere, we decided to continue working together in a longer-term capacity, and ultimately landed on the title general manager. We chose this title because I hoped to be for Rashaun + Silas what Nancy Umanoff, general manager for the Mark Morris Dance Group, was for Mark Morris—chief organizer and partner in visioning. I had seen Nancy in action during my time as Mark's research assistant and later marketing intern and was impressed by her strength.[1] Mark had told me that much of his success was due to Nancy, and I wanted to be the kind of person who worked hard to help achieve artistic dreams.

The work of manager/producers, with its varying responsibilities and specific contexts, is difficult to define and operates under a variety of titles. In my work with artists I have held a variety of positions: project manager, general manager, administrator, and consultant. There are a myriad of other words that could also describe the work that I've done, and that are routinely used in the field: executive director, creative producer, project manager, company manager, agent, and assistant. Beyond these resume-worthy titles, other descriptive terms that gesture toward the roles that I play include strategist, dramaturg, therapist, salesperson, writer, publicist, and stage manager. The responsibilities of a manager/producer vary depending on the artist and the project, and change over time. On any given day I could be drafting a contract, sitting in on rehearsals, reconciling a budget for a recent performance, organizing tour logistics, facilitating a visioning conversation, or writing a grant. I often describe my work as wearing many hats, and there are moments when I literally change costume—shifting from grubby pants and sneakers for last-minute errands to a sleek dress for preshow remarks. The ability to articulate these different skill sets, have the awareness to know when to apply them, and quickly transition between them is a core strength of manager/producers.

The titles manager or producer themselves are slippery, and also take different meanings in varying contexts—from independent productions, company structures, and institutional arenas. Within an independent production a producer works for an artist, supporting the ambitions and desires of the creative impulse. Producers working directly for an artist are often working on their own and thus cover a wide variety of responsibilities, though they may be occasionally accompanied by other administrators hired for specifically allocated tasks—for example, a bookkeeper or a grant writer. Within a company structure—say the dance company A.I.M by Kyle Abraham—a general manager will specifically focus on touring and the successful organization of new works with dance company members, contractors, and collaborators.[2] A.I.M has specific departments for marketing, development, and finance with multiple employees—supporting greater specialization and ensuring support for greater demand and larger-scale initiatives.

A producer at an institution—whether it be an organization like Jacob's Pillow or a museum like MoMA—similarly works on the creation and presentation of performances, but focuses on the institution's mission and financial bottom line, rather than that of the artist. While institutional producers negotiate with an artist to determine a set fee or commission and collaborate with the artist to ensure a successful production, they ultimately are holding the broader needs of the larger festival or presenting platform in mind, and serve as a broker with the artist. Although the context helps define the responsibilities and orientations of each producer or manager, ultimately all of these administrators are colleagues working to support the dance field, albeit from various positions.

For the purposes of this essay, I will focus on manager/producers working with dance artists who work in experimental, independent practices based in the USA.

- Manager/producers—People who work directly with living artists creating new productions.[3]
- Dance—Movement-based performance practice.
- Experimental—Creative exploration developing new modes and ways of being through investigation, trial and error, and continued curiosity.
- Independent—Nimble structures that are often, though not exclusively, project based. Structured in a variety of ways, independent artists and managers resist institutionalization and usually do not have ongoing general operating support, full-time employees, and/or building ownership.
- USA—Turtle Island, the land now known as the United States, specifically circumscribed by limited government arts funding and broad precarity for dance artists and arts workers.

> There is no single way to be a manager/producer. The challenge and joy of this work is in its carefully crafted mode specific to each relationship. The text boxes throughout this essay include excerpts from interviews I conducted with members of the LMCC Manager/Producer Group to depict a diversity of perspectives and practices.

Crafting Relationships and Modes of Support 93

> Miranda describes her process working with presenters grounded in transparent accounting and open dialogue, and how these practices lead to trusting partnerships that collectively support artists.
>
> **Miranda Wright: Founder of Los Angeles Performance Practice and the Live Arts Exchange [LAX] Festival**
>
> *Successfully negotiating a contract means that we are getting everything that we need and that the presenter feels like it's fair and justified. For example, once when planning a tour for an artist I went through my regular budgeting process and proposed a budget that would cover our expenses with a small contingency. Ultimately, additional expenses came up, mostly related to freight and visas. We also had to replace an actor, so we had to do some advance rehearsals before going and that added some expense too. Because I dealt with the presenter fairly early on, I was able to go back to them and say: "Hey—these extra things came up. Do you have any spare budget you could help us with? Otherwise, we're going to be at a loss." And they came up with extra support.*
>
> *There are some presenters who are really doing the best they can, and once they assign you a number, it's really difficult for them to add more to it. There are also many cases where I know presenters, particularly smaller festivals, don't have the enormous budgets that a university presenter will have. It's always my priority to make sure the artists are getting paid something along the lines of a liveable wage, and there are presenters whose budgets just don't allow for the kind of support that we're trying to get for artists right now. In those cases, I lay out what I'm trying to do for the artists, and I break down an example of an artist fee into an hourly rate to recontextualize it for the presenter. Often, I'll try to work with the presenter to assist in additional fundraising to come up with the balance. At the end of the day, the presenter and I work as colleagues to support an artist in bringing a performance to the stage.*

Not surprisingly, many of the manager/producers within the dance field have a background as dancers. This experience, beyond giving them an in-depth and embodied understanding of their field, develops strong skills in attunement as dancers learn how to partner, improvise, and collaborate with others. Dance training also instills determination, attention to detail, and the ability to pick up material quickly—all of which are assets to a manager/producer.

Some manager/producers have specific training in arts administration courses, though I have found that these programs more often train individuals for institutional positions, rather than independent work.[4] Most manager/producers have a bachelor's degree, from which they derive organizational, writing, and speaking skills. These strengths are often honed in internships or work-placement programs in institutional settings that give manager/producers insight into the specific contemporary dance context, which they can later adapt and apply to work directly with artists. For me, Barbara Bryan, Laurie Uprichard, and Megan Kendzior—all senior managers and administrators—were critical mentors, and taught me professional skills and ethics in this line of work. Artists I worked with supported my professional development by helping me attend annual conferences like Dance/NYC or Dance/USA, which kept me up-to-date on emerging practices on local and national levels, and provided critical opportunities for networking.[5]

~

In August 2013, Silas Riener sent me an email titled "question about project management this fall," which ultimately served as the catalyst for partnership. Silas had been one of my dance technique teachers at Princeton University the previous spring, and we stayed in touch as I moved to New York City following graduation and took on many part-time jobs, trying to make ends meet and to figure out my way in the dance world. He wrote:

> rashaun and i are tentatively looking for someone to help out with handling logistics and sort of general organizational support for our show at Danspace Project in mid November. does this sort of work interest you? it would be paid, we are still waiting to see how much (Waiting on a grant application...) but hopefully enough that it would at least be able to be a priority the 2 weeks preceding the show, and maybe enough to attend some meetings and rehearsals in september/october. i know this is a shot in the dark, but let me know if it's an interesting proposal, and we can maybe try and talk more about it.[6]

That shot in the dark hit home, and following the Danspace shows we agreed to keep working together. With the support of a New York Foundation for the Arts Building Up Infrastructures for Dance grant that gave funds specifically for administrative support, I became the general manager for Rashaun + Silas in 2014.[7]

Choreographers often start to work with a manager/producer to help them navigate the field and create new work. Given the resources it takes to train, pay, and maintain a relationship with a manager/producer, this means of working is not accessible, or palatable, to all artists. Most dance artists begin their careers independently and start to work with a manager/producer when they have enough capital and need to warrant it. For many artists a significant grant, their first national tour, or multiple simultaneous engagements prompts a search for a manager/producer who can help handle the increased workload and, hopefully, parlay modest success into more robust demand and support for their work. Most artists see this transition to hiring someone to manage the organizational details of creating a new work as a significant step in their career. Some artists hire a manager/producer specifically in hopes that this individual might change their career—helping them gain new commissions, receive additional grants, and better budget productions. While these outcomes are possible, an artist's success cannot be solely derived from the manager/producer, and is ultimately a mix of strong artistic creation, savvy stewardship, and the appropriate contexts. In a best-case scenario, manager/producers are allies and strategists in collaboration with the artist.

Aaron describes the creative partnership with an artist as a collaboratively crafted collection of outfits. His relationship with Beth Gill was built on a deep understanding of creative practice (which came in part from his own dance training) and its articulation in language—critical skills for a manager/producer.

Aaron Mattocks: Producer for Beth Gill, 2015–17

In some cases, the artist has approached me to ask if they can access those skills, and in some cases, I have approached an artist and offered access to the skills that I have. It feels like building a wardrobe. We ask: What do you already have in your closet, and what are you looking for me to bring to try on?

My relationship with Beth Gill as her producer began because she got NDP (National Dance Project grant) for the first time. We had previously met when I was commissioned to be a NYLA (New York Live Arts) context notes writer when she premiered New Work for the Desert in 2014. She said to me after the process: You rearticulated for me what I was telling you I was trying to do with my piece. The way that you wrote about it helped me see the end.

> *She saw me try to grapple with her work in language and when she got NDP, she reached out for help with administering her tour.*
>
> *As we worked together, our conversation shifted from solely tour management to developing structures to support a piece that doesn't exist yet and needs to be built from the ground up with touring partners in the mix from the beginning, which was different from how Beth had ever worked before.*
>
> *I think that the choreography of shapeshifting is being able to be a grant writer in some instances, because that's the only thing that a person might need, and then in some other cases, being a creative strategist.*

There is no standardized way to establish a working relationship between a choreographer and manager/producer. Most choreographers find an administrative partner through word of mouth, relying on relationships and the experiences of others to direct them to someone. In other instances, a choreographer may have a relationship with an individual as an artistic collaborator, student, or writer in the field and inquire if their skills could be applied to the role of a manager/producer, even if they have not previously done that particular kind of administrative work. Some choreographers formally advertise a position for manager/producer, writing a job description and clarifying a desired working model up front. Alternatively, some manager/producers actively seek clients—advertising their services or reaching out directly to artists—seeking to be in dialogue with a particular artist or type of work.

~

Manager/producers organize their work in a variety of ways. Many of us work as independent contractors and negotiate with artists directly for a set rate based on hours worked, monthly increments, or a project-specific fee. Some people work with a variety of artists and cobble together multiple freelance clients to support themselves. This method, while giving the manager/producer freedom to craft their own schedule and working conditions, also often puts the onus of insurance, office space, and professional development on the individual. Many manager/producers working in this manner can only do so for a few years before shifting to full- or part-time employment. Many cite significant burnout and fatigue from managing many artists simultaneously without support structures or colleagues.

Independent producers like Miranda Wright, founder of Los Angeles Performance Practice, organize their work with multiple artists under their own

Crafting Relationships and Modes of Support 97

nonprofit or business structure. This format supports standardizing practices across artists, and, depending on fiscal structure, can open opportunities for the manager/producer to apply for different government grants or business loans.[8] Other organizations like Pentacle and ArKtype work with multiple artists simultaneously on a larger scale, supporting over ten artists with multiple full-time staff members and long-term initiatives that collate financial, fundraising, and producing support.[9] Others, like myself, balance independent manager/producer work with other jobs.

I have found it helpful, both financially and professionally, to work an institutionalized job simultaneously with my freelance work. Working as an employee gives me benefits like health insurance and retirement savings, a relatively regular schedule and workplace, and taxable income, which is an important counterweight to freelance contracts. That being said, it's a balance that can be difficult to manage in terms of time management and conflicts of interest.

> Nora models open communication, renegotiation, and transparency in communication with an artistic partner. She demonstrates the importance of crafting a model that is specific to each artist, and the ways it is reevaluated and changes over time.
>
> **Nora Alami: Producer for Jasmine Hearn, 2021–Present**
>
> *Jasmine and I have been working on short-term contracts, which can align with the length of a project or span of available time in our schedules. In these contracts we outline the job description for what I'm doing, how we'll communicate together, and deadlines. Then at the end of each period we revisit the contract and talk about what worked and what didn't. As we write each new contract we then have a record to reference and build from. Each contract builds upon a set of agreements we created together, detailing ways of collaborating built from lessons we've learned from others and values we center in our relationship. We call this choreographies of care. While the term "choreographies of care" has many histories, we engage choreographies of care as a spell, recipe, and poem that builds on the ways that Jasmine Hearn has been in witness with their mom and aunties during the development of their project Memory Fleet. We chose to collaborate this way because it enacts our ethics of antiracism and transparency in the work that we do.*

I once tried to describe my work and relationship with Rashaun + Silas, and after going through a long list of duties, the person sitting next to me, a little befuddled at how I could be both in charge of negotiating contracts and doing laundry at the end of each show, shook his head and said, "I see—so you're the one who gets the job done." Embarrassed, I argued that no—it was a team effort. This is a crucial distinction: I cannot do my job alone. Crafting, tending, and navigating the relationship with the artist is the work itself, and it is never done.

There is a constant navigation of power and reorientation with each other in manager/producer relationships. I bristled when I found myself saying, "I manage Rashaun + Silas." Manage used as a verb feels regulatory and laden with hierarchy, recalling the stereotypical manager of a newly emerging pop star who is tutored and preened by a superior. I also found myself a bit uncomfortable with the phrase "I do contracts and grants for Rashaun + Silas." The word "for" flips that power dynamic and makes it seem as though I passively receive a list of tasks to complete. Sometimes I went for a compromise and said I "support" Rashaun + Silas. That statement is true, and while I appreciate its active phrasing it still feels shortsighted. While its one-way course feels appropriate—after all I was being paid—it ignored what I gained from the work, and the ownership I took in it. I like the preposition *with*. I do my work *with* artists. That's not to say that my work is always hand in hand with artists, but that it navigates all of the betweens in dialogue *together*.

～

My work is keenly attuned to orientation: how I am oriented to the artist, how the artist is oriented to me, and the distance, temperature, and terrain of the space between us. Sometimes I am in front of the artist and I act as a shield, director, or deputy. It can be advantageous, particularly when negotiating a contract or navigating a dispute, for me to receive feedback and advocate on behalf of the artist. This distancing can preserve an artist's time and bandwidth, and can also provoke different transparency in conversation with funders and/or presenters, who may want to preserve a more focused creative relationship with an artist, and keep financial negotiation and logistic discussions separate. When I manage a project, I often see myself as being in front, putting in place plans and affirming details in advance of an artist's arrival to smooth their way. When I am in front of an artist, I am visible and vocal. Conversely, when I am behind an artist, I take an offstage role and support from

Crafting Relationships and Modes of Support

the wings. This work can be as literal as feeding artists lines and as broad as completing directives they have defined. Rarely, though, is the orientation between the artist and myself so binary, but I've found these poles a helpful way to identify the spectrum of positions.

I often strategize about this positioning with the artist, and we rely on each other to notify and pull the other into position as needed. Similar to the tension needed between two dancers in partnering, this positioning only works well when there is strong attunement to the space between us and the forces at play in transitioning from one orientation to another. There were moments when, for example, a presenter might reach out to me directly to invite Rashaun + Silas to present a new work. Reaching for my partner, I would then have a conversation with the artists before I responded to the presenter, and then depending on the artist's desires, would bring them into the conversation. Similarly, Rashaun + Silas would loop me into a conversation, bringing me into parallel beside them, or swing me in front so I could manage dialogue. As we pulled each other back and forth, we were also aware of the distance between us. There were moments when we were too close, stepping on each other's toes as we both responded to emails or each thought the other was doing a task, or too far apart, becoming uncommunicative or straying from the determined path. Tuning in to each other, and to ourselves, is a deft and detailed process that is continually rearticulated and refined.

Chelsea offers another revision and rearticulation of the metaphor of manager/producer as performer, drawing particular attention to the collective work of the performance process. She advocates for new practices of collaboration and mutual support to counter a culture of overwork and burnout.

Chelsea Goding-Doty: Independent Producer for Kaneza Schaal and Others, 2020–2023

You can see the whole making of the production as one performance and each person has a role in it. Sometimes you move individually and sometimes you move as a group; sometimes you're supporting and sometimes you're standing still. Choreography applies to the role insomuch as the manager/producer needs to know when to go, when to hold, when to step out front, and when to sync in with the group. They need to have peripheral vision to be able to see and take a cue from someone else off on the side. I perform

> my role as the performer performs their role—it's a group effort, there is no singular accomplishment that doesn't reflect on the entire group.
>
> It makes me uncomfortable to imagine myself as a buffer, because buffers are meant to be worn down. My gripe with the field is that people are wrung out to the last drop and tossed away. I think if there is a moment when we need to brace for something or we need to protect ourselves against some discomfort, it's important that we be standing beside each other.

It takes time to establish working methods and to build trust. When starting a new working relationship, each partnership begins to articulate expectations, planned projects, goals, and communication styles. Developing a rapport together and learning how to tune in harmony takes time and honest dialogue. Means of tuning can also change over time, and regular check-ins, not solely at the start of a new working relationship, are critical.

This way of working together is complicated and compelling to me, and I often feel that it is many things at once: a creative practice, a job, and a caring relationship. There are times when I describe this process as a practice—something I am continually honing and shaping as a creative endeavor. The word practice feels linked to collaboration, and points toward the way my practice weaves together with the artistic practices of artists. This language leads me down a pathway that is both literal and metaphorical—we are crafting a complex choreography that combines well-rehearsed movement sequences with scores and improvisation. There are other times when it just feels like work. At the end of the day, I negotiate a pay rate and structure and hope to collect enough income from it, and many other forms of employment, to keep moving. And there are other times where it feels like love; when it is love. Rashaun + Silas and I take care of each other. Our relationship extends into shared friendships and family and to tender places of vulnerability and intimacy. There are moments when they have been my friends, my brothers, and my mentors; sometimes all in the span of a single conversation.

It is precisely this dense, intricate navigation that draws me to management/producing. This work gives me a way to be thickly involved in creative practice, and I have found over time that I am just as excited to be a part of a performance backstage as I am as a dancer. It is satisfying to orchestrate discernible progress and to be the central spoke for action to ensure forward momentum. Perhaps most of all, management/producing is care-oriented, and gives me a feeling of being needed and offering support that I crave.

In my work with artists over the last decade, I have toggled between prizing invisibility and seeking recognition. In my first show with Rashaun + Silas at Danspace Project I felt I had done my job best when I was hidden backstage, working in the dressing room and on email to keep focus squarely on the performing artists. As my work has evolved, and as I have matured, I have increasingly sought acknowledgment—both for my own professional advancement and as broader advocacy within the field. Crediting is important, not only in terms of acknowledgment, but also in terms of education—so that the field sees, appreciates, and supports the many types of collaborators needed for a project.

> Marýa shares how her own consciousness and framing of her work as a producer has changed over time, and in dialogue with artists. She gives examples of how she speaks openly about working practices with artistic partnerships to improve and differently articulate her visibility.
>
> **Marýa Wethers: Creative Producer for Edisa Weeks / DELIRIOUS Dances and Others, 2014–2024**
>
> *I feel a sense of responsibility to my colleagues, particularly coming out of the LMCC cohort. The public needs to know what it actually takes to do this kind of work. It's not just rehearsing in a studio and the artist shows up and they do a show; the work necessitates these long-term, multifaceted partnerships. It has also emerged from myself coming to a new understanding of the role in the last ten years. I inherited that practice of not being seen, that we're supposed to erase ourselves because the spotlight is only so big—a martyrdom way of being in service to artists. Now I'm realizing: no! That's not what I'm doing, that's not what I want to do, that's not sustainable. And so then learning how to assert that in different ways, and a starting point for those conversations is with the artists themselves.*
>
> *I might say to them: "Well, when you do this you've negated my involvement in the process. When the presenter only emails you, you need to add me to cc, tell them why I'm there, and tell them to make sure I'm always there."*
>
> *We still need to talk about it and go over: This is how this is operating. This is how I feel about it. This is what I'd like to have happen. Approach it with*

> respect and good intention. Most of the time when I brought things like that to any of my artists they usually respond and say, "Well, thank you for telling me," which speaks a lot to the kind of people that they are, that they can take that in and understand.

In 1969, Twyla Tharp sent the National Endowment for the Arts a concise two-sentence grant: "I write dances, not applications. Send money. Love, Twyla."[10] Her retort was successful, which feels impossible in today's world where artists are increasingly expected to do it all—make dances, garner funding, and independently produce their work.

In the last twenty years, initiatives like Creative Capital and LMCC's Extended Life Dance Development program have supported artists with professional development opportunities and classes in accounting, grant writing, marketing, and new work development.[11] Harnessing the neoliberal rise of the individual, these programs sought to bolster artists by giving them tools to navigate a field marked by scarcity and competition. These programs, much like the NCCAkron Creative Administration Research program, place emphasis primarily on the artist, rather than the complex ecology of the field. This is not to say that artists are not creative administrators, or that they shouldn't have access to these tools and supports—they absolutely should. The idea, though, that artists are the only people who should receive access to these supports is shortsighted. If organizations truly want "to think beyond the boundaries of known, traditional models and 'best practices,'" as NCCAkron notes, then they need to acknowledge the critical role that manager/producers play in creating new work and provide resources specifically for them.[12]

In other parts of the world, producers are valued differently with specific grant support, advocacy groups, and caretaking. Dance Umbrella in the UK runs Producer Farm, a free weeklong residency for producers to gather, rest, and consider future projects. Organized collectively with presenting institutions like Bristol Old Vic and producing organizations like In Between Time, this program exemplifies the field's support specifically for producers, both those working in presenting organizations and those working independently.[13] In Yokohama, the Japan Foundation annually funds Next Generation: Producing Performing Arts, which supports travel and participation in TPAM

(Performing Arts Meeting in Yokohama) as well as a conference presentation where fellows share their practices and build relationships across Asia with other emerging producers.[14] Performing Arts Connections Australia's Local Giants Regional Producer Platform similarly supports producers through annual convenings, professional development, and grant support.[15]

In the last five years, amid the COVID-19 pandemic and increasing calls for consideration of inclusion, diversity, and equity, the dance field has begun to recognize and differently appreciate the role of the manager/producer. In 2017 APAP, the leading national advocacy body for performing arts, changed its name from the Association of Performing Arts Presenters to the Association of Performing Arts Professionals, embracing the diversity of the performing arts field.[16] Founded in 2020, the Creative & Independent Producer Alliance (CIPA) has emerged as a strong advocate for producers developing live performance.[17] Creating New Futures, an "arts worker-driven effort speaking to the dance and performance field," notably included producers as part of its creative team, and considered how manager/producers act as critical intermediaries between artists and presenters, particularly within contract negotiations and revisions to long-standing force majeure and cancellation policies.[18]

∽

In the LMCC Manager/Producer group we discussed the impact of our meetings together, and how for many of us our regular conversations had been a critical lifeline during the tumult of the apex of the COVID-19 pandemic. Together we shifted our own perceptions of what was a siloed, undervalued role into a community-sustained, esteemed leadership position. Just as we craft contexts to support the artists we worked with, we are imagining specific care structures for ourselves. In asking questions we collectively consider and envision the future:

What would the US dance field look like if it saw the administrative practices of manager/producers as creative, and endowed them with the same support available for artists? What new work might emerge if artists could receive support to hire manager/producers, and thus focus more intently on their craft? How might the ecosystem move differently if it saw support structures as teams of intersecting relationships, rather than artists forging through a competitive landscape alone?

Administrative Experiment

- Choose a dance artist and trace their career trajectory. Have they worked with a manager/producer? If so, when? Are you able to discern differences in the times they worked with a manager/producer and those without?
- Select one of the manager/producers mentioned in this essay and research their practice. With whom and how have they worked over time? Can you identify how and why their methods have changed over time?
- Imagine you are a choreographer hiring a manager/producer. How might you articulate the job description? What title might you use? What working relationship and structure of compensation would you employ?
- What choreographic skills have you developed that are also manager/producer skills? Practice being a director, a soloist, a member of the corps—how might that manifest in an administrative practice?
- Craft an improvisation with a partner or small group. How does your navigation of movement together—following, mirroring, and proximity—reveal different modes of orientation? Reflect on how you might orient and reorient within a manager/producer and artist relationship.

PART III
CAPITAL

Beg, Borrow, Steal (Back)
How US Dance Artists Fund Their Work—Excerpts from the podcast *Are You For Sale?*

Miguel Gutierrez
with amara tabor-smith, Antonio Ramos, Cynthia Oliver,
Rosie Herrera, and Michelle Fletcher

In 2018 two significant events occurred. First, I received multiple grant rejections for a new dance piece, which sent me into an emotional and administrative spiral because I couldn't readily imagine another way to fund my work. Second, I read Edgar Villanueva's book *Decolonizing Wealth: Indigenous Wisdom to Heal Divides*,[1] which critiques the American philanthropy sector as a vestige of settler colonialism and slavery. This sent me down a rabbit hole of study into the history of philanthropy and federal funding, and into conversations with many dance artists about the financial conditions they face when creating their work.

This subject matter became the focus of a podcast I started to release in 2021, *Are You For Sale?*, which looks at the ethical entanglements between money and art making.

The following are excerpts from Episode 6, "Beg, Borrow, Steal (Back)— How Dance Artists in the U.S. Fund Their Work."[2] I interviewed colleagues in various locations throughout what is currently called the United States, throughout the summer of 2020. Together we examine what it means to operate inside a system of scarcity and success. The episode features conversations with Cynthia Oliver,[3] Rosie Herrera,[4] Antonio Ramos,[5] and amara tabor-smith.[6] The excerpts begin mid-episode, with a conversation between my manager, Michelle Fletcher, and me.

MIGUEL

[voiceover] How much does it cost to make a dance? Well, let's start with how long it takes to make a dance. In my experience, it really depends on how an artist works. In the experimental scene, it's pretty common that you work in chunks of time stretched out over longer periods of time. So for example, most of my evening-length pieces [and evening-length just means a piece it's like forty-five minutes or longer]. They take about twenty to twenty-five weeks of rehearsal spread out over the course of about eighteen months. I don't work in ballet, but I know that those choreographic working periods are much shorter, like you might get three weeks to make a new piece. So we're going to do a thought experiment where we build a budget for a piece that takes ten weeks to make. And for this budget, we're going to talk in ideal numbers mostly. And to do this, I'm going to bring in my manager, who's also the managing producer of this podcast, Michelle Fletcher.

MIGUEL
Hello.

MICHELLE
Okay, let's do this. How many people are in your piece besides you?

MIGUEL
Let's say four folks.

MICHELLE
And you're in it too, right?

MIGUEL
Yep, that seems like a good amount.

MICHELLE
So how often do you want to rehearse?

Beg, Borrow, Steal (Back)

MIGUEL
Let's say the rehearsals are like five hours long because in an ideal world, you get to go to dance class in the morning or whatever. Ten to twelve and then you go to rehearsal like one to six.

MICHELLE
How many days a week?

MIGUEL
Five-day workweek, just like the rest of the world.

MICHELLE
How much are you going to pay people?

MIGUEL
How much did I pay last time?

MICHELLE
Twenty-five.

MIGUEL
Okay, well, we should be paying at least more than that.

MICHELLE
Thirty bucks an hour?

MIGUEL
Yeah.

MICHELLE
Everyone's getting paid the same, including you?

MIGUEL
For this. Yeah, sure. Okay, that's that's that's enough, right? Like, okay, the time has come for us to…

[*music: Violent Femmes, "Add it up!"*][7]

MICHELLE
Five performers, five hours a day, five days a week. That means a day of rehearsal cost $750.

MIGUEL
Okay.

MICHELLE
Which means one week of rehearsal cost $3,750.

MIGUEL
Okay.

MICHELLE
Which means that ten weeks of rehearsal with five performers cost $37,500.

MIGUEL
I think we could do that.

MICHELLE
Um we're not done. What about the lighting designer?

MIGUEL
Yeah. Oh, yeah.

MICHELLE
A composer? Is there any kind of set?

MIGUEL
We're gonna like, activate sculptures or something?

MICHELLE
Costumes?

MIGUEL
Sure.

MICHELLE
Do you want to bring in someone as a dramaturg? Or an outside eye?

MIGUEL
What are you trying to say? Like, I have to get someone?

MICHELLE
Is the composer working alone or with other musicians? Are they performing live?

MIGUEL
Live?!? You're funny.

MICHELLE
Okay, I'm just putting down 5K for all that. The set designer probably needs to get materials to make a set with, right?

MIGUEL
Sure, I don't know, it's like the same amount.

MICHELLE
5K.

MIGUEL
Okay. The lighting design is going to be super involved, though.

MICHELLE
Okay. 3K. Are they renting any equipment?

MIGUEL
I mean, they usually do, right?

MICHELLE

Okay. 2K.

MIGUEL

Sure.

MICHELLE

The costume designer needs some kind of budget. Unless everyone's naked.

MIGUEL

Well, that's definitely cheaper. I don't know. $1,500?

MICHELLE

Okay, but they're gonna need to get paid for their work.

MIGUEL

Okay, so like, I don't know, $1,500 again?

MICHELLE

Seems kind of low.

MIGUEL

They're gonna just have to, like get stuff from the thrift store. We're not gonna like ask them to sew…

MICHELLE

I thought you said, this was ideal.

MIGUEL

Okay, okay. $2,000.

MICHELLE

Dramaturgs should be at rehearsals for a pretty decent amount of time, right?

MIGUEL

Yes, sure. But like, I don't know. Like half…

MICHELLE
Okay, $3,250. Oh, and me. Who's paying me for all of this?

MIGUEL
Well, I'm—I mean, I'm paying you. But wait, how much do I pay you?

MICHELLE
Thirty-three an hour.

MIGUEL
That's pretty good.

MICHELLE
No comment.

MIGUEL
So like five hours a week for like three weeks of work. That's what you should be doing?

MICHELLE
We're applying for five grants. Do you realize how long that takes?

MIGUEL
Okay, okay, like fifty hours. So like, $1,500? Wait, can I get paid for that—

MICHELLE *(INTERRUPTING)*
You have to get photos. That's at least $500.

MIGUEL
Okay, but did you hear my question about paying money—

MICHELLE
And you got to videotape it?

MIGUEL
Yeah. Okay. Wait, how much is that?

MICHELLE
Well, are they editing it too?

MIGUEL
Yeah, I think so. Because my friend said he wasn't gonna do that for free anymore.

MICHELLE
Okay, so that's $2K.

MIGUEL
Wait, where are we gonna rehearse? We only have that one two-week residency.

MICHELLE
I thought you said this was ideal.

MIGUEL
Yeah, ideal. Sure. But not, like, delusional.

MICHELLE
Twenty-five hours a week for eight weeks at $15 an hour.

MIGUEL
Woah, you found a place that's only $15 an hour?! Where are we rehearsing, a walk-in closet?

MICHELLE
That's $3,000.

MIGUEL
Okay, so let's see where our budget is now?

MICHELLE
$65,750.

Beg, Borrow, Steal (Back)

MIGUEL

That's not like that much. Right?

MICHELLE

The theater is asking if you have insurance. Do you have insurance?

MIGUEL

Ummm…

MICHELLE

The costume designer needs to order cars for when they come to rehearsal because they have to carry all that shit. And so do the set and lighting designer, they're gonna need a truck.

MIGUEL

A truck?

MICHELLE

And you're gonna pay for an ASL interpreter. Right? You got all that text, Mister Interdisciplinary?

MIGUEL

Yeah. Okay, of course. I mean, how much is that? Wait, shouldn't the theater pay for that?

[music: Violent Femmes, "Add it up!"][8]

MIGUEL

[voiceover] Thank you, Michelle. And that was us, ACTING! [Archival Recording of: Uta Hagen "It was just superb, truly."][9] Well, thank you, Uta. [Archival Recording of: Uta Hagen—"I can tell you love the character."] Welllll, I wouldn't go that far. So that was a crash course in what a budget might look like. There's a bunch of stuff we didn't even factor in. But you see how quickly the numbers add up. And I'll be super transparent and acknowledge that the $25 an hour number that I cited, that's real. That's the most I've ever been able to pay folks for hourly rehearsals and it is not enough. [Audio: Cardi B talking—"I'm glad you brung *it up. Because I've been dying to talk about it for fucking hot minute. First of all…"]*[10] *A $70,000 project budget may sound like a big number. But when you break it down, you realize that it's really not that much when you're talking about a ten-week rehearsal period and paying upwards of ten folks. By way of comparison, did you know that the average cost for a thirty-second national television commercial is $115,000? So yeah, $70,000, it's still not enough to pay performers what they should be getting paid as experts in their field. But I'm gonna guess that there are some dance artists and performance makers out there who are listening to this episode, who are now thinking, "Hey, I'm never gonna get $70,000 together for a project." And statistically, sadly, you're probably right, especially given that the highest project grant amount that I know of that you can apply to is $50,000. And that organization only accepts applications for dance-based projects every few years. And you can only get it once.*

Antonio has for years now been applying for pretty much everything out there without much success. I ran through a list of national funding possibilities.

MIGUEL
Did you apply for MAP?

ANTONIO RAMOS
Nada.

MIGUEL
Did you apply for National Dance Project?

ANTONIO RAMOS
I have applied for that.

MIGUEL
Did you apply to the National Association of Latino Arts and Culture?

ANTONIO RAMOS
Nada. They're really, really, really conservative.

MIGUEL
How about Creative Capital?

Beg, Borrow, Steal (Back)

ANTONIO RAMOS

Uh huh, nada as well.

MIGUEL

How about the National Endowment for the Arts?

ANTONIO RAMOS

Yes, I have. But they're like weird about like, cause I don't have anybody producing me somewhere. Is that the one?

MIGUEL

Yeah, you have to have support.

ANTONIO RAMOS

Yeah.

MIGUEL

Okay. What about a fellowship? The Guggenheim Fellowship?

ANTONIO RAMOS

I have applied, nada.

MIGUEL

What about one of those nomination-based awards like the Alpert Award? *[voiceover] Yep. That Herb Alpert? [Music: Herb Alpert and the Tijuana Brass, "Spanish Flea"]*[11] *Has he been nominated for that?*

ANTONIO RAMOS

Six or seven times?

MIGUEL

[voiceover] No luck there either. Then we talked about more local funding possibilities.

MIGUEL

How about the New York Foundation for the Arts Fellowship?

ANTONIO RAMOS
Nada.

MIGUEL
New York State Council for the Arts?

ANTONIO RAMOS
I think probably next time I got something, like, really super small.

MIGUEL
[voiceover] He also got some support from the Brooklyn Council on the Arts.

ANTONIO RAMOS
It's like $3,000.

MIGUEL
[voiceover] Once we went through that list, we took a moment.

ANTONIO RAMOS
You know, I'd be like when you look at the picture in general, I feel like I should be quitting a long time ago. I should have. Because it's like so—it's frustrating, just being in that field for so long—I keep reapplying and feeling like there's not an audience or there's (only) conservative people, who'd actually be a little more open to the kind of work I do.

MIGUEL
[voiceover] Yeah, and that's a lot of unpaid time applying for grants. I'll also add that on paper, those different granting sources, if you do get them, are allegedly supposed to go to different aspects of your artistic life. Income source division yet again! There are project grants that are supposed to be just for your projects. There are fellowships which are sometimes research focused or like awards, they could just provide money for you to live for a while. For example, amara, Cynthia, and Rosie have all been recipients of the $50,000 United States Artists Fellowship. Theoretically, it's not meant to be used for a project. But...

ROSIE HERRERA

You know, a second ago, you mentioned the United States Artists Award. And I have to tell you, every time somebody brings that up, I'm like, I should have bought a house.

MIGUEL

But it's not enough money to buy a house!

ROSIE HERRERA

I know! And I live in Miami, it's like, there's not—it's not enough money to buy a freaking apartment. But I just I, you know, as I get older, and like, rents just increase and increase and increase and increase, and I keep getting pushed out of every single neighborhood. I just like, really, I couldn't, that was the most amount of money I've ever gotten. And, you know, like, I'm never getting that much money again, I should have, you know... but that money was spread out over many years to help support a variety of works that were my heart.

MIGUEL

[voiceover] I asked the artists how they manage their expectations, once they apply for a grant, and how they deal with rejection.

ROSIE HERRERA

Kind of such a fucked-up thing to say, but the truth is, I just never expect it. Just assume that it's not gonna happen. And not because I've been rejected so many times. I'm just so used to working outside of that grant system that I'm like—I'm making or dreaming in a different way.

CYNTHIA OLIVER

To this day, I never anticipate that I'm going to get something and maybe being a young dancer and auditioning teaches you not to get overconfident. Because of the amount of rejection that you know, dancers get early on in their careers, or, you know, ongoing in their careers. There's never an expectation, there's of course, the hope that I will get it because I am also not a prolific artist, I'm not one of those people who does a new work every year. That's not how my head works or my life works. So when I have the inspiration, and feel strongly about doing something, then I'm hoping that that connects with whatever panels are operating at the time, because that's the other reality of the... depending on the panel, you may or may not be the selected artists. So there's never... I never expect.

The other thing is I've always thought of myself, and I said this, to the US Artists people, I always thought of myself as like a B artist, right? So like, there are the A-listers in film. And then the B-listers, that... and the C-listers and all that. And I always thought of myself as, you know, B or even C-level artist and I was okay. I reconciled myself with like, I'm not going to be one of those people. And they are, you know, they absolutely deserve where they are. But I'm going to just keep toiling away at what I do. There's an audience that loves my work, and I'm happy to see them, they seem to be happy to see me when I do something. And I'm fine with that. It works in my life in a fine way.

The other part of that was that I also elected not to pursue a 501(c)(3) status. I had conversations with a number of people about it, because there are certain funding opportunities for folks who choose to do that, that the others don't have. As an independent artist, you cannot apply for some things if you don't have that status. But I chose to do that because I did not want to be a business, an official business. I didn't want to have a board that I had to answer to. I didn't want to have workers' compensation that I had to figure out how to pay for even when we're not working. I—there are all these complications that I didn't want to have so that when I'm not making a work, I could just let myself rest and recover and regenerate and think toward the future work.

MIGUEL
[voiceover] And finally, at the end of each of my conversations with the artists, Rosie, Cynthia, amara, and Antonio, I asked them what they wished were different, what sort of changes they would like to see in terms of funding.

ROSIE HERRERA
Wouldn't it be wonderful if there was a way to support an artist's life versus going piece by piece, it's like, you know, constantly like on a hamster wheel trying to prove that you are still relevant, or that you have something to say when that has been clear.

Miami has wonderful, wonderful training programs. We produce phenomenal artists. I just like the work here better than everybody else. The work being made here, the dancing that's happening here is so amazing. But we don't necessarily have the best track record for keeping artists here. And when I look over time, who stays and who doesn't stay, and what's the price that they pay, and who has access to continue to dance full time or continue to make work full-time, it's very challenging, and those statistics are pretty freakin bleak, you know? So a lot of artists leave. And more sad than that, a lot of artists struggle with having families, and the choices that have to be made when you have a family, you have to support a family, and what that does to your career as a dancer. So I think to myself, like, man, wouldn't it be cool if those artists that are making amazing work, and that are checking all the lists, you know—getting the national recognition, doing the work with the community, diverse, beautiful ensembles of people working for them, creating jobs—had support to stay.

What if it was the bigger organizations that were like, "Here's a fund that you can apply to buy a freaking house"? "Here's a fund that you can apply to support the work of touring mothers," so that artists can stay, artists that are amazing artists can live. And I'm not even saying like live well! I'm just saying just like live in this place, and still be able to make work. And this is coming from the most privileged, probably, choreographer in Miami, who's probably getting the most support and the most funding and the most national recognition. And I still am struggling to make my life and still, you know, obviously have that—I don't know if you've had this, like every six months you're like, "Will I ever have a family? Could I ever have a home?" You know? Is the price of this life a little too high?

CYNTHIA OLIVER

One of the things for me has been... that I feel like, there was a flash moment when a number of the powers that be realized that it wasn't that I was failing at imitating white artists' aesthetics, it was that I actually had another set of values and aesthetics at play. And I think that moment was key. And so if that realization happened much sooner in the funding community, perhaps there would be a different way of thinking about what people are doing, as opposed to presuming it from a deficit, a place of deficit, "Oh, these artists, they're not as good creatively or aesthetically," as opposed to: "What are the aesthetics that they're operating from?"

AMARA TABOR SMITH

There's enough money for all of us to get what we need. There's enough, it's just we're just not getting it. There's enough money for everybody to get what they need. Everybody. And so a friend and curator and art person, Ashara Ekundayo, she says, "Artists are first responders." And I think that artists can perform a kind of first response in terms of, you know, responding artistically, to whatever's going on. If we're the forward thinkers, if we're the, you know, if we are part of the visionary team of people that are like imagining what it could be, then let us, you know, let like… listen to us. Listen, and believe us when we say, you know, believe that this work, believe that all of our work is important. Believe that art is really, you know, is, is… is necessary. We have never been without art. So nobody knows, like, "Oh, could you live without art?" You've never had to. You've never had to! Value artists and pay us. Pay all of us. Even like, the art that you don't like, pay those artists. Because you know, what we like is, it's subjective, it's, it's so individual, and there should be room for all of it.

ANTONIO RAMOS
We should all get something out of the pot, my fantasy is that we can all receive a portion enough to survive in this, especially in times like this.

MIGUEL
[voiceover] In the last few years, Antonio has been traveling to Peru to study plant medicine at a spiritual center run by an indigenous family.

ANTONIO RAMOS
Like I mean, at the end, we're all fucking connected and, and we forget about this. And I feel like this is one of the things that I have learned from the indigenous people and from their beliefs, it's like, if you go into a forest, the forest is connected with all of the trees that are there, the roots, and the microorganisms are all connected to themselves. And when something happens to one of them, one of them is either dying, or has a disease or has anything, they actually bring nutrients to that tree, and they support the life of that particular tree. And also, they send information to the forest, like, to tell them, "Yo, this tree is suffering from this, let's help them but also let's keep them alive." And I just feel like we kind of have forgotten about that within all communities. Like it doesn't matter, gender, and race, and color, and shapes. Like I feel like we all deserve to be supported by each other. And we forgot that.

How I Built This
Dance Church®
Kate Wallich

CASE STUDY: STUDIO KATE WALLICH + THE YC

    My mother ran a daycare out of our basement, so I had access to dancers, starting from a very young age. I'd like to think that I formed my first dance company there. I was always making the dances happen: organizing the rehearsals, choreographing the moves, styling the costumes, doing everyone's hair and makeup, and inviting everyone to the show. I even remember having my first collaborative negotiations in this setting—discussing what choreographies were best for the Britney Spears song and sharing artistic ownership around dance moves. I was very passionate. Everything I did was always highly designed, and I wanted everyone to pay attention. I didn't even care so much about being the performer myself, I just wanted anyone who was watching to intently watch and I wanted every detail around the performance to be perfect.

After I graduated from Cornish College of the Arts, I had just left dancing for two choreographers I was apprenticing for who couldn't afford to pay me. They also were not the best at cultivating the healthiest working cultures. I was in Seattle, and I did not have the resources to leave and go on a European audition tour to try and get a dance job in a company. At that time, there was a very small technique-driven class-taking culture in Seattle and concurrently, I was not overjoyed by the styles that were being practiced—no one in Seattle taught a specific technique but rather they created their own eclectic systems influenced by the lineages of Lynn Simonson, Joan Skinner, Irmgard Bartenieff, and other improvisation and somatic pioneers. And contextually, I was stuck behind a false narrative that I had to go try to be a "dancer" and my ego at the time did not consider dancing in Seattle as "successful." I was lost, stuck up, and poor.

I reached out to my mentor, Tonya Lockyer, for advice and she helped me come up with my plan. I was going to start making dances, and she was going to try to bring new ideas and perspectives that were being practiced on an inter/national scale to the regional Seattle dance community. This was the beginning of the Israeli-based Gaga "movement language" craze,[1] and the rising international fame of choreographers like Pacific Northwest native Crystal Pite.[2] Both of these approaches centered on the mover's movement expressivity by focusing attention on very specific body regions and metaphor-driven explorations. I loved this point of view and wanted to explore more of it. I never thought I would immediately start choreographing after my education, but I had strong values guiding me from what I had learned in the past, and I started forming my vision of what I wanted to do. It was inspired, and fueled, by the same passion I had when I was a kid: I was going to make work, start a company, and be part of the building of the Seattle dance community.

Then Tonya Lockyer invited me to join a tiny co-op movement space she founded, RED, in downtown Seattle and I began working. After hundreds of hours processing through my own body, I eventually found the desire and confidence to begin transcribing what I was discovering onto other dancers. But I needed money to pay rent and pay the dancers. So I started a class on Sunday mornings open to everyone, not just dancers, and made it donation-based. The class was our warm-up for rehearsals, which guaranteed that there would always be at least five people in the class. This was key to making newcomers feel welcomed and like there was already a togetherness around the experience. News of the class spread through word of mouth and amateur marketing campaigns I would post to the internet. Eventually, it got some traction and the students named it Dance Church, their Sunday morning ritual and—unknown to me at the time—the seed of what was to become not only my soul realized, but the backbone to my fiscal freedom as a dance artist.

One of the artists I began working with was Lavinia Vago, my now long-term collaborator of over twelve years. Lavi and I met at Cornish, and we had the same level of passion for dance and life, which is rare to find at that age. She and I became strategic partners in a sense. She left Seattle to dance in New York and Montreal with choreographers like Sidra Bell and Victor Quijada and was braiding into the dance community in New York. Meanwhile, I was in Seattle choreographing, applying for grants and festivals, staying consistent to Dance Church, and expanding into the artistic community in Seattle. I would use the funding from grants and classes to fly Lavi back to Seattle whenever we were working on projects.

Within the next year, Tonya Lockyer became the artistic/executive director of Velocity Dance Center, Seattle's home for contemporary dance, and invited Dance Church to join their curated class schedule. (For a more detailed examination of Velocity during that time, and RED, you can read Lockyer's essay in this book.) Velocity's physical space was in Seattle's arts district, a true neighborhood vibe with coffee shops, restaurants, and local retailers—key ingredients to building a community.

Alongside teaching Dance Church, I started teaching a contemporary class, rehearsing at Velocity, became an intern (which gave me free space), and began creating and presenting work at Velocity alongside other Seattle festivals. Velocity was becoming a strong institutional relationship of mine. I ended up self-producing and curating my first show, *Split-Bill: Wallich, Hankins,* at Velocity alongside Portland-based artist Allie Hankins under the name Company Wallich. This was the official premiere to Seattle as a "dance company" and was also a marker for my coming successes as a dancemaker in Seattle and beyond. With the support of Velocity's accessible presenting platform and a successful Kickstarter campaign—the earliest form of my company was born.

The impact of *Split-Bill: Wallich, Hankins* was unprecedented—it's the reason I received my first evening-length commission from Velocity Dance Center, how my work was seen by On the Board's then artistic director Lane Czaplinski, which later led to two, large-scale evening-length commissions; dance company commissions started rolling in, and it's also how I procured an invite to be an artist-in-residence at the Robert Rauschenberg Foundation's Residency program.

When On the Boards asked for my program notes for my first large-scale commission, *Splurge Land,* they asked how I wanted to be identified for the season. We had already been going by The YC, but the artistic director said, "Why do you want a company? Your work should just be your name." That spiraled me and I said, "They need a name. They are not just me." The name The YC was born from a commission I received from Portland-based dance company Northwest Dance Project, in which I titled the piece *Yacht Club.* The work was a dreamy and iconographic dance on themes of desire and idealism. In directing the mood and energy of the world to the dancers, I would reference photos and imagery saying "This is the vibe of Yacht Club... it's very YC." As a modality and way of communicating direction with dancers, YC became a symbol of expressing and embodying the works I was making. When it came time to make a decision and put a name on the program, I told On the Boards: Kate Wallich + The YC, and rest assured that this was in fact the name of the company.

Between the years 2010 and 2020, Kate Wallich + The YC went on to make five evening-length works and many more short-form works commissioned and presented by world-renowned arts institutions including Velocity Dance Center, On the Boards, Seattle Theater Group, MASS MoCA, The Joyce Theater, ICA Boston, and the Walker Art Center, among many others.

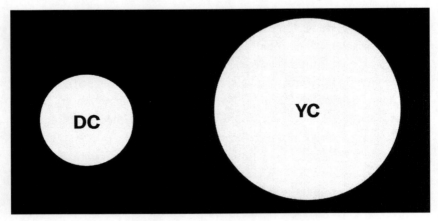

CASE STUDY: STUDIO KATE WALLICH

At some point, I realized that I was in fact making some money from Dance Church and I had more and more commissions and artist's fees coming in as well. All of this revenue was helping fund the work I wanted to make with The YC and also, it had the potential to fund myself and the dancers. I had

How I Built This 127

1099s flowing in from every direction, transactions from Dance Church® coming in via cash, Venmo, check, et cetera, and I had one personal bank account. I had an accountant, but it became very clear that I needed to make a major business decision.

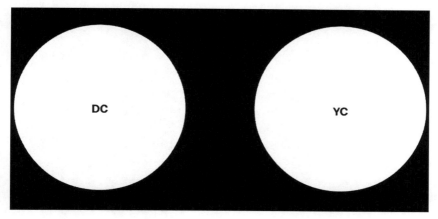

For years, I had heard people in dance talk about how challenging it was to apply for and get status as a nonprofit. For a long time, I believed them, until I researched what was needed to start one. Turns out, all you need is a mission, vision, and values statement; plus, a community of people who want to support those things, e.g., a board, patrons, and community members. Up until this point in my career, I had dancers, people willing to help me out and give me advice, institutional support and relationships helping to procure donors, and people coming to our shows, and I also had fiscal sponsorship through Fractured Atlas.[3] Having nonprofit status would essentially cut out the middleman of fiscal sponsorship and bring everything together under one umbrella, giving me the autonomy to develop donor relationships directly and fundraise for the mission and vision on my own terms unattached to any specific institution.

At this time, I wanted three things: to continue making work with or without institutional commission support, a more direct line to community fundraising and donor cultivation, and to make and envision something that I did not see existing around me—a large community of artists and the public supporting uncompromising dance projects. As my community expanded into design, visual art, fashion, and tech I wondered why the dance audiences in Seattle didn't look like the people in audiences of other fields. I began to realize how niche Dance was, and I wanted to make it more accessible and relatable to masses of people.

Starting a nonprofit, or starting anything as a business, means that you now have a container that separates you as a person from the things you are making. This was a major step for me and all that I was trying to do at the time—build community and make dances.

Studio Kate Wallich (SKW) was officially formed in 2015. Our programs were The YC: a collaborative, research-based dance company comprising world-class dance artists, premiering new works in Seattle, New York, and touring internationally; YC2, created in partnership with Velocity Dance Center: a platform for emerging dance artists to receive consistent paid training, mentorship, and professional performance opportunities with the goal to empower young dancers to become change-makers in the field of dance; and Dance Church: an all-levels movement class that offers a fun and inclusive approach to dancing.

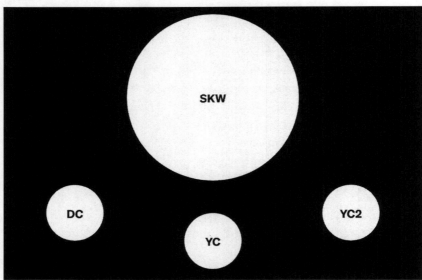

Between 2015 and 2020, Studio Kate Wallich supported nineteen world-class dancers, four composers, eight musicians, production staff, graphic designers, wardrobe stylists, and seventeen Dance Church teachers. We reached thousands through weekly attendees of Dance Church in five cities across the

How I Built This 129

country plus pop-ups in many more. We engaged thousands with countless performances around Seattle, across the country, and on other world stages. We produced over twenty-five new performance works through The YC, YC2, and our continuing education programs. SKW was an era in Seattle—it had a vibe, style, and was hugely successful in fulfilling its mission and vision between the years of 2015 and 2020.

CASE STUDY: SEPARATION OF CHURCH & KATE

There is a term in business called Product/Market Fit, which essentially describes a scenario in which a company's target customers are buying, using, and telling others about the company's product in numbers large enough to sustain that product's growth and profitability.[4] For Dance Church, this first happened between 2015 and 2017. Classes were a consistent twenty or more people every week for the first five years, but then around 2015 they started exponentially growing to the point where a typical Dance Church class in Seattle averaged seventy-five people a class. On the one hand, this became a very positive (and lucrative) thing for Studio Kate Wallich—we were making more money. On the other hand, as Dance Church® began to grow, the studio severely lacked the operational and business expertise for what was developing.

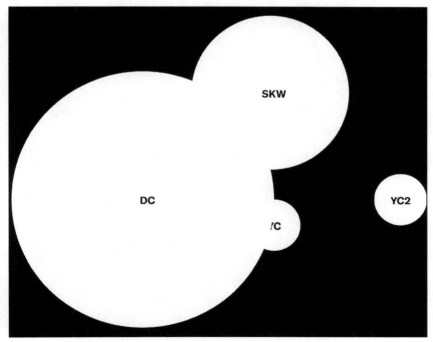

Grassroots expansion and reactive scale in part created this situation. People loved Dance Church—dance artists were asking to get trained in the format and community members were asking for it to launch in their cities. Between 2017 and 2020, I experimented with expanding Dance Church inside and outside of Seattle. Seattle went from one class a week to seven classes. Portland was the first experiment with regional expansion, starting with pop-ups and eventually training two teachers to lead the community in weekly classes. We then expanded to New York and Los Angeles, and eventually Salt Lake City and Indianapolis in a similar format. Each of these expansions had its own unique partnership relationships with dance organizations and business models that we were experimenting with.

This was a good problem and a bad problem.

1. From a business perspective—I had built a model for Dance Church's income to support the operations of a nonprofit that was generating dance works. The problem was, the dance works were not bringing revenue back into the organization. Fundraising, in theory, was supposed to help fill that gap, but that wasn't happening because all of our efforts were in managing Dance Church and a touring company. Dance Church was using expansion to increase our revenue, but expansion costs money and takes time. Plus, The YC's work was beginning to tour, and touring is extremely expensive. Fundraising efforts needed to drastically increase but, owing to a lack of business expertise from leadership (me), a lack of time (one other full-time staff member), and an inexperienced board, ultimately this led to the realization that this business model was not sustainable.
2. From a community perspective—It looked and felt like Dance Church was growing and becoming more available to people via added classes and cities. Thanks to a highly skilled graphic designer, everything looked very professional and well put together from a forward-facing perspective. In retrospect, I think this gave a look and feel that we were more together than we actually were, because what was really happening is that we were consistently in the red, our new cities were taking too long to grow, and our star cities were

How I Built This

moments away from the floors caving in because so many people were coming to class. Everything was a walking liability.

3. From a teacher's perspective—The lack of operations, systems, and structures was taking a toll on the teachers, and ultimately, they were not receiving the support they needed from the organization to show up and do their jobs. Everything was ad hoc and reactional. To put it frankly, scheduling was happening via text messaging and I once trained a teacher in a juice bar over green-drinks. Not okay.

The decision was made to separate Dance Church officially from Studio Kate Wallich and formally stop producing and using the Dance Church trademark for SKW-hosted events. What this meant was that SKW no longer was receiving the income from Dance Church, which ultimately cut SKW's funding by about 90 percent. This devastated SKW as a model, but ultimately, the model was not sustainable in the fashion in which it was created. What came from this separation were two completely separate business entities—a nonprofit organization and a for-profit S-Corp.

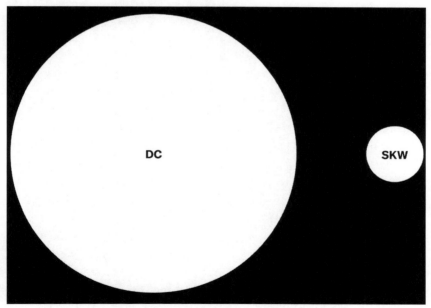

CASE STUDY: DANCE CHURCH INC.

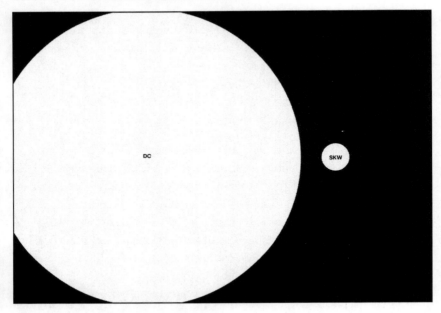

In March 2020 when COVID-19 hit, Dance Church made a giant pandemic pivot-turn. As Seattle was on the early front lines of the virus, I panicked, knowing the implications for our community and teachers. I activated the community I had formed in design and tech and together, we were able to launch Dance Church Go, a live-streamed version of our in-person experience. The community we had been building for ten-plus years across the country followed us to the internet and we had viral success in the course of a weekend.

Our mailing list jumped from zero to forty thousand people, we were streaming classes with upwards of ten thousand people dancing together online, and we were even presented to the director of the World Health Organization as an example of hope and resilience in response to the pandemic. It truly was a phenomenal moment in such a dark and scary time. We were able to continue supporting the Dance Church teachers and providing for our community who rely on Dance Church for their mental and physical health.

As the pandemic continued to not go away, and Dance Church Go was continuing to grow, I realized that once again we were in the same situation as we were before Separation of Church and Kate. I very clearly saw that we needed help and expertise from people with business and tech knowledge and fast, because I also knew we needed big money to keep up with music licensing fees, production costs, and legal fees. We had essentially gone from being a grassroots community movement to an unintentional tech company overnight.

I started to do research and began to realize that Dance Church could really get major financial and operational help in a venture capital-backed[5] way, with what had been built over ten years and the success we had online. I reached out to Pioneer Square Labs,[6] a start-up studio and venture capital fund in Seattle, and ended up partnering with them to help rebuild the infrastructure of Dance Church from the ground up to prepare it for true, intentional growth and scale.[7]

With the help of PSL, we launched the Dance Church platform a year into the pandemic featuring a subscription, video-on-demand library of Dance Church classes. We soon hired a CEO, Clara Siegel, to lead the business operations and scale of Dance Church. Together, Clara and I raised a $4.7 million seed round of funding, led by MaC Venture Capital, with participation from PSL Ventures, Crush Ventures, KID Venture Capital, Spike Ventures, and Graham & Walker Venture Fund. Upon the raising of capital, the company entered build mode, growing and operationalizing the team and launching new features to the platform. These included Dance Together, a feature that enables our community to synchronously stream on-demand classes, and a proprietary event registration system[8] to integrate in-person classes on the online platform, as well as launching the ability for Dance Church Teachers to post their own content to the platform and tools to directly connect to their community members.

∼

Dance Church currently employs thirty-five dance artists and growing, eight staff members, two design agencies, and one software engineering company. We host ongoing classes in over ten major cities across the country, and host pop-up events nationally and internationally. We subsidize classes for dance artists and BIPOC artists, and we keep our Sunday live-streams free for those who can't afford our membership price. We've partnered with well-known brands like Nike, Alaska Airlines, Nordstrom, and Outdoor Voices and arts organizations across the country including Mark Morris Dance Center, the Frye Art Museum, LA Dance Project, Gibney Dance Center, and the National Center for Choreography-Akron, among many others.

Three years into this journey, I will say three things:

1. Creation exists beyond any one person. The practice of separating yourself from the things that you have birthed is a useful meditation in letting go of control and allowing others to be generative and owners of growth.
2. Leadership is a skill. Skill sets can be learned. Learning takes time. Time is what you make of it.
3. Dance is inherently universal. It is as old as humans. That is a very large TAM[9] and there is huge potential in that—for audiences, for support, for engagement and money.

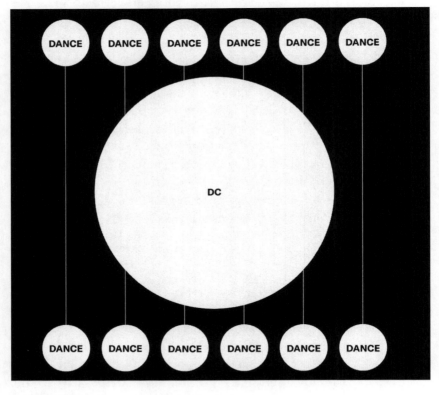

Administrative Experiment

What is your "Dance Church"?

RECOMMENDED READING

Moshe Feldenkrais, *The Potent Self: A Guide to Spontaneity* (Harper San Francisco, 1992).

Ben Horowitz, *The Hard Thing About Hard Things: Building a Business When There Are No Easy Answers* (Harper Business, 2014).

The Practice of Questioning and Generating Revenue

Delphine Lai and Christy Bolingbroke

In 2012, Deborah Hay, an experimental dancemaker and founding member of Judson Dance Theater, debuted a solo performance entitled *Turn Your F^*king Head*.[1] Hay later explained the premise for the piece as part of a performative lecture titled *Reorganizing Ourselves*.[2] She noted that a choreographer or dancer may walk into a studio or rehearsal space for the first time and ask, "Which way is 'front'?" By beginning with that question, Hay argued, the answer creates a paradigm of a fait accompli and prevents any additional questioning or discovery. Her advice to the artist is to "turn your f^*king head" in order to really see the room, every corner, every opportunity, in order to make an informed decision or determine the next question. This practice of questioning is not necessarily to acquire answers, but to adopt a conscious effort to unlearn in order to ask new questions instead of only seeking the same answers over and over again.

How can dancemakers extend this practice of questioning beyond the studio to the business of arts administration, and specifically toward revenue streams and fundraising? Both in the studio and in the office, our practices are grounded in history and assumptions. What unlearning must be done for artists and administrators to design creative environments for more effective and generative interactions? Questioning can help us truly see "the room" and its potential rather than only operating with decisions already predetermined.

TWENTIETH-CENTURY PRACTICES: UNPACK THE ASSUMPTIONS YOU INHERITED

For over fifty years, the dance field has built up a series of best practices that reinforce institutionalized approaches to arts administration and that assume all artists best thrive as organizations. However, prioritizing institutionalization and its accompanying practices has persuaded many artists to limit themselves to traditionally incorporated business structures with outdated fundraising practices. This pursuit of stability has resulted in dance artists and organizations operating under a narrow definition of success rather than tapping into the many creative possibilities.

There are a lot of practices across the professional world that we employ because we think it's what we are supposed to do. We continue to have conversations with choreographers peppered with statements like "I need an executive director..." (even though they have no other staff) or "We need money" (without identifying who might give and why, as well as how those relationships will be managed). Those kinds of declarations are presumptive conclusions or solutions. Instead, artists should identify what they really might be looking for in administrative support rather than starting with a position's title or pursuing individual donations without thinking of relationship-building with the communities that they want to reach. Our field, our leaders, and our workforce in and outside the studio already have creative tools. But we need to unlearn or question the best practices that we think we should be doing in order to develop custom tools and thinking that more accurately mirror our artistic goals and more effectively support our art.

Twentieth-century thinking around art and money implies that fundraising is a simple path: when dance artists need money to create or share their work, those dance artists need to start fundraising. This fundraising path seems straightforward and linear. If you hire a fundraiser, this person will do some research, ask individuals for donations, maybe write a couple of grants, host an event, and then you will have money for your project. But today's arts organizations, artists, and nonprofit administrators will quickly agree that revenue never comes so easily, regardless of the artwork, tax distinction, operating model, or geographic location. This twentieth-century approach to fundraising is predicated on two major assumptions:

1. Resources = Money; and
2. The artist has an incorporated nonprofit model with full-time staff to do the work.

This approach is based on centuries of giving to churches that carry the same nonprofit tax distinctions (and tax benefits for donors) as large cultural institutions, as well as centuries of unequal wealth distribution (from Renaissance Europe to Southeast Asian Kingdoms)[3] that resulted in the practice of arts patronage in the United States—individual wealthy patrons supporting artists. This approach also is rooted in an outdated visual arts model where a single artist just needs materials and time to create new work, so money = supplies, and artist + supplies + time = new work.

The dance field is moving beyond singular choreographer/artistic director models; embracing ethnically diverse dance forms and a wider variety of training, as well as artistic activism/artivism; and questioning national tours, home seasons, and a full-time company as the goals of artistic practice. In 2016, the New England Foundation for the Arts (NEFA) National Dance Project published *Moving Dance Forward*,[4] a report marking twenty years of their funding program. Of the artists who participated in the research surveys, 80 percent reported they were operating on a project-based model, likely meaning these artists were fiscally sponsored, conveniently incorporated, working under a limited liability corporation, or otherwise organized.[5] These artists were likely paid on a contractor basis rather than on salary, and these artists were likely working double duty as both choreographer and administrator. Some artists may have configured some sort of contract team to assist with administrative work, but they most certainly did not have a full-time administrative staff, and they possibly were not even pulling down a full-time salary for themselves. These project-based choreographers were living and working from grant to grant, gig to gig.

As the dance landscape continues to evolve, fundraising practices need to evolve as well: project-based artists don't have full-time staff; artists need to fundraise for resources beyond money; and you don't need to hire a fundraiser. You need to start asking new questions.

QUESTION THE ROOM: INSTEAD OF "HIRE A FUNDRAISER" ASK "WHO KNOWS THE WORK AND CAN ADVOCATE FOR THE WORK?"

In twentieth-century thinking, fundraising is a singular specialty. A conventional organization would have a fundraiser solely focused on individual donor identification, solicitation, and management; grant writing and grant management; and/or special events to solicit donations. However, the fundamental part of fundraising should be working with artists, directors, and project leaders to assess resources, research opportunities, and make connections. For this reason and perhaps especially in smaller, project-based operating environments, *everyone is a fundraiser.*

The twenty-first century is reinventing the fundraiser. So we challenge you to abandon a search for a development director, grants writer, major gifts officer, campaign consultant, or membership manager. There are such people, but do you want a career fundraiser? Or do you want someone who genuinely cares about your art and who can tell your story? It's possible to find a career fundraiser who knows your art and will advocate for it, but if you have to choose between the two, choose the person who already knows and cares about your art. Although there are development professionals who work full-time for nonprofit organizations, fundraisers can be and should be anyone in your network, including choreographers, dancers, production staff, lighting designers, costume designers, board members, office staff, finance directors, accountants, booking agents, presenters, and so on.[6] Many fundraisers are now project-based individuals or contractors who often hold multiple roles at an organization.

Fundraisers should advocate for your artistic vision, increase awareness for your goals and financial needs, and identify opportunities to grow your revenue and your community. Fundraisers do raise money and other kinds of donations for an organization. Nevertheless, if you limit yourself to seeing fundraising as raising money, then all gifts are transactional and all support is temporary. You are losing an opportunity to build your community. A single project might be funded but where does operational support come from during the following year? The gift, the fundraiser, and the funder will come and go. A good fundraiser focuses on understanding artistic vision and building relationships to support that work. Fundraising is not about getting money—*fundraising is building relationships.*

~

As we move beyond the twentieth-century job description of fundraiser as solicitor, at NCCAkron we challenge artists to think of fundraisers as additional dramaturgs for long-term artistic vision.[7] Regardless of title or responsibilities, administrative collaboration requires that everyone be a dramaturg in this work. Plays, musicals, and operas utilize dramaturgy, but dramaturgy in dance is still a relatively new idea, and dramaturgy in development pushes the term even farther. In theater, a dramaturg ensures that all pieces of the production are working together to tell the same story. As an organizational dramaturg, the fundraiser will witness and then tell your story, whether to appeal to a funder in writing, to a presenter on the phone, to a potential individual donor or board member at a performance, or to social media channels. This dramaturg understands your vision, retains the details of your story, and can translate your message.

If everyone in an operating model is responsible for fundraising, perhaps the twenty-first-century model for non-siloed, artist-centric ways of working means *everyone is a dramaturg too.*

QUESTION THE ROOM: INSTEAD OF "GET MORE DONORS" ASK "HOW DO WE BUILD AND CULTIVATE OUR FAMILY?"

For venues or organizations with buildings, the front questions in their marketing and development efforts have historically been about getting people through the front door. First, a person may buy a ticket to a single performance. Then, the cultural entity's marketing department tries to entice that person to come back, maybe the membership department tries to upsell a series subscription to that person, or the development department asks for a year-end donation. Over multiple years and visits, a relationship forms. The development department (usually staffed with multiple full-time employees) will identify this individual as a prospective major donor, and then research whether this individual or this individual's family has the capacity and the interest to get involved at a greater level. This prospect may be asked to cochair a fundraising gala or even serve on the organization's board, and eventually, a development officer may invite this person to make a major gift. But how do artists who work on a project basis (80 percent of the dance field, per NEFA's *Moving Dance Forward*)—and who have no full-time staff nor a building—cultivate individual donors in this manner? With the COVID health and safety restrictions that begin in 2020, established organizations and less conventional artists were suddenly in the same set of circumstances—no one could welcome people through their doors.

In response to the pandemic, Jacob's Pillow pivoted to an entirely virtual festival with eight weeks of performances during the summer of 2020.[8] Participation trends showed 80 percent of the online viewers were new to the Pillow family.[9] In all likelihood, these people will never make the trip to Becket, Massachusetts, to experience the festival in person, even in nonpandemic times. For an over eighty-year institution like the Pillow, the digital season introduced an opportunity to engage a new group of potential audience members. Even with the sheer volume of performances each summer and the longevity of their programs, there was an untapped market of additional demand with whom the Pillow could engage but not using the tools and practices they had relied on up until that point.

In contrast, Dance Place, a more intimate performance venue in Washington, DC, received very different feedback from their digital pivot to a virtual presentation series in Spring 2020.[10] In a reflection on the successes and shortcomings of these live-streamed performances with the board, then executive/artistic director Christopher K. Morgan shared that a single weekend of digital programs reached approximately four hundred viewers.[11] Board members were surprised that viewership was not higher. Morgan had to explain that four hundred people exceeded the number of patrons that Dance Place could host in a sold-out weekend (typically two shows with a maximum capacity of 144 patrons per show) in their physical theater space. His point was that just because they put a show online where there are more people than in Dance Place's immediate neighborhood did not mean there was additional demand or even awareness of what they offer.

Both examples reveal different responses and adjustments in an organization's thinking around the conventional pipeline of individual cultivation. The Dance Place example shows a nonprofit organization keeping and maintaining their existing audience. Perhaps there were a few outliers who tuned in remotely, but the number of people reached was only slightly larger than for their traditional, in-person performances. If Dance Place wants to reach new people, they will need to adjust their messaging and put in some additional labor/energy/resources to identify new audiences and to determine how to communicate with these new folks. The Pillow example shows a nonprofit organization reaching a whole new group of people with an interest in dance and the Pillow's program. Moving forward, if the Pillow wants to keep these new audiences, the Pillow will need to determine how to build a relationship with this audience and how to continue engaging them as part of the Pillow community even if these new audience members may never step foot on the festival grounds. Like Jacob's Pillow and Dance Place, individual artists and small dance companies need to question who comprises their audience and whom they want to reach, regardless of tax status and regardless of operating in a dedicated bricks and mortar setting or not.

Working through the pandemic and continuing to move forward as a field, many artists and arts organizations have extended their work to the internet, building out websites and social media channels. For project-based artists, online platforms can become a primary tool to directly find, expand, and keep audiences. Unless artists are self-producing and in charge of their own ticket sales, artists are usually not in direct connection with their audiences. A venue or presenter primarily holds audience relationships in between performances, so the artist's community often includes only immediate people in their life and work—close family members, current and former students, collaborators, the occasional institutional funder that supports new dance works. But by focusing on online efforts and using the metrics and data available through various media platforms, artists can identify their current digital audience (FIND); build out strategies to either identify similar groups or reach different ones (EXPAND); and develop tools or means to funnel offline audiences to engage with them directly in between performances (KEEP). Rather than following the traditional practice to just "get more donors," look for questions that will lead to more generative action. Who has seen your work? How do you engage with those people? How could you engage with them more? How would they want to interact with your art? Online or in-person? As a witness or as a participant? Where is your current audience located? Are these audience members located where the art is created or performed? Who is missing from this community? What is the best way to reach those people? How would you keep these new people engaged? Why might they give to you? Asking more questions will help inform any possible fundraising strategies or campaigns rather than just meeting a monetary goal.

QUESTION THE ROOM: INSTEAD OF "RAISE MORE MONEY" ASK "WHO DO WE WANT TO REACH?"

When JPMorgan Chase first launched their Community Giving challenge in 2009, the nonprofit community outwardly welcomed this new opportunity because JPMorgan Chase claimed to be giving power to the people—any Facebook user could vote for their favorite nonprofit and help distribute $5 million in corporate giving. What was not visible behind the scenes was the extra time and labor that nonprofits took to be competitive in that space, and ultimately the opportunity cost of throwing one's hat in the ring.

For their 2009 Community Giving campaign, JPMorgan Chase promised $25,000 grants to the 100 charities that received the most votes through the Chase Community Giving Facebook page. Those 100 charities would then be eligible for a $1 million grant (again decided by Facebook votes) with the five runners-up receiving a $100,000 grant. All nominated nonprofits would also be eligible for $1 million in grants that would be decided by the Chase Community Giving Advisory Board.[12] Small and midsized single choreographer companies that had jumped through the institutional tax hoops of incorporation shifted all their social media and email marketing efforts to convince their relatively small listservs to go to corporate portals and nominate or vote for their arts organization. Even large dance companies did not have a large enough volume of followers to yield the necessary traction to secure a $25,000 award. Arts organizations were competing with national nonprofits in the areas of education, housing, the environment, and health and human services[13]—the arts are a small fish inside that philanthropic pond. Many national nonprofits have regional chapters or networks that can create a groundswell of support for their campaigns with corporations, not to mention the lack of demand and societal value for the arts.

Rather than communicating and messaging about its artwork, the dance field was using its limited time and resources to promote the Chase Community Giving program. While these efforts generated an increased number of witnesses for Chase's philanthropic giving, the 2009 Community Giving program provided minimal support for the arts, and no support for dance.[14] Dance artists and organizations leveraged their networks to vote, but a financial contribution never came, and no new potential audience members were engaged because Chase did not share the names or the contact information of the voters.[15] What this spectacular failure in the arts and culture sector did demonstrate was the ongoing hunger for increased access to alternate revenue streams and the potential to activate the "social" in social media.

In the last two decades, online fundraising has become more prevalent with digital crowdfunding platforms such as GoFundMe, Kickstarter, and Facebook Fundraising that target individual donors. With new digital tools to ask for money, executive directors at conventional arts institutions were quick to direct their marketing and development staff to add a crowdfunding campaign into their development plans. What they quickly found out from their staff and their communities is that large arts institutions were not competitive in these fundraising waters because of their relative Goliath size. These crowdfunding tools are more compelling platforms to support individuals rather than organizations. For project-based choreographers who do not have any full-time staff, much less a dedicated fundraising or development person, the crowdfunding tools can be a more realistic means to an end.

Both project-based choreographers and large dance companies would benefit from the process of questioning before pursuing crowdfunding, a corporate grant, or any revenue opportunity. What person or community are you trying to reach? Do you already have a relationship with that potential donor? Why would that person/community want to be connected to your art? Do you already have a relationship with that person/community? How would that person/community like to contribute? How would you like that person/community to contribute? Does that person/community prefer interacting in person or through letters, phone calls, email, or social media? What would motivate that person/community to make a donation to you and your art? Questioning can help determine if a revenue stream will result in additional resources and if that revenue stream will align with both your artistic vision and your operational capacity.

QUESTION THE ROOM: INSTEAD OF "CHOOSE A BUSINESS MODEL" ASK "WHAT CAN WE LEARN ABOUT OURSELVES FROM EXPLORING A BUSINESS/FUNDRAISING MODEL?"

In 2013, Michael Kaiser and Brett Egan[16] published *The Cycle: A Practical Approach to Managing Arts Organizations* as a framework for arts organizations and nonprofit leaders.[17] The book explains the key components of operations as well as outlining the interdependent relationship between them. The Cycle's thinking organizes the four key components as the face of a clock. Straight up at twelve o'clock is ART. Moving clockwise ninety degrees is MARKETING. Straight down opposite ART is FAMILY. Another ninety degrees is $ or RESOURCES before circling back up to ART. Rather than presenting fundraising as a one-way linear path from money to art, Kaiser and Egan present an expansive loop where each item is dependent on or somehow in conversation with the next.

At NCCAkron, we constantly work to truly "see the room" per Deborah Hay and embrace questioning within our programming and organizational infrastructure. Seeing the room may result in challenging artist assumptions

The Practice of Questioning and Generating Revenue

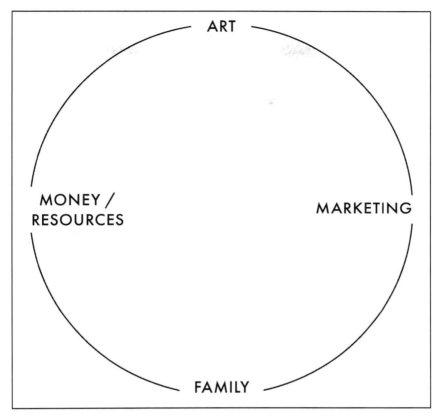

From *The Cycle: A Practical Approach to Managing Arts Organizations* by Michael M. Kaiser with Brett E. Egan

about having to teach or produce some kind of work-in-process showing as part of their engagement with the Center. As we codesign programs with our guest artists, we will ask artists, "Is that something you even want to do?"

For our Creative Administration Research (CAR) program, we engaged nineteen Artist Teams to reevaluate their operating environments and challenge administrative best practices, including fundraising. CAR Artist Teams are composed of a lead choreographic artist or collective, a curated Thought Partner to create momentum and accountability in this work, and NCCAkron team members. NCCAkron also self-identifies as the unofficial twentieth

Artist Team among this think tank, since we are still a young, burgeoning organization developing and learning alongside artists. One exercise that NCCAkron practices internally as well as with all the CAR Artist Teams is to try on The Cycle according to Kaiser and Egan.

NCCAkron asks how this framework might work or not work for even smaller cultural operations—project-based artists working across the ecology at large without full-time administrative staff or assistance, much less an incorporated 501(c)(3) status. The Cycle suggests that for every arts organization, these four elements are required for success, and all four hold equal weight and importance. When digging in, many CAR Artists discovered that applying The Cycle's four elements to their own work leads them to existential questions about their own administrative and artistic practices:

- **What is ART?**—Being a process-based organization with rarely public-facing offerings itself, NCCAkron usually reframes this element as "creative output," which could include live performances, gallery happenings, dancing in the streets, teaching at studios, teaching at universities, writing about dance, or even Instagram live feeds. For CAR Artists, creative output could be all of those things and more, or just one or two. In your individual operating ecology, what falls under your ART or creative output?
- **What is MARKETING?**—CAR Investigative Retreats promote both the institutional and programmatic marketing recommendations from The Cycle. Programmatic marketing is a specific call to action or transaction—buy a ticket, sign up for a class or intensive, book my company. Regardless of tax incorporation status, institutional marketing references your longer artistic arc and continuously conveys your vision or value in between performances and activities. Understandably, some artists push against embodying nomenclature like MARKETING because of its capitalist connotations. At that point, we reframe the term to be storytelling, communicating, or messaging—any way the artist and others can talk about the ART. Think about the above question "Who knows the work and can advocate for the work?" Operating from a position

where everyone is a fundraiser and a dramaturg, these witnesses inside and adjacent to your creative process can provide the best input regarding messaging around artistic work. Whether for archival purposes or future newsletter copy, how are you collecting information from these shared experiences? Who is the audience you are trying to talk to about your work?

- **What is FAMILY?**—More conventional, nonprofit leaders and grantmakers may use broad, monolithic terms like audience or community served. More expansive thinking about FAMILY includes ticket buyers, board members, collaborators, dancers, funders, staff, students, and many others in and around the artist's orbit. FAMILY can be anyone who is inside your operating ecology and may interact with your ART at any level. The term FAMILY raises less existential concern among CAR Artists because of its interpersonal nature as well as its flexible way of thinking outside of nonprofit arts management and conventional business, for example, a birth family as well as a chosen family. If anything, artists need to not remain too comfortable or close to home with their FAMILY, and instead think of whom they may want to welcome into their networks. Think about the above question "How do we build and cultivate our family?" Do you know who is currently in your FAMILY? Do you know why they engage with your work? How are you using that information to inform how you keep, find, and expand your family? How does this information relate back to your communications strategy and content?

- **What are RESOURCES?**—Of course, RESOURCES include money, but RESOURCES can also encompass so much more. RESOURCES can be relationships, access to space, past creative output, institutional memory, community invitations and connections, grants, and opportunities that lead to new or more creative output. In conventional nonprofit environments, board members and volunteers may bring specific skill sets and donate their labor as contributing RESOURCES. Think about the above question: Whom do we want to reach? As we continue to be (sometimes painfully) more and more aware of wealth disparity, we know and feel there is more financial capacity out there in the world. Rather than chasing the funds or any opportunity, how are you selectively choosing strategic partners and deciding where to place your energy for cultivating specific FAMILY members and securing RESOURCES? How are you maximizing those RESOURCES not only to make your next project, but to also move your business operations forward?

Most of the CAR Artists are project-based, and as they tried on The Cycle, many realized that their project-based thinking has them stuck in a small loop operating primarily between ART and RESOURCES. They came to understand that they may remain in this small loop without additional capacity, effort, or wherewithal to consistently build out a communications plan, cultivate a network of support, or evolve their individual operating ecology.

The Cycle empowered these project-based artists to see how they may have been blocking themselves by seeing funders, presenters, and other gatekeepers as large geologic resources that we must build operations around, rather than seeing these entities as FAMILY. By adding questions about whom you want in your FAMILY and how you want to engage with them, The Cycle enabled many CAR Artists to better understand and potentially redesign their operational pipeline, so that their administrative work (including fundraising) made sense to them and their artistic vision.

Some CAR Artists also began to experiment with rearranging The Cycle and re-imagining whether each of the four elements should be the same in size and weight, or not. For example, a community organizer might bring people together through just one artistic performance every three years as a result of long, deep work within communities. So for that CAR Artist, FAMILY is more central and important to their reason for being, while MARKETING, RESOURCES, and ART are secondary.

For NCCAkron and the CAR program, The Cycle has become one means for self-reflection. The internal analysis can identify underutilized assets, unexplored corners of the room, and ultimately new ways forward in the shape of revenue streams or other useful resources. Rather than seeking the exact business/fundraising model to use, many CAR Artists found that trying on The Cycle provided a lens through which to play and experiment; to better understand their own artistic and administrative work; to connect the artists' administrative thinking as it relates to the creative work; and to communicate why or how certain administrative tasks and fundraising efforts speak to a larger strategy for long-term sustenance.

TWENTY-FIRST-CENTURY PRACTICES: WHAT TO CARRY FORWARD

The term "nonprofit" is a tax distinction, not an operating model. Whether you decide to incorporate as a nonprofit organization, operate as a limited liability corporation, or acquire fiscal sponsorship as an individual artist, how do you want to do business? How might your business practices and your fundraising practices reflect your artistic values and thinking?

To all our creative colleagues who work behind the scenes and to the choreographers and artists who simultaneously tackle artistic, administrative, and fundraising responsibilities—we challenge you to embrace your whole self and to extend the practice of questioning to the business of arts administration. As each of us finds our own way through the intersection of art and business, we advocate for the practice of questioning in order to ensure that all work stays grounded in the ART. By staying grounded in the art and artistic practices, we uplift our business practices and our fundraising practices. And we also uplift our art.

So, creatively interrogate your operational practices, instead of assuming they are best or professional, as if there is only one way. Instead of assuming that hiring a fundraising professional will solve all revenue needs, what are your resources? Where can you experiment with fundraising and other long-held business practices? You don't need to upend all your practices tomorrow. Feel free to start small. Identify opportunities and deadlines beyond your control, but also make space for experiments with grant research, individual giving, earned revenue, in-kind support, network development, and strategic partnerships.

Because creativity should extend beyond the studio and the stage, and because the generation of revenue should always be aligned with artistic vision. Stay curious, experiment, and ask new questions instead of seeking the same answers.

Administrative Experiment

QUESTION THE ROOM

The practice of questioning can help determine if a revenue stream will align with your capacity, your long-term administrative goals, and your artistic vision. Not every revenue strategy is a match for every dance artist or for every dance organization. A strategy may be appropriate at a certain point in your administrative or artistic trajectory but not at other points. So prior to pursuing (or letting go of) any revenue opportunity, unpack your assumptions and "question the room" in order to better determine if a revenue strategy is a good match.

Consider these two twentieth-century assumptions that many dance artists and organizations still hold:

- We need to have a national tour and home season every year.
- We need a major individual donor/foundation/corporation to give us money.

As you reflect on these two assumptions, ask yourself these questions beyond the potential for earned income or contributed income:

- Who are the people you are trying to reach? Is this the best method to reach and engage those people or that community?
- What are your resources to support this opportunity? Do you have the human capacity and the time to plan, engage, solicit, and cultivate long-term relationships?
- How will this opportunity strengthen or build your family?
- How will this opportunity support your art?
- How will this opportunity reinforce your marketing and storytelling?
- What are the likely benefits? Is it worth the investment of your time and resources?
- Does this opportunity align with your artistic vision?

After this first set of questions, push the practice of questioning even farther for each specific topic:

- *For Touring or Home Season Performances,* consider the places (cities, organizations, or venues) that you have engaged with as part of your creative output and engagements, such as performances, teaching, research, residencies, and so on. How many places have you been more than once? More than three times? Are those the places where you want to continue to invest your energy, or are there other places you wish to develop further? You might decide to concentrate on a single location, a couple of locations, all of them, or none of the above. All avenues are valid, but a strong sense of your past output and relationships will give a reflexive internal analysis to inform programmatic decisions and revenue strategies beyond the financial ramifications.
- *For Foundations,* consider whether a relationship with these potential family members is realistic and beneficial. Beyond the possible financial award, is the institution aligned with your mission or your artistic vision? Do their interests and/or geographic focus complement where you would like to deepen or expand your network? If you apply this year, does the grant period align with your creation timeline? If the grant period doesn't align with your creation timeline, would you still benefit from engaging with the foundation or applying anyway to gain feedback and initiate a relationship? There are many valid paths for engaging foundations. Even though many foundations outline a strict calendar for letters of intent and proposals, many program officers offer information sessions, and foundation staff are often open to conversations with artists as long as you aren't contacting them immediately before a deadline. So rather than feel limited by the foundation's next deadline, think about what foundation relationships make the most sense for your art. The path will be different for each foundation, for each artist, and for each situation.
- *For Corporations,* consider the reach of your events. Corporations want recognition, and they operate much more transactionally than artist-centrically. Many corporations give because they are trying to offset their capitalist reality, gain a tax break, and

improve their corporate image, not necessarily because they believe in the nonprofit or the art. Their community giving program often exists within their marketing, communications, or public relations departments. Is your community the target audience that the corporation wants to reach? Are your audience numbers large enough for the corporation? Do you have any connections to top-level management at the corporation? Securing corporate grants or sponsorships can be significant, but these gifts also require significant resources and networks.

- *For Individual Donors*, consider family connections and storytelling strategies year-round, especially when exploring internet avenues like Giving Tuesday or crowdfunding campaigns. People give to people, not to a solicitation letter or an email. Have you developed a family for your art, beyond your immediate friends or birth family? How do you engage with this extended family in between performances and donation solicitations in order to deepen their connections with your work? What is the capacity of your family to ask others for donations? How can people contribute beyond just money? Twenty-first-century solutions, like crowdfunding portals, have made fundraising more accessible to project-based artists, but these revenue streams come up short if you don't utilize these tools inside a larger, long-term strategy.

Both in the studio and in the office, by questioning and unlearning, we strengthen our artistic as well as our administrative potential. So let questions be your starting point. Through the practice of questioning, you can leverage learning, uncover resources, and better evaluate revenue opportunities. Rather than seeking the same answers, question and experiment to find the revenue streams that work for you and your artistic vision.

PART IV
PATHWAYS

CHOREOGRAPHY, PERFORMANCE, AND THE ABSOLUTE TRUTH ABOUT BEING AN ARTIST[1]

Raja Feather Kelly

THE STORY ABOUT HOW DREAMING IS IMPOSSIBLE

I was recently at an artist gathering.[2] It was incredibly inspiring—artists from all over the United States gathered and wanted to be gathered. They were paid for their time, fed, and transported. There were no obligations other than to talk to each other, agree to have conversations documented, and respond to a lofty proposition. We were posed to use our imaginations to make possible a radical future. It occurred to me that this was a proposition that we as artists are not asked often. And the answers, in my opinion, were all small, possible, and not radical. Care, Support, Inclusivity, Agency, Community, Collaboration, and Equity were among the top repeated responses. Why is this? Are these variables truly radical? While they are not as radical as I wish they could be, perhaps they are radical because while often reaching for the stars, we don't ground our visions in what we need rather than what we want.

WHY DO WE DREAM FOR WHAT MANY WOULD SAY ARE THE FOUNDATIONS OF ART MAKING?

In a world where the artist is the producer, the HR department, the marketing director, and the lead fundraiser—is dreaming impossible?

TEN THINGS I DARED MYSELF TO SAY OUT LOUD.[3]

1. Artists always say: "*Time, Space, and Resources*" when asked what they want, because that is exactly what they want and need. It's that simple.
2. I bet you an artist wouldn't say this out loud, but when we are asked, "What are the desired outcomes of your proposed [residency / grant / project / or proposal]?" 99 percent of the time we lie with our answers. We don't know. We're artists.
3. I truly believe there is no such thing as a target audience, because, if artists could really choose who or where we wanted to present our work—we'd either already have the money or not need it.
4. The first sentences in each of the questions you respond to on your grant applications are the only sentences that matter.
5. In America, artists have to ask for permission to be artists.
6. More than 60 percent of grants are lottery even though applicants are led to believe they are not.
7. Getting an award is like currency, like a VIP Pass.[4]
8. You are only as good as how many tickets you can sell.
9. If you don't take the high-profile, low-budget, less than average, mediocre, once-in-a-lifetime opportunity that comes once a year, someone else will.
10. Every artistic opportunity is a one-night stand.

THE HISTORY OF MY ARTIST STATEMENTS
2009

I consider myself a theorist. I see myself as a chemist with small pieces of the world at my fingertips; small pools of my imaginations flooding a war between what I see and what I touch. I am a sponge, a chameleon sponge looking for a secret. What here is at my disposal and what change is at my expense? What is a vision if not merely a failed dream, one you forgot to have, one we spend too much time trying to recreate and re-live in. What am I if not the dynamics of music and the influence and product of the infinities between years, sunrises, hours and handshakes? Is there a future for my broken shapes and lines convoluted by mixed messages and Picasso pieces? There is a message in here somewhere. Am I standing on it, in it, or is it in my hands, or feet rather, grounding itself becoming perennial?

2011

I consider myself an image-maker. My experience as an actor, dancer, writer, filmmaker, and administrator has given me no label to concentrate the work I create. I am inspired by and work through collecting and combining images—provocative images emblematic of the beauty I see in pain, deceit, and motivation. As a little boy I have always been drawn to the life of Andy Warhol—its depictions of rawness, the personal and the private, as well as borrowed and exploited ideas. I have spent a significant time studying the work of Anne Sexton, her inclusion and development of what we know as confessional poetry. Sexton created images that readers could find empathy with and her work became an archetype for artists doing work for communities of feelers needing permission to take risks. Connecting these two platforms for making work through the medium of dance is my focus in making dance/performance work.

2012 (FEBRUARY)

I am interested in exploring work that is ridden with understanding the human condition—I recognize the human condition to be the distinctive and patented landscapes of being human, particularly existentialism, fear, and desire. I am interested in creating multifaceted artworks by organizing the layers of history, philosophy, literature, and the arts that lead us to understanding the human condition. It is my goal to bridge common psychologies and philosophies behind the human condition and the creation of referential and investigative physicality as an entry point to my aesthetic, theories, and plots. I plan on developing a line of work individually and collaboratively which includes performance, written texts, audio works, and photography/film focused on the questioning and considerable answers to the human condition.

2012 (SEPTEMBER)

My artist statement is as simple as the words: Do you hear what I hear, do you see what I see, do you feel what I feel? Or the children's game of "telephone."

2013

I have been developing my body of work as movement-based performance essays. My artistic process begins with physical games, puzzles, systems, and strategies and develops into research-driven, iterative performances. A fully realized work requires engaging in these open-ended practices over time. An ongoing theme for me is POP-ART. Andy Warhol says that movies have been running things in America since their invention—showing us what to do, when and how to do it, how to feel about it, how to look and how to feel about how you look.[5] My current explorations and collaborations are wondering if this is true. I want my collaborations to extend beyond what we see as ordinary, especially in respect to movement vocabulary, the line between personal and private, and duration. My research-driven, iterative process questions when the audience becomes necessary to the achievement of the work, and by what means it is the most appropriate to communicate to said audience: movement, video, text, prop?

2016

I am obsessed with the life and work of Andy Warhol and the development of Popular Culture over the last thirty years. I use performance-making and exhibition as a way to promote empathy. My artistic practice identifies and magnifies opportunities where popular culture and human desire intersect. My practice imitates the structures, themes, and aesthetics found in reality television, celebrity culture, and social media (YouTube, Instagram, Facebook) and deconstructs them. The work I create addresses how we are taught to interact with different human themes through television, movies, music, and art. My performances combine fashion show, gallery exhibition, dance performance, drag-ball, stand-up comedy routine, minstrel show, and stage-play into a single, overwhelming, over-saturated Gesamtkunstwerk—in which artists and audience alike recognize their shared humanity.

2017

I am obsessed with the development of popular culture over the last thirty years. I am inspired by repetition, iconography, and cinematic sensibilities. I am invested in amplifying mundane and pedestrian movement so that it becomes scientific and virtuosic. I use performance-making and exhibition as a way to promote empathy. My practice identifies and magnifies opportunities where popular culture and human desire intersect. Two parts: The work unabashedly appropriates structures, themes, and aesthetics found in reality television, celebrity culture, and social media. Then it deconstructs them into new works which combine dance, theatre, and visual media. The aim: to challenge audiences to recognize their own implication in popular media: how media has trained and molded our desires, relationships, and identities. My movement-based performances combine fashion show, gallery exhibition, drag, stand-up comedy, minstrelsy, and stage-play into a single, overwhelming Gesamtkunstwerk—in which artists and audience experience their shared humanity.

We bend, but don't break, the specific formal rules of each genre we appropriate. We deconstruct each genre from within the genre's own internal rules and contradictions. All of my training and background—Speech and Debate, Musical Theatre, social dance styles of the 90s, my academic study of Modern/Post Modern Dance, and English Literature—have prepared me for the unique way that I rehumanize my over-mediated experience of reality. Though I use text and elaborate costuming, the forefront of my research is the research of movement as the language which represents all bodies, cultures, and ideas. For me, the body is one of the only vessels that can both represent and abstract ideas.

2020

I am obsessed with the development of popular culture over the last forty years. I am inspired by the philosophy and aesthetics of repetition, iconography, and cinematic sensibilities. I am invested in amplifying mundane and/or pedestrian movement so that it becomes scientific and virtuosic. I use performance-making and exhibition as a way to promote empathy. My practice identifies and magnifies opportunities where popular culture and the human condition intersect. The aim is to challenge our audience to recognize their own implication in popular media: how media has trained and molded their desires, relationships, and identities. I rehumanize our over-mediated experiences of reality.

With my company, the feath3r theory (TF3T), I collaborate with dancers, actors, filmmakers, musicians, photographers, and designers, with a mission to broaden the space for unheard voices and repressed histories, to bring into the theatre those sometimes left out, and to use theatre to provoke much-needed public conversations. The work of TF3T synthesizes dance, visual media, fashion, drag, standup, minstrelsy, and narrative theatre into virtuosic, expansive, radical and surreal large-scale pop-culture phenomena or an overwhelming, over-saturated "Gesamtkunstwerk" in which artists and audience alike experience their shared humanity. We are committed to addressing pressing social issues through Dance, Theatre, and Media with an emphasis on LGBTQ themes.

THE ONE ABOUT BUDGETS

So I remember back in 2016 I took a course on budgets.[6] The refrain that I remember hearing over and over was: "the budget tells a story, the budget is a story, the budget is the work."

So here goes:

> I recently had a show to be produced, but the theatre was too small. So the presenter partnered with another theatre to put up the show and everything came down to the budget. Even though the show had already been created and premiered months before this production, both theaters together couldn't quite come up with enough money to present it. They kept saying THIS was the show they WANTED.
>
> The theaters made several unsuccessful attempts to ask me to change the show. Then they said: Let's just look at the production budget and make adjustments as necessary. We'll squeeze tech rehearsals down to two days. You will come into the theater a week before and pre-focus your lights, and we will make one person on our staff hold two jobs that week: technical director and lighting technician.
>
> Do you see where this is going? If I agree to this, what then is my work?
>
> Does this sound genre-pushing, community-building, fashion-forward, culture-leading, humane, and provocative?

CHOREOGRAPHY, PERFORMANCE, AND THE ABSOLUTE TRUTH

I AM MY OWN PRODUCER

Hey, It's Raja,

I wanted to reach out to let you know that I am putting you in touch with the people that you need to be in touch with. Person A needs to be put in touch with Person U and they are both in this thread.

Also, I was able to move things around in my personal budget to make room for the marketing budget line that you promised me that you would most definitely provide.

Oh, I will record the show myself to make sure we have a document of what we did.

Please let me know if you saw my edits for the copy for the press release, and the list of all the press agents I know. I was also able to get the contracts out to the cast and creative team. Yes, I was able to hire a photographer.

Lastly, I got quotes on all the load-in and load-out labor, I created and ordered the programs, I booked and catered the afterparty, and I made a spreadsheet so we can follow up with the presenters that come and other V.I.P.s.

If you could just let me know you got this email, we'd be all squared away. My assistant has got everything else covered.

Thanks again,
Raja

MY THREE MOST POPULAR/SUCCESSFUL SHOWS HAD NO GRANT PROPOSALS

Three of my most successful works were shows that I made when I had no idea what I was going to make. I was given a time frame, space to do the work, and money to do it.

In 2018 The Bushwick Starr[7] said, "We have space for an eight-week residency and performance." I took the opportunity and said I wanted to make a solo. I hadn't made an evening-length solo before, but I knew I wanted to make something, I knew I wanted it to be about my experience, and I knew I wanted to make an experience for the audience. The rest was a timeline. I moved into The Bushwick Starr and 8 weeks later I created something I was truly proud of. I had no showings, no one checked up on me, and no one told me if it was good or not good before I had a chance to perform it. I didn't have to ask for permission. It was within the budget I was given. I didn't have to reconcile a production narrative or write about if I achieved my goals or not. The shows were sold out, it was featured in the *New York Times*, received a Princess Grace Award,[8] and toured internationally.

In 2020 during the COVID pandemic, my show at New York Live Arts[9] was canceled. New York Live Arts asked me what I wanted to do; they said we have space, budget, marketing support, and a slot eight weeks from now. I said I will make something. I knew I wanted to create something that was performative, digital, and experiential. That's it. Because of COVID guidelines, I had to work mostly alone. Because of COVID, New York Live Arts said they weren't overly concerned with ticket sales, so I didn't over-advertise. The COVID restrictions allowed me to think about showcasing my work in alternative mediums that I often work but seldom have the opportunity to exhibit. The result was a three-part exhibition in New York Live Arts' Ford Gallery and a three-camera film, created by my design company, that was live streamed. I was so proud of the results. The show was featured in the *New York Times*, had two re-presentations in New York City (which is rare), and had a seven-city international tour.

In 2021, Karl Regensburger, the artistic director of the ImPulsTanz Vienna International Dance Festival,[10] asked me if I wanted to perform the above two works (*Ugly Part 1*, and *Ugly Part 2*) at the festival and asked me if I wanted to make it a trilogy. I accepted the offer and only knew that the work needed eight weeks and double the budget of the last project. I needed space that was all my own, and a budget that could expand as I learned more about how the work developed. I was given six weeks. My design company[11] was flown to Vienna, Austria, to work with me. I was most scared about this work because I really didn't know what I wanted to do, only that I had to do it, not because of the commission, but because I felt this deep in my soul. This sentence would not be accepted as a grant proposal although it is often what I feel when I know I need to make work. And all I need is the space, time, and resources (money, accommodations, props, production tools) for me to attune to my gut and create what needs to be created, and a way to design an experience for an audience to encounter these ideas. The result was *UGLY Part 3*[12]—one of my most successful works to date and a major catapult of my now regularly performing internationally.

HAS ANYONE ASKED AN ARTIST WHAT THEY NEED?[13]

It's Monday, May 4, 2020, at 6:20 p.m., and about two months into the New York City lockdown as a result of the COVID-19 pandemic. I start a text chain with ten artists I find on my phone. I'm at home, I am bored, and I am in this sort of limbo with myself. Dusty Springfield has been on repeat. In my head. My love-letter-slash-sad-love-song to New York City right now is her song: "I just don't know what to do with myself."

Usually, I work all the time and I work as much as I can, and it almost feels like a disease. But I also love my work. I get up before 6 a.m.; go to the gym; clear my inbox and get on the subway. I work for three to four-hour slots between different gigs, jobs, and commissions, and in between, I take phone meetings and Skype calls, and I field hundreds of text messages. At some point, I'll eat something. When the evening hits, between 5 p.m. and 6 p.m., my workday is done and then I go to rehearsal until 10 p.m. with my company. There is a warm-up, conversations about everyone's feelings (we don't have an HR department), and then we dance, we make theater, we record some media and we work until someone kicks us out. I have a complicated relationship with this routine. But, as an artist, this is simply what the hustle looks like.

I start a text chain with ten artists (Broadway choreographers, celebrated teachers, well-known performers, and those who have made great contributions to their art communities). No one is asking me what I need right now. I asked my colleagues, "What do you need? Who's got your back? And, What's next?"

What followed was a series of responses that explained that they haven't been cared for, had no offers for support, felt uninspired, hopeless, and homeless, and while this was during COVID, it seemed these feelings were ongoing, continued, lasting since before COVID-19.

When I ask myself these questions, 'What do I need? Who has my back? What's next?' I think: "I'm trying to lean far back into why I do this. This art thing." I never wanted to do this for money. And yet I need money to keep doing this. I don't know if anyone has my back if I can't offer them something in return. I think I might not know who has my back until it's too late and I'll either die or be surprised by who catches me.

> To Funders, Presenters, and those alike:
> Please note that money will always be at the core of our needs, but sometimes we need something else, or something more. To know that we matter, and to know that our contributions are valuable, and to know when you say, "We're going to get through this together" that we are a part of that "We."

Let's think deeply about what we are going to return to after the pandemic, and what that will mean for us artists. More applications, more competitions, more fundraisers, and more needs. We are not machines. Give artists homes. And mean it. What is next is a choice. Each choice we make today designs our world for tomorrow.
Please hear me loud and clear:

Artists are a force for change. Artists carve the path forward. Artists will design the plan for the reclamation of culture. Artists are here to transform, challenge, and to make meaning. Artists are here to constantly reimagine our world and show us what our world could be. Artists are here to bring people together and build communities. Artists have been here for entertainment AND culture time and time again.—Raja Feather Kelly

LONGEVITY V. SUSTAINABILITY

Sustainability in our field has been a survival mechanism; an ever clawing at the gate, or gasping for air when artists are at the end of our capacity for holding our breath.

I sometimes think to myself: "to sustain is to avoid."

But can sustainability be a pathway for artists to take care of themselves so that we're not taking away the possibility for others to take care of themselves?

I believe the way I was taught to think about sustaining is the antithesis of the ideas that make up a company, organization, field, or community. I believe the term sustainability is too broadly used "to indicate programs, initiatives, and actions aimed at the preservation of a particular resource." There are four commonly recognized pillars of sustainability: human, social, economic, and environmental.[14] When we combine these four pillars of sustainability; can sustainability mean the capacity to endure?

When I think about dance and the dancing body specifically, I would never want my body to be sustaining. Would you? A body requires durability—the ability to withstand wear, pressure, or damage; and flexibility—the willingness to change or adapt. Don't we want our bodies to appear to have permanence while we're performing?

Perhaps our bodies want longevity. Longevity holds the performance of permanence strong. We're in an ephemeral art form and we are in an ephemeral world. Don't you desire longevity?

Our companies and our work want to have Longevity; a long adaptable life with the human, social, economic, and environmental support/resources that allow us to do so. After being given the task to consider an alternative to a scarcity mentality that makes one believe that sustainability is supreme, I offer Longevity as an adaptive practice for artists, producers, presenters, institutions, and foundations to consider and realize.

Long Live Longevity!

HORROR STORIES AND PERSEVERANCE

It appears to me that I spend a lot of my career fighting for a kind of integrity that would allow me to live and work the way I *want* to. While I have more horror stories than stories of success, I believe that I am slowly moving the needle. When I arrived in New York City there were nearly twenty companies of my size and determination. I imagine there are just three of those companies still active today. Perseverance is real. But chasing perseverance with a long dose of integrity is a kind of relentlessness so few of us can fuel.

THE CASE FOR "NO"

If success consists of going from failure to failure without loss of enthusiasm, then Art should not be measured by the number of "No's" we get, but by the number of times we can say "no."

WITHOUT ME FUNDERS WOULDN'T HAVE A JOB

This was a mantra that I had to tell myself for months. I needed to put myself in a position of power. I have agency. I have art, I know how to make art, and I am a collaborator. I am not inferior. When I really think about it, the world WANTS AND CRAVES ART, and I am dedicated to being a cultural leader. Money is filtered from corporations to foundations, to organizations, and *then* to artists. The one category of people where the buck stops is the artists. So, without me and artists like me, then what?

SAME PAGE OR SHARED EXPERIENCE

As the pandemic began to shift, I began to rethink my experience as an artistic director, as a culture leader, and as an artist. As a part of a Creative Administration Research program with the National Center for Choreography-Akron,[15] I convened with my board to think about our "next steps." We needed to talk about who we were as a company; what we wanted to be doing;

and how we were going to do it. But we were eager to do this differently than we knew how to, we were determined to "get on the same page" after this meeting. It occurred to me that the idea of all being on the "same page" was absurd, minimizing, and impossible. This was the email I shared with my board:

> Hey Friends,
>
> I realized that after I left you all yesterday in a flurry to make my flight, which I did, that "Same Page" perhaps is the administrative term for what we call an Artistic "Shared Experience." While the same page suggests that we all think and feel exactly the same about a way forward or about a specific situation, perhaps it actually is meant to acknowledge that we all just did a thing, at the same time, and have taken a year (or several) to do that "thing" with intention.
>
> Bordeaux, San Francisco, San Diego, Ohio, the at-home working spaces of New York, and lobbies of New York's finest artistic institutions have held space for where the art really happens—the exchange between people; a designed shared experience.
>
> I am so grateful. Actually, inspired and indebted to the time you took to do so. If anyone is like me, I am ALWAYS angling to get out of a meeting or a zoomer or another thing unless it holds a great deal of merit for me, something I believe in, something I can stand behind, something with meaning and fortitude.
>
> Nobody got time to just be wasting.
>
> Thank you.
>
> While much of the artistic process of creating this new work is about a group of people attempting to travel to the sun to cover it with mud, I am eager to consider that administratively we are working backward with this metaphor.
>
> So much is stacked against us. Time, money, and all of the hills, brush, and mountains in between achieving these resources. The personal, the political, and that which is unseen.
>
> Our work, administratively, is about *uncovering* the sun with the mud that keeps it from shining. Art is a light, art is a pathway, and art is (at least for me) the sun.
>
> Sun: a star around which Earth and the other components of the solar system revolve. It is the dominant body of the system, constituting more than nine-

ty-nine percent of its entire mass. The Sun is the source of an enormous amount of energy, a portion of which provides Earth with the light and heat necessary to support life.

Art: energy around which people and other components are revolving. It is the dominant body of culture, constituting more than ninety-nine percent of human interaction. Art is the source of an enormous amount of power, a portion of which provides the earth and its beings the strength and vitality necessary to support life.

Thank you for sharing your experience of the last two days with me. I look forward to more.

Administrative Experiment

MY LIFE THE BOOK

I invite you to consider that you are exactly where you need to be. That where you are right now is not good or bad, but that you are on a journey...

With that in mind, imagine yourself twenty-five years from now. Imagine that you have done exactly what you wanted to do with your career, life, interest, and hopes, and imagine all of the dips and valleys, and people, and situations that got you there.

Now imagine that you have to recount what you have done to get to where you are, and you have been tasked to write an autobiography.

1. What would you title this autobiography?
2. What would the title of each chapter be?

You can stop here... or you can keep going.

3. Write a short synopsis of the book.
4. Write a paragraph about what happens in each chapter.

You can stop here... or you can keep going.

Answer the following…

Where are you in that story now?
What happens next?
What gets you to the next chapter that ultimately gets you to the end result of your unfinished and unpublished autobiography about _____, _____, and *your* absolute truth about being a *successful* _____?

You can stop here… or you can keep going.

Now do that.

Do the thing that gets you from where you are now to the next chapter.
And remember…

You can stop here… or you can keep going.

Sharing Resource Stories
How Did I End Up Here, and Where Is Here Telling Me to Go from Here?
Makini

I offer this chapter of sharing. I offer it, hopefully, in service of encouraging more sharing of the like. To provide a deeper contextualization into the story of my arrival to this point—wherever this is... midcareer artist? established artist? on the precipice of a career shift and/or midlife crisis?—at least from the perspective of the material, communal, and spiritual resources that got me here. Especially while working as a younger, professionalized artist, I often felt both quiet and loud encouragements toward privacy in relation to resource/economic history. From various folks who were more established within the professionalized art world, I felt an agreement to adhere to a collective hush about the foundations of our material resources, if we had any, in order to prevent others from tapping our current resource wells or exposing our unearned advantages. Like so many industries, our art worlds and the folks who sustained them were often guided by a conservative fear of scarcity, of resources coming to an eventual end. A privacy ethic, it seemed, would help competitively protect personal and/or narrowly communal interests from other hungry competitors who are also looking for a meal on a table of quickly disappearing food.

Especially as a younger artist, I had immense curiosity about how other artists were making their own economic decisions, receiving financial support, and being buttressed by wealth resources. Now, at the age of forty, after having toured my live performance work nationally and internationally, after having received residencies, grants, and fellowships on local, national, and international scales, I am eager to assist younger and/or differently positioned artists to navigate through this art field with more information at their disposal, with a wider scope of the engines that fuel those who have achieved a certain level of recognition within the field. I am a Black, queer artist who grew up within a socialist pan-Africanist community,[1] and those identitarian and ideological foundations continuously orient my desire to contribute to joyous futures especially for Black and Indigenous queer & trans professionalized artists who have yet to receive our owed reparations from what is currently called the United States. And, in general, I believe that expanding a rigorous joy and love ethic throughout our species will lead to abundant health and care. My desires lead me in service of supporting visions for interdependent worlds in which individual and collective accountability are embraced. My transparency in relationship to my personal resource history is a further act in service of nurturing those worldviews.

For me to be able to do anything that I do, I am lifted by the support of those who have mentored, looked after, and loved me. My families—blood and chosen—are implicit in my choices, my gifts, and my responsibilities, even if I do not name them specifically within a given moment. This sharing that I do is also not anomalous and is in conversation with the work of so many other folks who are doing their own work toward more interdependent futures. I am often inspired by Sydnie L. Mosley's artistic and activistic work, and she has been engaged in her own sharing practices on her website.[2] Miguel Gutierrez's podcast *Are You For Sale?*[3] (also, see Miguel's essay in this book) helps demystify the function of charitable foundations within the professionalized art world, and what that has to do with the success, or lack thereof, of artists who seek their resource support. Angel Edwards's,[4] Jonathan González's,[5] and Dakota Camacho's[6] artistic work often encourages me to think more deeply of myself in relationship to larger systems of care and of oppression, and how artistic work itself can directly engage as a roadmap toward practices of collective liberation. Amy Smith's[7] work with artists to help interpret and subvert tax systems and manage money has been extremely informative for me, offering immediate tools to help transform thinking about resource and money. I am grateful to be in the company of these folks, and so many more.

PROFESSORSHIP

My parents both currently work at Lincoln University, each with a long history of engaging with pedagogical practices as educators, administrators, and organizers. My maternal grandmother was a teacher of English literature and English as a second language for many years. My maternal grandfather was a Baptist pastor, and when my siblings and I visited his church, we were always involved with the weekly Bible school youth sessions. Education and academia have been significant presences in my life for as long as I can remember, so chasing an MFA in dance with a position as a professor of dance felt in some ways like an obvious blueprint. Also, in 2007 when I entered academia as a professor, it seemed the obvious—and possibly safest—conclusion of a terminal degree in the arts.

In May 2018, I concluded my final course taught at Swarthmore College after a ten-year position there as a 3/5-time assistant professor of dance. This fraction, in a given semester of the school year, equated to, for example, teaching a choreography class once a week for three hours (1 credit), teaching a studio practice/technique class twice a week for one-and-a-half hours each session (0.5 credits), attending dance faculty meetings every other week, and agreeing (at will) to advise students' independent study projects or guided reading projects. For those ten years, Swarthmore was my sustainable income. When I left, my gross salary as a 3/5-time assistant professor was about $52,000 per year, and I had access to up to about $2,300 a year in research support and travel reimbursement for conferences.

My decision to leave academia was largely due to having a lack of freedom in determining my teaching schedule in relation to the work I did outside the college, and also feeling like I could do better teaching outside the limits of a department curriculum. The decision also came at a time when I was feeling less responsibility to be financially available for others (more on that in the FAMILY section below). It felt like I had enough information about how to navigate through the professionalized art field and through life as an adult to make such a significant financial decision. I had enough information and support to trust that I could continue to avoid the threat of becoming a starving artist—a threat that has continued to subconsciously scare me since I first threatened myself with the dream of being an artist, a threat that is nestled firmly in the deep recesses of any artistic dream that I may dream, even with as much navigational acumen as I have accumulated and collaboratively whittled.

LOANS AND DEBT

I sold my car when I left Swarthmore. I wanted to get rid of the $260 monthly car note that would have lasted until 2021. When I bought my next car in 2021, I bought it outright with money that I had made from the sale of my car in 2018, and money I had saved from a surprisingly high previous insurance settlement from when a drunk driver had totaled a previous car.

My undergraduate degree (BA from Swarthmore College in English literature and Black studies) and graduate degree (MFA from Temple University in dance) continue to cost me about $154,000 in student loan debt (current amount after several interest years). They are all federal loans that I pay on a federal Income-Based Repayment[8] program. Most of the loans are from graduate school—each year, I think I took out the maximum amount to go toward living expenses. The second and third of my three years were supported by graduate teaching assistantships. I first entered into a master's program that was not eligible for fellowship support from the university, and when I switched into the MFA program after a semester, there were no possibilities to apply midyear for MFA fellowship support. While completing my BA at Swarthmore College, I believe that full tuition and housing costs were in the mid-$30,000s. Because of my family's household income at the time, most of these fees were paid by grants from the college. The remainder of my financial aid package included federal Stafford grants, the maximum federal Stafford loan allowable per year, and a family contribution portion of maybe around $2,000 per year. This contribution was often covered by my mother's parents, with my own parents contributing to this when they had the money.

I currently have no financial debt other than these student loans. At the time that I went, graduate school felt like it was a good decision for me, but were I to make the choice again, I probably would not attend without full fellowship support.

CREATION MONEY AND PAYING MYSELF

Upon leaving my professorship at Swarthmore College, I was interested in following a growth in momentum I had been feeling for the previous several years toward more touring with performance, teaching, and choreographing of my artistic work. At the time, I was working toward the culminating performances of *Let 'im Move You*,[9] the series of projects I developed in partnership with my friend and collaborator, Jermone Donte Beacham. Beginning in 2016, we applied for and were awarded several national grants and prizes, accumulating money toward a multi-hundred-thousand-dollar series culmination (a project called *This Is a Formation*), and eventually touring through several cities in the country with that project.

In addition to touring work, almost all of the money to create my art has come from foundational support (grants, residencies, or commissions). When I taught at Swarthmore, I also used my salary to subsidize my creative work.

Beginning around 2013, there was a period when I stopped applying for foundational support and chose to focus on smaller projects that I could subsidize entirely through my income. At the time, I felt a growing interest in my work from funders and presenters. I also felt growing desires from funders and presenters with whom I had professional relationships to advise me and aid in the shaping of my work and career decisions. I felt like I was being herded in a direction I did not quite understand, toward a particular vision of career success that I had not articulated as a desire for myself, and at a pace faster than I was able to reflect on what was happening. I decided I needed to take a step back and reevaluate how and with whom I was sharing my work and its stewardship. I needed to slow down. To the pace of paying deep attention. To the pace of being in relationship at the rhythm of getting to know someone, not at the rate of transacting business with someone.

After a few years, I began again to apply for foundational resources and develop new relationships with art presenters, but I felt much more grounded in the facts that:

1. I was applying for resources for which I should not even have had to apply;[10] deviously acquired resources[11] that should not even have been gate-kept by the administrators at the foundations whose founders deviously acquired them.
2. The institutions that fund or present my work would not *always* be collaborators in nurturing the worlds I wanted to help imagine. I should have clarity about this at the onset of each new relationship, whether it is a collaborative visioning project with someone with whom I am to make community together, or whether it is a transactional relationship with a gatekeeper of resources that I need or want, and the resource is at the center of what defines our relationship together.

Generally, the decisions about collaborator and administrator wages in relation to my creative work are made via conversations with the collaborators about the budget I have assembled, what I propose as fees based on this budget, and what they can accept. I have a single-member LLC[12] that is federally classified as an S Corp, allowing me to pay myself and others as employees through the LLC.

I work with a managing producer, and we typically make final budget decisions after some amount of conferral together. Although we share budget and resource information openly with collaborators within creative processes, our artistic collaborators have historically been invited into the process after the budget is fairly settled, leaving some room for later flexibility, but not much. Granting organizations require budget narratives and spreadsheets as part of their funding application processes. Historically, the success or failure of that process has determined whether our projects will be possible to make at the envisioned scale, or at all. The budget monies have already been abstractly allocated by the time our funds are secure, and our artistic collaborators are invited into the process.

While we have typically been able to revise budgets to a certain degree, I am currently committed to devising new systems that allow artistic collaborators to take part in the collective creation of project budgets. Especially in the face of COVID-19 and its aftereffects,[13] various grant organizations have been loosening attachments to the stated budget goals identified at the beginning of an application process, recognizing that necessary shifts are a part of any creative process. My managing producer and I are also currently working with a consultant to research cooperative organizing models as we rethink our systems in the direction of collaboration on all levels from artistic to administrative to fiscal.

We are trying to design collaborative project work that is better supported, less susceptible to the instability of tour schedules and budgets that artists often endure within the professionalized art world. COVID-19 revealed some of the systemic fragilities that come along with being a contract worker, which is how most independent artists are hired when they commit to creative projects.[14] For the tour of *Let 'im Move You* in late 2021, we were able to hire all of our principal collaborative artist workers as temporary employees for the period of the tour, taking care of tax payments, and contributing to Social Security and Unemployment. After the tour, I remained on as the only employee of the LLC, my managing producer preferring to be paid as an independent contractor. Until leaving Swarthmore College, I did not consider paying myself through the work I produce, since all of my financial needs and many of my base desires were covered through my Swarthmore College part-time income.

Additionally, I have frequently done projects under the direction of other artists, generally taking these jobs based solely on my desire to participate in them—regardless of pay rates. Rarely have I had to take gigs just for the money, but every once in a while I would do so if I had a specific personal project to fund (buying a new computer, paying for an upcoming trip, and the like).

Upon leaving Swarthmore, I had to think more consciously about how to pay myself through my projects and teaching work; and what I wanted to pay myself, based on what principles. Utilizing a model from Philadelphia's Artists U organization,[15] I established ideal hourly, daily, weekly, and monthly rates for myself. The Artists U model, informed by Creative Capital's[16] desires to support artists in fostering sustainable artistic careers, encourages artists to review the previous year's tax return, thinking about whether they have made enough money to do the things they have needed to and wanted to do (basic necessities, affording time off, emergency money, discretionary income desired, and so on). Adding to (or subtracting from) that figure to find an amount of money per year that they would like to be earning, they then have a foundation from which to establish base rates of payment for their work.

The Artists U model looks at a typical white-collar full-time position that would demand forty hours a week, probably for fifty weeks a year (2,000 hours). They encourage artists to work toward 3/4 of this amount of work (1,500 hours per year), to allow ample time for the reflection and dreaming that artists (and, really, humans) need to do. The artist's ideal yearly income is then divided by 1,500 for an hourly rate. From that hourly figure, multiply by eight for a daily rate, forty for a weekly rate, and so on.

In 2018, I did a version of this—taking the amount that I want to be making per year, and then dividing it by forty—establishing a rate that accounts for working forty weeks out of a fifty-two-week year, and also imagining that a lot of the work that I would do would be paid on a weekly rate. From there, I divided that by thirty-six hours to find my hourly rate, since I wanted a work week to consist of thirty-six hours. These base rate figures helped me make decisions about when I needed to subsidize my wage to take a job that I really wanted, or when I should increase my rate to subsidize my ability to take on projects with smaller budgets.

Since using the Artists U model, I have been impacted by consulting with, and occasionally assisting, dance artist, tax preparer, and financial planner Amy Smith. I have also been influenced by the conversations that I have had with collaborators in creative processes, and with peer artists whom I have helped with financial organization. Based on the "Valuing Your Time" worksheet that Amy Smith designed,[17] I developed the spreadsheet "Designing Your Fees Worksheet"[18] as a means for people to consider their expenses to design appropriate wage rates for themselves—as opposed to wages based around market rates. For me, it is important to consider the wages that I work toward in relationship to the communities I want to live in, the world that I want to help to realize, the capitalist systems that I want to help eliminate.

FAMILY

I grew up living with both my parents as well as my four younger siblings. We lived in various California cities until I was fourteen, and then in Philadelphia from age fourteen forward. Throughout my childhood, before leaving for college when I was seventeen, there were periods in which various extended family members would live with us as a moment of rehabilitative pause from other life struggles. For many of my years before leaving for college, my parents were students. My mother received her bachelor's degree when I was in the middle of high school and began working as a teacher. My father finished his PhD when I started college and began working as a professor.

When I entered my MFA program, directly after completing my bachelor's program, I started living in the house in West Philadelphia that my family owned at the time (via several refinanced mortgages), but from which they had recently moved to be closer to Lincoln University, where my father had just gotten a faculty position. Our oil radiator in the basement had imploded and sent up soot throughout the entire house (called a puff back). I moved back into my family's house, just as the homeowners' insurance-funded renovation process was beginning, with three college mates. While I was in the MFA program, my parents allowed me to live in the house while overseeing the long (multiyear) renovation process and managing the property. In exchange, I did not have to pay rent until I graduated. When I graduated and did start to pay rent, the rent I began to pay was slightly below market value I would have had to pay in my family's West Philadelphia neighborhood.

Some years after my 2007 graduation from the MFA program, I began to brainstorm with a couple of my siblings and my parents about how we might be able to mortgage a multi-unit house together and rent at least one of the units as income to help with the mortgage. Home ownership and management of rental income is something I have thought about since winning a Pew Fellowship for $60,000 in 2012. The following year, I was very close to buying a triplex in the Kingsessing area of Philadelphia. Less than a week before closing, I pulled out because I did not have a clear plan for myself about how I could go through with it and still work toward a just housing system, and against being a pawn in the familiar gentrification system of dislocating homeowners in the

Sharing Resource Stories

area.[19] This is the area of Philadelphia that I and my family had lived in since I was fourteen, but my plan didn't feel rooted enough in community-mindedness to feel like I would really be doing much good with my purchasing decisions—even for myself. My family's West Philadelphia house was always so tied up in debt that, in high school, I used to worry daily about the bank delivering a foreclosure notice to our doorstep (this may have happened once…twice?).

I am still thinking of home ownership and am slowly organizing ideas around contributing to the purchase of a cooperative compound of residences and art spaces.

Slowly.

I am far less excited about the notion of rental property at this point. The notion of renting space to tenants felt like it would help me contribute to my individual sustainability while within an art industry that makes future-planning so unpredictable. However, I have not yet been introduced to—or created—a rental model that can contribute to more justice, love, and interdependence within my world.

I always recognized my family as a significant support system for me, even despite growing up in a large, often underresourced (cash-poor) household. In addition to being able to move back into my family home postgraduation, I was never in serious fear of being put out by my family for being queer, a luxury that other queer peers of mine did not have. Feeling surrounded by love through my family has consistently been a resource and privilege for me that has allowed me to have stability even in my less stable moments.

Growing up, I felt a significant sense of responsibility to be independent enough not to take resources away from my younger siblings, and also to have enough money available to aid one of them, my parents, or extended family members if any should need financial support in a given moment. At this point, my youngest sibling is thirty, and each of my siblings is able to independently resource their own lives, as well as their respective families'. Every once in a while, I will feel called upon to financially assist an extended family member, but the urgent sense of responsibility I felt when I was younger is significantly alleviated.

At this current moment, I am forty years old, single, and have just started a life project with a dear friend of mine from college. She invited me to be a sperm donor in late 2020, and I was excited to agree. The more we talked about how we wanted this project to proceed, the more we realized we were envisioning something that looked much more like coparenting than sperm donation.

Recently, I moved to Durham, North Carolina, where she was living in the house she owned via mortgaging, and I began to split time between there and Philadelphia when I was not otherwise traveling for work. While I still live with my friend in her house, our person-making project has been put on hold for the time being after many unsuccessful trial months, many with clinically assisted IUI,[20] and some of those sessions with hormonal intervention. Her mother contributed principally (by far) to the IUI and medication payments, and my friend's health insurance also supported costs. We have established a time limit around an upcoming trial of IVF,[21] also supported by my friend's mother, which will be our final attempt to carry through with this project. If it works, wonderful. If not, I know that I will continue my parenting journey in ways that I already have been—parenting/mentoring/supporting other family (blood and chosen) through their growing.

I do not offer this sharing as a blueprint for how one makes a living as an artist. I do not profess to have "the way forward," and I would not be able to define that individually, without community collaboration, anyway. In all truth, I am at a moment in my life in which I am confused very often, looking perplexedly toward the futures as I try to define my own way forward. I know that I would like to be making more money. Earlier this year, I choreographed a film that my sister directed,[22] and I would like to be doing more work within the Hollywood industry as a means to significantly subsidize the other work I want to do. At the conclusion of this writing, though, I am hoping that I have been as clear as possible, with as little self-conscious explaining as possible. I strive for honesty when I am sharing—an honesty that is different from telling the truth, or different from *just* telling the truth, as one might if on the stand in a court trial in which a goal is to tell as much of the truth as is necessary to refrain from lying. Here, I offer honesty in service of demystification, and hopefully in service of exciting other folks into similar sharing. Interdependent worlds are collaboratively derived, by their nature, and I hope this writing is enticing enough to rally some new collaborators.

Administrative Experiment

Thinking about how doing some sharing of your own can be a brick on the path toward the worlds you are manifesting? I can offer some questions that can help you get started:

Will sharing information on my current economic status and background lead to embarrassment, guilt, and/or shame?

Do I have or am I working toward building community that can help me process those reactions to sharing?

In general, I will encourage toward confronting the discomfort, navigating the instability, and asking for support as you traverse terrains of tension. Having embarrassment about a lack of financial and/or resource support is a pattern that is systemically supported by scarcity mentality, especially if you are of one or more groups of people who have been historically and systemically excluded from macro power systems. If you are concerned about feeling guilt in relationship to sharing, this may be a part of the work that you need to be doing to collaborate toward more interdependent worlds—*especially* if you are of one or more groups of people who have historically and systemically excluded others from macro power systems. If you feel like you could recognize yourself as both an excluder and an excludee (many of us can), I recommend Olúfẹ́mi O. Táíwò's *Elite Capture: How the Powerful Took Over Identity Politics (and Everything Else)* to help you navigate through the entanglements. And I also recommend community to hold you down, lift you up, and jostle you.

With whom should I share this? For whom would this matter?

These are consistently useful questions for me. Identifying the answers has also encouraged me to consider having different versions of what I share, so that the tone, vocabulary, content, and direction can really be in conversation with the folks with whom it is intended to converse.

What are the significant sources of resource support that I have and/or have had?

From where did those resources come? Are they owed to me? Does that question make sense to me?

These questions can help ground the narrative, and your ideological relationship to the narrative—both the background, and the future directionality.

Who else's stories might I have to tell in order to effectively communicate my own?

Talk to your people. And it is not always easy. Talk to your people. And it might not lead to an eye-to-eye resolution. Talk to your people. They are your people. And, if they are not your people, well…

What economic strategies have I tried already on my journey toward the worlds I want to help build?

Remember to remember the steps you have taken already. Even if there have not been many. Even if you now know better. Part of the spirit behind my own sharing is encapsulated in the notion of Sankofa, from the Akan Twi language of Ghana. The word itself means "to retrieve," but the larger cultural meaning has to do with looking back in order to go forward. I am less interested in attaching an idea to the term of an accumulative future built on the sum total of past events. I am more interested in an act of expansive remembering as a means of being accountable, of buttressing honesty, and of giving propulsion to informed imagination. These feel like necessary tools toward achieving more and better interdependence.

The Fruits of Dissatisfaction
Julia Antonick and Jonathan Meyer

Maybe it's hours of unpaid admin time to land a grant that can only be used to hire a $150-an-hour consultant who offers you generic "best practices" that don't fit the particular sub-sub-niche of dance you inhabit, or who regales you with the same things that have long stymied your to-do list, because you're too busy applying for grants like this one to get them done. Maybe it's a lighting designer showing up late to a technical rehearsal, texting during hang and focus, getting paid four times as much as the dancers who've labored a grueling half a year on the project with no one questioning this inequity because that's just "how things work." Maybe it's hearing another artistic director complaining about the lack of professionalism of their guest teachers, whom they aren't compensating, although they pay themselves $100,000 a year. Or knowing that the executive director of a granting organization is paid $80,000 a year, plus benefits, to be the gatekeeper for dance artists who can't even afford health insurance. Or reading that just three dance companies in Chicago receive 56 percent of local dance funding while nearly two-thirds of dancers in Chicago earn less than fifteen thousand dollars per year.[1] It usually starts like this: dissatisfaction.

As the codirectors of Khecari, a Chicago-based dance company, there's a lot we've been told to accept or expect that has felt both emotionally and rationally dissonant, counter to what would create a more vibrant and healthy dance ecosystem. As artists, we've cultivated the rigor of cutting or altering what doesn't serve the work. We sought to level the same positive ruthlessness to our administrative practices. We began to listen to our frustrations and ask: Really? Does it need to be that way? Why? How can we do it differently?

Dissatisfaction. We've hit a wall. We can't continue doing what feels wrong.

So we commit to figuring out something new, however imperfect and ever-evolving. We put our heads together, engage that pleasurable volleying back and forth of ideas, winnowing the chaff of the preposterous and impossible. Conversations squeezed in between rehearsals, grants, Medicaid wrangling, backed-up toilets, a crying-at-three-in-the-morning baby, until the telltale energetic release says we have something to work with. An idea. A seed.

From such seeds, we have created a set of interrelated practices for Khecari. Here are three:

EQUAL PAY POLICY

We first implemented our Equal Pay Policy in 2010. It took years to apply it consistently—the greatest challenge was raising enough money to stop volunteering our time as directors—but we achieved the goal: dancers and artistic directors, executive directors and administrators, consultants and costume designers, accountants and composers were leveled at the same hourly pay rate. Underlying this policy are core beliefs. We are all of equal worth. Everyone on each project is irreplaceably important. Everyone's time should be respected. No one's contribution is worth more than anyone else's. We will plan and budget such that the policy is never sacrificed to expediency. We are all worth far more than it is possible to pay us. If we can raise the money to pay more, we will all get equal raises at the same time.

Here's common practice in the dance field: Pay dancers stipends while expecting an unspecified and potentially ballooning number of rehearsal hours. Pay those less involved—costume or lighting designers, administrative staff or consultants—a comparatively generous hourly wage. The directors might also pay themselves handsomely. They might volunteer their time, because they are economically privileged, or because they're young and obsessively dedicated. If the dancers are doing their math when the project wraps, they're seeing two dollars an hour, maybe. A conventional wisdom persists that one must shell out for a good executive director in order to get the talent needed. It suggests that said expensive ED will so brilliantly fundraise that everyone will benefit. But can a dance company afford such a gamble? And if it can, should it? Do we want to value the ED's time more than the dancers'?

If this is common practice, why does it remain largely undiscussed? In the few conversations we have had, we've heard guilt, even shame. The apathy of impotence. The exhaustion born of obsession. The righteousness of dedication. This is a knell of caution: when we didn't pay ourselves equally, it was easy to miss the creep of stealth expectations. As if those who danced for us should make sacrifices equal to ours, because we felt the work to be compelling.

Let's be clear: this is not about paying well, it's about equity. Many of us start out paying little or nothing because that's all we have to pay. Some continue paying little or nothing because it's an impoverished field. But is everyone getting paid little or nothing? Or just the dancers hired by one who's well-compensated?

We need to air these things out. We need to talk with each other.

The Equal Pay Policy changed how we worked. There were former collaborators who wouldn't work at this rate, and others who worked harder and were able to become more dedicated to the work because they saw that their old flat-rate fees they used to quote us were being exceeded by the hourly pay under the new policy. There were new people who were as excited about the policy as about the project. There were lean times when we would have to backburner a group project because we could only afford a duet project. Sometimes people would say, "My time is worth more than that." And we'd say, "Yes, but so is everyone else's on this project, and if we paid you more, we'd have to pay them less." "Them" being the sine qua non, the dancers.

It is not as if we could suddenly just pay everyone equally. Khecari was only able to pay us full-time as directors after fifteen years of our working half-time at minimum-wage jobs and donating forty hours a week to the company. That Khecari now enjoys a relative and insecure sustainability (that sounds oxymoronic but is simply endemic) is predicated on the unsustainable practice of early years of self-exploitation.

There is conversation in the field about how pay rates need to be unequal to be equitable. At times this appears to simply obfuscate an entrenched hierarchy of worth. Language borrowed from affirmative action justifying a higher salary for a director or consultant. But also we know that women have frequently been pushed out of the field when they have kids. We know that Black artists have been oppressed, underrepresented, and expected to conform to Eurocentric and white supremacist standards. We believe in the Equal Pay Policy as a central ethic, so we've chosen to address other issues through other means. We've set aside an Access Fund for Khecari collaborators that can be used to pay for childcare or an ASL interpreter. We've created a Commute Fund knowing that one of racism's expressions in Chicago is geographic segregation, and our location on the far North Side of Chicago plays into that.

Through these and other practices, we can acknowledge historic inequities while responding to individual needs and situations.

We believe cleaning toilets matters as much as crafting choreography. This ethic works for some folks, not for others. Prepping for *The Cronus Land* included shoveling five hundred gallons of fallen plaster from a derelict Roaring Twenties ballroom. For us, that's as much "the work" as dancing. The felt sense of space was exactly what that piece was examining. But people have to know what they're getting themselves into and say "Yes" to it. The Equal Pay Policy is about this, too. We're all of equal worth, we all work equally hard—digging or dancing, we all get paid the same.

In our own little sphere of agency, it ameliorated the pain of inequity and struggle.

TICKETING PHILOSOPHY

What are we worth? What makes us worthy? Who gets to decide we are worthy? What are the metrics that give us this particular valuation of worth?

By 2015, Jonathan had sent half a dozen fundraising letters to a proverbial Rich Uncle before he finally just called him and asked him to donate to Khecari. There was a beat of silence, and then he said, "Well, Jonathan, I think if someone has to ask for money then it amounts to a hobby."

As working artists, it is no secret that grappling with our perceived value constitutes an unfortunate amount of time and energy. It seeds defensiveness, insecurity, egotism, and self-aggrandizing alike. Even when we eschew such thoughts to buck systems of judgment and gatekeeping, they slip insidiously into every aspect of our work that involves money. From fundraising to ticket sales, grappling with our perceived value flavors our relationships with the other side of our community—the audience, whom we feel deserve to know more than they do about why we ask for money. As does every performing arts organization in the country, including the operas, ballets, and symphonies Rich Uncle loves and lauds. He's in no way obliged to support us, but there's this misconception that artists don't know how to be business people: if they could manage things better they wouldn't need to ask for support. As if the for-profit companies he's negatively comparing us to don't receive disproportionate aid through tax breaks and incentives.

What are we worth? Recently, we had just missed a show we'd been wanting to see. We asked the director of the space how it went. "It was a great show," he said, "but no one showed up. It was priced too high, twenty-eight dollars."

The Fruits of Dissatisfaction

On the heels of the Equal Pay Policy we looked at show ticketing. In our niche, one sets a ticket at twenty-five or thirty dollars and discounts from there. Why? Because that's what's done. With *Oubliette*, we came up with a simple math equation to determine what a full-price ticket would actually cost if we only relied on ticket sales:

Total cost of the show divided by the number of available seats equals a full-price ticket.

Put another way, if we could sell out, with all seats as full-price tickets, we would not need donations or grants to support that project.[2]

Full-price tickets for our show *The Cronus Land* were 250 dollars. This is the often hidden reality. It costs that much. People often don't realize what is involved in making projects like we do. Six months is a short rehearsal period; typically, it's years. There are so many hidden aspects: the time involved in lighting design, location scouting, recording music, budgeting. By using this math equation and labeling the full-price tickets as such, we could both educate (this is what it actually costs) and advocate (it is worth this much).

At the same time we're fully committed to financial accessibility. It's ethically critical, not to mention we personally couldn't begin to afford tickets at that price. *The Cronus Land* had tickets priced at zero, 10, 25, 50, 100, and 250 dollars. Instead of saying "free" or "discounted," we called them "fully subsidized" or "90 percent subsidized," for example. We set the smallest number as full-priced tickets, and the largest number were 25 dollars.

This ticketing structure also gave us a chance to talk about how much we were paying our artists, and how much time they had committed to the project. It also demonstrated how much work is required of the artists themselves to subsidize others' ability to see their work. We have to commit a great deal of time to grant writing and garnering individual donations in order to make the work affordable. The vicious cycle here is apparent: the more time we spend fundraising, the more expensive the project becomes. How much grant money is simply used to pay for the writing of grant applications? Nevertheless, we're happy to put in the work to make it affordable, and we're careful to frame the ticketing language in a way that can educate and advocate, but also encourage people to feel good about claiming a subsidized ticket.

There was a wholly unanticipated benefit. Since we had a specified number of tickets available at each price point, rather than a sliding scale option, we put the word out ahead of time: tickets go on sale tomorrow, there are only so many fully subsidized available, etc. Those sold out in a day, and then we said, okay, there are only so many 90 percent subsidized tickets left, move fast. And those sold out fast. This approach has driven early and robust sales. And more than once, we've had a person buy a partially subsidized ticket, because that's all that was left, and then donate the difference back because they wanted to support the full price of their seat.

So in the end we felt we could educate folks about the true costs of dance-making, and advocate for the worth of what we were putting out into the world—and the time all the collaborators were committing—and also really promote financial accessibility for anyone who needed it, not just prefab categories like student or senior, and also drive ticket sales more successfully than we had done previously because there was transparency that showed worth in a time-release ticket-selling format. We've kept using this model ever since.

DEGROWTH

Imagine a painter or writer working under a board of directors. The 501(c)(3) model was created with large foundations in mind.[3] It can be a good fit for a big repertory company, but many small dance companies are really individual artists making their work. In our case, with Khecari, it's a two-person collaboration. It functions: we get donations and grants, and these keep us afloat. But there's this strange way in which you're expected to pretend. As if you are not an artist making your work, but an employee working at the pleasure of a board who are remote to the work of artmaking.

It creates assumptions and pressures. One of these is to grow. The American capitalist economic model is based on growth. Holding steady means sinking.[4] It's embedded in our language: "to grow as an artist." For many years, Khecari's board members asked for reports that demonstrated we were growing. Granting organizations expected to see proof of growth and plans for future growth. We questioned this. Does Khecari need to be bigger? Do we need a bigger budget, more staff, larger productions? Then we came across Degrowth, both a movement and a collection of political, social, and economic theories that critique the very notion of growth, asserting that infinite growth is unnatural and unsustainable, and that its pursuit is detrimental.[5] This has given us a better framework and language for ideas we'd long been chewing on. Instead of growth we speak of sustainability. Not because we have any assurances of Khecari's longevity, but because this feels like a healthy goal to guide planning.

We famously—if arguably—live in a global village. If true, it is a digital, virtual village. There is a theory that homo sapiens, having evolved in small villages and tribes, have the capacity to interact in a meaningful way with about 150 people—those we can know by name and consider a friend. When the agricultural revolution concentrated populations, it made social organization the job of governments and of cities themselves, rather than the result of relationships.[6] With Khecari we try to function as much as possible in that direct and interpersonal way, because that is the heart of the work we do. We make live work for live bodies in a shared place. We are frequently asked to justify based on numbers. Granting organizations want to know, "How many people will this project reach?" A development grant asks, "How will you grow your audience?" Yet for us, the point of presenting performance is in the lived experience between people sharing space, and the quality of interaction that occurs. It is knowing audience members by name, conversations that span years. It is the ineffable but inarguably felt resonance, a feeling that cannot find its way to words, much less metrics, but vibrates in the air when the curtain falls.

What can aid sustainability? Despite dwindling resources, we are increasing our hourly Equal Pay Rate, because our collaborators are critical to the work and we all need the support in our own lives. We continue to try to reach out to new audience members and to communities who have been underrepresented at our shows, but we do this in order to establish new relationships, not to "grow our audience." Increasingly, our small audiences hung around after performances to talk and stayed in touch by email. Increasingly, we stood up for the value of the quality of our relationships with the people who see our work, above the number of attendees, when we felt the pressures of growth from the systems we interfaced with. We've pruned from our production calendar the classic large galas but kept small fundraising parties, where we can see the little circle of people we know, stay connected, deepen relationships, and meet new people brought in as friends of friends, not anonymous bodies at big events. This is the village we want: actually connected, with a smile, a hug, our voices resonating in each other's bodies.

ALL THAT WE STILL DON'T KNOW

This is what dance training programs should be saying: It's really hard. There's so little money. Few remain in the field long-term. Those that do, do so mostly despite poverty, or due to alternate sources of income.

We are now in our forties and fifties. For most of our lives we've each lived on about twelve thousand dollars a year. For the couple of years that Khecari could pay us full-time, we earned about twice that, but between diminished funding and the realities of child raising and health concerns, we're back to part-time work and the struggle to not throw in extra unpaid hours to keep up with deadlines. And despite all of this, in the context of the dance field we're more privileged than many, and we're doing better than many: we have in-kind rehearsal space, modest local name recognition, and grant money and donations enough to make work, pay artists, and pay for some admin assistance. We're still here, because it's what we're meant to be doing, because we couldn't conceivably do anything else. And we're still trying to figure it out, trying to use our dissatisfaction to find ways to make things better. Because how things function in the dance world is not okay. It's not good enough.

In the studio, as choreographers, we have a practice: to always say, "It's good enough... and how can it be better?" This is the practice we bring to the office, too. This is how we attempt to live in a place of constant uncertainty, by relishing the possibilities inherent in not knowing. This is how we attempt to accept limitations, and instead of anxiety, guilt, or stress, to feel gratitude for what limitations can teach.

We look for how to do better because that's what is exciting, that's where it's juicy. How to make better work, how to be more efficient with limited resources, how to be kinder and fairer. Look at what is, what's given, and utilize it where it works; accept what is imperfect but functions when that's the best thing to do. Improve it where it can be improved, radically rethink it when you're butting up against frustrations or impossibilities. Or just tweak it a little bit each day. Reach out to the people around you, peers and elders, ask for advice, information, help. Offer it back with resource sharing, mentoring, being available for that advice and information and help. Butting up against impossibility and magically finding a secret door—this is what we're doing, all the time, as artists and as administrators. It's a practice, a learned skill, a challenge and ever-present curiosity.

Administrative Experiment

Write down the first three administrative tasks that pop into your head as you read this sentence—reflexively, without consideration.

Look at each one and consider, why did you write that one? Did it feel like the easiest, or most accomplishable, or most enjoyable? Most urgent, dead-

The Fruits of Dissatisfaction

line-wise? Most necessary, for example, in order to have the money to pay the bills? Most frustrating, irritating, or unaccomplishable?

Then think thoroughly through your arts administration to-do list and pick three tasks that didn't pop into your mind before, but stand out the most now.

Why did you write those three? Perhaps it's something you simply keep forgetting. Or something you've been backburnering for months or years. Or something you unconsciously avoid thinking about because it makes you uncomfortable.

Among these six tasks, choose the one that feels the most ambivalent: that which feels most important, yet most uncomfortable. See if you can reimagine this task. Here are things to try:

- Write an "either, or" statement that captures that ambivalence. ("Either I make myself ____, or I don't get to ____.")
- Write down the positive and negative aspects of the task. ("I like thinking through ____, but I hate calculating ____.")
- Write down the assumptions or best practices attached to the task. ("You need an elevator speech to be able to ____.")
- Assume that for any task there are many ways to approach it. Write down new possibilities. Don't censor yourself to what's realistic or even possible. The impossible idea might be the first step toward something better, however imperfect.
- Find someone who cares about your success but won't mince words with you. Share your ideas with them and ask for conversation and curiosity. Put your heads together and see if you can find that pleasurable volleying back and forth of ideas that leads you somewhere new.

Administrative Points of View from Creative Living

Rashaun Mitchell and Silas Riener

MIDDLING

SILAS RIENER

I call it Middling. I use this word not for what it has come to mean, as a synonym of mediocrity, but for what it might suggest about movement through the world, through time, through a career. A gentle back and forth, pinging off the sides. Neither good nor bad nor stopping to reconsider, but continuing to continue.

I am writing to you from the middle of this story. At least I think I am maybe somewhere near the middle. It's hard to know for certain where I actually am. It's surprisingly hard to tell where one is *without relating to something else*. For most of our human history, it has been very very hard to tell where one is, especially at sea.[1] It is clear I am no longer *emerging*; *I have emerged*. Where that leaves me is uncertain, but for sure it is not-still-at-the-beginning. This is not about how I got where I am, or how I am trying to get to some next place, but instead how I move in multiple directions, and how I have navigated a life and career as a dance artist. So far.

What is happening in the middle (in this story, in my career, in my life) is the yawning gap—in funding, in forms of certainty.[2] What got me to the middle seems no longer so relevant, the ground shifts underfoot, and my values

Administrative Points of View from Creative Living

have changed. Daily training classes in the city and ambitions to have sold-out shows are replaced by project-based rhythms, and questions about long-term viability, and healthcare. Improvisational modalities which focus on the way a decision is made take the place of premieres with new sets of concepts, new choreography. This is a natural progression from a first idea, a local idea—making a show which happens twice only in New York City—to a body of questions, an international idea—a conceptual framework which can move in any room, or forest clearing, or body of water. So, I am in the middle. No longer the fresh new thing but not yet wizened or sage, I have learned some few things, but I do not know how to tell where to go from here. What path forward should I cut?

A *trailblazer* is actually a person who cuts a trail, literally with a shovel into a hillside, making it clear *this* is the way to follow. This is done by putting up little tokens, flags, or spray paint—*blazes* of color which stand out and indicate which way to go when it seems unclear.[3] You can always see the next one from the one you're at.

Being a dance artist feels to me like walking in the woods where there is no evidence people have been there before. The brush is thick and there aren't any distinguishing characteristics. The only thing to do is hack and tromp through, clear a space around yourself until something seems like somewhere to go, a path to follow. So being a dance artist is also bushwhacking.

Some traces of a way forward come into view. And, as a white and male-bodied person, I benefit from much privilege and much opportunity. I do have some certain forms of certainty—I know I want to continue, and I know there will be another show. If I look back at the last fifteen years of dancing and making work, I see patterns in the blazes through the forest I have walked past already. I see decisions where at the time, in the viewshed of my experience, I saw none. I see now how one thing led to the next.

While the building of it began far earlier, Rashaun and I began Naming, and Keeping Track Of, what we would come to call Desire Lines in 2017.[4] A *desire line* is a term used to describe paths worn into existence out of use, rather than planning.[5] They represent an accumulated record of disobedience in public space. We have applied it to our creative practice as a way of Naming and then Keeping Track Of the pathways of decisions (in time, in space, in relational orientation, with language, with objects) that get made in the kinds of improvisatory structures we work with in making dances.

Naming What Happened so it might be retrievable or shaped in further iterations is often referred to as a form of emergent strategy.[6] Pulled from the Background of Things That Happened While Improvising, it populates what becomes a kind of fabric or structure of the work.

Rashaun and I began working on dances together in 2009. At first it was nailing jelly to the wall. Move for a while, and reconstruct the good parts. Hone them to a gem-like shine. We have shifted our creative practice away from the repetition of dance steps and fully toward the creation of improvisatory containers. Now in our work the honing happens in real time, in front of the audience. The work is made from the honing of honing.

Rashaun and I live together, we make dances together. We began working-on-while-living-in-this-house together in 2017. It's all together together, everything is everything else. He is a great repurposer in our grant writing, and I use "old work" in our renovation. Taking apart a house means deciding which of all the different-sized pieces of wood will be *useful*, worth saving.

It was natural for the kind of thinking we used in our creative practice and then in turn in our remaking of this house to smear over into our administrative practices because they are all facets of the same form of thinking about utility: Everything which can be salvaged is reused and repurposed and shoved somewhere until it's needed.

We have not set out to make dances with a road map, with a destination in mind other than to be able to Keep Going. We wanted to be able to make things differently, and make different things. We wanted to dance outside, and out of bounds. We cut the path as we went, and followed it down to the proverbial shore's edge of our creative certainty, out into open water. Deep water. Deep enough to make big choices.

Now from the middle we gaze back at our wake and can see by transposing its shape forward in time how things might look in the future with subtle shifts in direction. Allowing your past to shape your future when your present is already in motion. Not possible to stop and evaluate—the *deliberation time* is overlapped with the doing. You have to think about it and do it simultaneously.

When you're on a boat in the water you can't just make a hard right turn, or pivot. The Newtonian mechanics of stopping is complex. Some ships on the ocean take days to stop. Mostly what we are all doing is careening.[7]

When you're on a boat and you can't stop, you only have what you have—a limited number of spare parts, at best. You're going to need something you don't have, and you're going to use something for a purpose other than what it was made for.

Like all things involved in making dances, and making a life as a dance-maker, it's completely made-up, and held together with paper clips and glue, chewing gum and shoestrings, spit and baling wire. We have performed in the five minutes between classes at the student center. We showed up that day and figured it out on the fly. We used whatever they happened to have on hand—old rope, a cardboard tube, a shopping cart. We switched gears when it seemed like it wasn't working. We use our clothes as costumes, we reuse costumes from other dances. We reuse choreographic situations. We upcycle. We borrow from Peter to pay Paul, we Jury-Rig. We improvise.

We really try never to do more work than is necessary, and we try not to make work for other people. If there is something that can be borrowed from somewhere else, it's better than making something new. To Jury-Rig is to use only what you have on hand to make something work for the day. This will work today. This applies to choreography, to administration, and to life. To propose an administrative perspective drawn from an artistic practice is using something not for what it was for, but repurposing it. It's a retrofit.

What did we do? We said yes to everything. We figured out a way to do it once we were already doing it. The way we train our improvisation practices is by alternating between hyper-focused execution and wild, expanded and experimental open-ended research. This way we are training from two opposite approaches from two opposite ends of a spectrum.

At some point we figured out how *not* to do everything for the first time, every time. We made shortcuts and switchbacks, and template contracts. We made mailing lists, press folders, and dossiers. We saved those fantasy budgets you make before you do anything and compared them to the actual budgets of money spent once the dust had settled. We worked with the same talented dancers in the studio, and the same talented technicians and production workers. We worked with Katy Dammers, our manager/producer, for nine years and her role grew and changed over time—in my opinion institutional memory is invaluable. We didn't have to start from scratch, even when our work shifted course. We could keep building our crooked house.[8]

How will we support our work and ourselves? How does the shape of the support for the work get made? I love having a good system, but all things change shape over time. At this point our heads are above water. We are in the black, we are afloat. We don't spend money we don't have. At first we allowed the administrative protocols to emerge much the way we would watch any improvisational structure take shape. Monthly check-ins, and a dashboard of things to Keep Track Of. Figuring out when to pass off an email correspondence either in the direction toward the artists or toward the administrator. The worn-in path of Experience shows us our patterns, and helps us understand what we needed four weeks out, two weeks out, the day before. Folders of photos. Subfolders of press-approved photos. Contracts. P&Ls.[9] More Contracts.

It works about the same as trying to figure out how to move twenty sheets of sheetrock, foam, and cement board from the garage to the house. Who goes backward down the stairs? When to swing around the corner and feed through the door? When to pivot grip so your arm doesn't get either crushed or dislocated while you are trying to open the door while balancing the end of a heavy thing on your knee? And importantly, how to pick up anything heavy off the floor and not have your back go out? How to communicate this to another person you are trying to do these things with while you are doing them. You have to find your rhythm by deepening the grooves of practice. Once you understand how to do what you're doing, you're done.

Administrative Points of View from Creative Living

I have never liked the expression "Don't Change Horses Midstream" but the message is clear.[10] Don't change your mind once you've already begun.

All I do is change my mind once I've already begun. It's how I live, it's how I navigate shifting terrain in an unstable field. Stopping time to perform a dead reckoning—to chart the projected course through velocity, trajectory, and pinpoint a destination in the future—is useful in the abstract, but it happens in a space out of time—stepping out of your own perspective to look back, and look forward. Strategic planning, goal-oriented milestones. It is not entirely clear to me that trying to get somewhere else (or somewhere else better) is a goal that should be held above others. We're past surviving, we subsist, we sustain. Can that be a goal? Just Middle yourself onward.

Maybe all my fancy navigation metaphors and terms collapse into some simple thoughts—Improve the way as you go. Stay organized. Watch what works, save useful things. Keep going.

UNDOING
RASHAUN MITCHELL

I like to think that I experiment by rearranging time. Of course, access to time is a privilege. Here, at an artist residency nestled on a mountain in Joshua Tree, the desert landscape gives a cue to perform a kind of timed waiting. The Sky is vast and the Sun does not sway from its relentless path. When the Sun is directly above, it's best to stop and take a nap. When the water bottle is half empty, it's time to return home. Hot noon here is a chilly 3 p.m. in New York.

As I wait here, The Roches' joyful tune "Quitting Time" plays like a confession, or a taunt, or a 1970s premonition. In 2021, I quit my job as a professor in an academic institution after nine years. Makes me wonder where the tiny toy cars on the distant asphalt are going. I imagine one in every three is driven by quitters, relocating to a less-populated area. Each car rolling by carries its own microclimate, thanks to the technology of air-conditioning. The noisy engines provide a bit of background bass to the twangy song.

"Now is the hour of quitting
Twilight paints the town
Old industrial skyline
How does the sun go down?
How does the sun go down?"[11]

The artist/academic professional role wasn't sustainable for me, and even though I had more opportunities than some, the fact that it didn't quite work underscores a reality that artists aren't really supported in our field. This is not a new story. Other colleagues and friends much older than I have shared similar tales.

The Great Resignation of 2021 is the climax of a decade-long trend of workers leaving their jobs, and as a person who isn't inclined to join large groups, I feel a fraught sense of belonging.[12] I prefer to think of myself as an outsider, loner, free spirit, so it hurts my ego to know that I'm a part of something so massive. Accumulation registers as truth over time though. Now I proudly belong to a flock of quitters who left for various reasons, one of which is the belief that not working is better than overworking.

Let me be clear—quitting was not the plan. The plan in place was perfectly good. Retirement plan! Steady growth, climb the ladder! Cumulative knowledge! Quitting my job was not easy. I had been there for nine years. I had relationships with people. My partner and I both relied on the income. But the plan was too product-ive, too populated.[13] Too industrial. Too greedy. Too hummingbird-time, not enough caterpillar time. It came with a kind of mincing of life.

I've identified at least three weapons against the tyranny of time: foresight, hindsight, and improvisation.

Did the artist Noah Purifoy have the foresight to understand that his land art—erected over decades on a plot of land in Joshua Tree—would decay under the harsh treatment of the desert elements in the most beautiful and heartbreaking way?[14] Did he understand that this would take many years and in the meantime his work would always be in transition?

Administrative Points of View from Creative Living

Did The Roches foresee the great resigned nation?

Foresight told me to decrease responsibilities and redefine professionalism as an imperfect, moving target. Foresight told me to prioritize maintenance, reflection, to trust in my ability to facilitate change.

The actual decision to quit was an improvisation. I dropped the ball. Now I practice dropping things, deliberately. Things that break. Things that make sounds. Heavy things and things that fall slowly. I drop my weight into the ground. I drop friends off at the bus station. I drop hints.

Dropping things returns my ability to act on impulse. I'm trying to keep the practice moving, lest I slide into the quicksand of sameness, or get seduced by the allure of expertise. I switch between drawing amateur architectural renderings, constructing poorly made objects, designing on intuition, moving by myself, rearranging my furniture, dancing for the wind, biking without spandex, swimming with foggy goggles, gardening without tools, growing things I forgot I planted, nurturing a collection of junk. In other words, a life— art as life, not art imitating life.[15]

Improvisation allows for impulses, desire, unknowing, and untrying to do the job. It is a call and response. Change is a constant, of course—its own form of quitting, a continual dropping of balls.

Dropping a plan or dropping the burden of expectation makes way for new relationships, new perceptions. Digressions, refusals, complaints, and the breaking of protocols are all forms of queer undoing. They stave off danger— subliminal survival techniques.

When a deer is trying to signal danger it lifts its white tail, flashing a warning sign. But you have to be behind it to see that. A female deer is sometimes referred to as a hind. Sensing the warning literally requires hindsight.

In hindsight, quitting my academic job was the best decision I could make as an artist. My work is better for it. My capacity is bigger. My contribution is clearer. In hindsight I can see the patterns—the reach to grow, and then the urge to destroy. I see the efforts to strip everything down to the studs. I see the interest in autonomy and wonder if this is libertarian or punk, or if it's just a survival response to the evasive properties of belonging in a competitive world with few resources. I see overconsumption as a tool used to distract us from ourselves.

I also see the way a dance gets made and then disappears. I see how that dance gets made again and again because it's never finished.

I see the cut and run. A refusal to stay in one line or to continue in the same direction. I see the subversive power in this. The game is never over but the deck needs to be reshuffled sometimes.

Time apart, time alone, time away from "work," has focused the artistic experiment. I now have the privilege to contemplate, to be out of time. Of course, the experiment requires a sacrifice. In my case that meant rescaling my life, eating into my meager savings, giving up my apartment in the city of dreams. It required that I make do with less and that I come to terms with financial instability. But it gave me the privilege to contemplate, to be out of time. I don't have to stay in place so the work can reorient and respond in new ways.

"Old industrial skyline
Drawing away from you
You are the one that's moving
You are the fool that flew
You are the fool that flew"[16]

Not enough people have flown the coop. Everyone should quit their job. We could all gather in the desert or the forest or on the shores and start anew without technology. Wait, we can't really do that, can we? There would be chaos and vulnerable people would suffer. So we just quit a little bit inside each day. Quit caring. Quit dreaming. Quit hugging. Quit dancing.

Instead we should quit exploiting people. Quit trying to get rich. Quit trying to be seen and celebrated for trying to get rich. Quit fossil fuels. Quit killing Black people. Quit war. But these are obvious.

We should also quit buying shit. Quit wasting shit. Quit believing shit. Quit dumping our shit in other people's backyards.

Who knows? We might have time for other things. Time for nothing. Time for resting. Time for being. Time for shuffling our feet in the sand. Time for listening. Time for wandering. Time to sit in front of the fire. Time to notice the first star in the sky. Time to watch the watermelon grow fat, to eat it and let the juices drip all over your chin.

We might have more time for time-based art.

Administrative Experiments

EXPERIMENT 1: NOTHING IS PERMANENT.
When I moved into our house I installed a reading bench in front of this perfect picture window. The rest of the design and layout of the kitchen came from that first choice. But after four years I realized that I didn't use the bench as expected and the kitchen had never felt balanced or organized in terms of space and flow. I tried moving the kitchen table, the wall-mounted cabinets, and even the oven and fridge until I realized that the bench was the problem. It now sits where the sink and adjacent counters live and the space is being used more. I enjoy the view often as I make the coffee and wash the dishes.

Renew your sense of belonging while moving new energy through your life. Rearrange a room in your home. This may be easier or more familiar for you; if so, just begin. If not, first assess what can be moved and what absolutely can't. Basically anything that is not attached to a wall or flooring can be moved. First, take away any assumptions about what should or should not go in any position. Lean into absurdity.

Start with the biggest object and end with the smallest. Use sliders or rugs to drag heavier things without ruining your floors or having to lift and hurting your back. Try to keep anything from touching anything else. It may feel counterintuitive, like you're wasting valuable space, but it will make your room FEEL more generous.

EXPERIMENT 2: DROP THE BALL. DROP WHAT YOU'RE DOING. BREAK THE SELF-INVENTED RULE. CUT TIES. END OF LINE. YOU'LL THANK YOURSELF LATER.

We're all holding on to something or many things. But let's imagine that guilt or shame or responsibility have no dominion here. Let's question the most fundamental assumption, the thing that everything else orbits around. That's a tall order. It can be counterintuitive but "Drop it". It can be as difficult as dropping a negative thought, or as easy as dropping household chores midway, in order to really listen to a loved one. Don't plan that you're going to drop it. Just make the decision right now and do it. And when you do it say "Drop," out loud.

You may choose to reclaim your action or return your material to its place in the end, but go through the experiment of removing it. This will implore you to reshuffle the deck. What are you holding on to? What is weighing you down?

Appendix
NCCAkron's CAR Investigative Retreat Toolkit

In designing the Creative Administration Research Investigative Retreats, NCCAkron practiced the following exercises with each Artist Team. Each exercise is a line of questioning that can lead to implicit thinking and behaviors around operations; or in other cases, identifying gaps where Artist Teams can be more explicit and intentional in their thinking and actions.

Similar to a physical practice where one comes to understand the physiological ways the body works, this line of questioning is meant to be reflexive as well as accumulative. We recommend starting with an internal self-assessment of how you make art, how you like to work, who is already in your operating ecology and let that lead to new questions and administrative experiments where you might dedicate your efforts. You can begin anywhere, but the questions are listed in the order NCCAkron noticed the conversations typically develop with each Artist Team.

To learn more about NCCAkron's Creative Administration Research program (CAR) and Investigative Retreats see the Director's Foreword.

WHAT IS YOUR ARTISTIC VISION OF SUCCESS?

- **Reflect on the past five to ten years.** What artistic achievements or highlights do you want to name? This does not need to be a list of everything you have done within the defined time period; just those aspects of your creative output that are significant accomplishments and somehow carry an implicit definition of future success as you move forward. Were these new works major engagements or opportunities? Did you work with specific communities?

- **Articulate your definition of success and how these landmark activities fulfill the brief.** How do you define success? Critical success from across the performing arts ecosystem? Quantifiable success in terms of money received or people reached? Frequency of new work premieres? Personal satisfaction or something else entirely?
- **Map out the people and resources it took to realize those achievements.** What was needed to make those things happen? Were there specific practices employed to foster the necessary relationships or opportunities?
- **Dream forward.** What are your artistic goals for the next five years? Whether it is a better world or the next work you want to build, are these new activities renewing or building upon those already tried? Are there possible micro-goals along the way to build toward some of your larger goals? Which practices are within your wheelhouse, and which need more intentional focus or development?

WHO IS ALONG FOR THE RIDE?

In conventional marketing and development departments of large nonprofit institutions there are studies about how finding and cultivating new audience members or donors requires more time and money than maintaining existing relationships. In CAR Investigative Retreats, we realized that while many artists toggle back and forth between artmaking and resource-finding, they often overlook two crucial elements for longevity: constantly communicating your story on your terms (see next tool) and identifying and cultivating where you want to work, and whom you want to engage.

- **Where:** Consider the places (cities or organizations) you have engaged as part of your work through performance, teaching, or creative output. How many places have you been more than once? More than three times? Is that where you want to

continue to invest your energy and/or are there other places you wish to develop further? Both options are valid but require different strategies.
- **Who:** In addition to those places, there are the people with whom you have engaged and interacted along your trajectory as an artist. Are they longtime witnesses to your work or acquaintances with room to grow a relationship? Maybe somewhere in between? Build out archetypal snapshots to name the roles they potentially fulfill in your individual operating ecosystem. How do you actively stay engaged or communicate with these people? If you and your work are not reaching the audiences you envision, where are they and how might you reach them?

HOW IS MARKETING AN EXTENSION OF YOUR ARTISTIC VISION?

Rather than just an administrative deliverable, marketing can be a creative exercise. Working outside conventional institutions, many artists do not spend enough time telling their own story because they are busy making their work. In CAR Investigative Retreats, we use the framework of WolfBrown's Arc of Engagement model as a starting point to consider ongoing communication strategies between new works and performances. WolfBrown's Arc of Engagement traces how the audience experience unfolds in five stages, from "the build up that occurs leading up to an arts event" to the "impact echo" that can last a lifetime.

- **Marketing as an artistic medium.** Marketing is a different format but a complementary medium to time-based performance. A one-minute social media reel may not have the impact of a fifty-minute performance, but how can it represent the spirit of that work? If you value, say, multidisciplinary dancemaking, how does that show up in your performances? How can those values show up in your images, social media posts, or other promotional assets?
- **Artifacts of the creative process as assets.** What meaningful artifacts might you share as marketing assets—before, during, and after the performance—to extend that Arc of Engagement?

Marketing and promotional materials do not have to be something only provided by request, but rather a part of the process. Creative detritus like video, images, written notes, and so on can be repurposed for storytelling purposes between shows.

- **Storytelling.** What words do you like to use to talk about you and your work? Are there words you don't like to use? How can you consistently practice this messaging across social media? In your website design, grants, press releases, program notes? Where else? How can you be ready to educate partners about how to talk about your work?
- **Artistic thinking as thought leadership.** Beyond finding out about your next show, why else might audiences and community members look to you? When might you communicate with people in your ecosystem other than when you want them to donate?

RECOMMENDED READING

Alan S. Brown and Rebecca Ratzkin, *Making Sense of Audience Engagement*, WolfBrown, 2011, https://wolfbrown.com/wp-content/uploads/Making_Sense_of_Audience_Engagement.pdf.

Hope Mohr, *Shifting Cultural Power: Case Studies and Questions in Performance* (University of Akron Press, 2021).

Notes

INTRODUCTION

1. I recommend Sharon Louden's *The Artist as Cultural Producer: Living and Sustaining a Creative Life* (Intellect Books, 2013) for a "contemporary art world" perspective.

2. See William Deresiewicz's *The Death of the Artist: How Creators Are Struggling to Survive in the Age of Billionaires and Big Tech* (Henry Holt & Company, 2020) for a deeply researched analysis of the changing role of the artist in society.

3. In April 1957, Marcel Duchamp presented a short paper, "The Creative Act," at the American Federation of Arts convention in Houston, Texas. See the full transcript in Robert Lebel's book *Marcel Duchamp* (1959). *Aspen Magazine* made a recording of Duchamp reading the paper. It can be found at Amazon Music.

4. Christy Bolingbroke quoted by Zachary Whittenburg in "Are Arts Administration 'Best Practices' Really Working?," *Dance Business Weekly*, May 19, 2021.

5. adrienne maree brown, *Emergent Strategy: Shaping Change, Changing World* (AK Press, 2017).

6. Alice Goldfarb Marquis, "The N.E.A. Plays to an Empty House," *New York Times*, February 24, 1996.

BUILDING AN AUDIENCE THAT CARES

1. United States Census Bureau, "Quick Facts, Akron, Ohio," July 22, 2022, https://www.census.gov/quickfacts/akroncityohio. In 2021, the estimated population was 189,347.

2. For more information about *The Black Card Project* you can visit https://shawentertainment.com/production/artie-and-the-black-card/ or watch the reel at https://vimeo.com/461896343/76e408dddc.

3. The term *black card* is slang used within the Black community for an imaginary object that "certifies" one's Black identity and membership within the community. It can be used either as a shield or a sword by anyone within the community to revoke based upon a certain set of behaviors.

4. "Design Thinking Resources," IDEO U, July 22, 2022, https://www.ideou.com/pages/design-thinking-resources.

5. Anyone who is interested in listening to the *inCOPnegro: Black and Blue* podcast can find it here: https://incopnegro-black-blue.simplecast.com/.

6. Pravenna Somasundaram, "Jayland Walker Was Shot Nearly 4 Dozen Times, Autopsy Results Show," *Washington Post*, July 15, 2022, https://www.washingtonpost.com/nation/2022/07/15/jayland-walker-autopsy-akron-shooting/. As I write this, I want to note that Jayland Walker's case is still an active investigation. The above citation is just one of many local and national articles on what occurred. The facts surrounding the case may change, but the outcome will not: a young man has lost his life entirely too soon.

CAUSING A SCENE

1. Benjamin Harkarvy Papers, 1910–2003, Jerome Robbins Dance Division, The New York Public Library for the Performing Arts, https://archives.nypl.org/dan/19835.

2. Diane Pecknold, "Heart of the Country? The Construction of Nashville as the Capital of Country Music," in *Sounds and the City*, ed. Brett Lashua, Karl Spracklen, and Stephen Wagg (London: Palgrave Macmillan UK, 2014), 19–37.

3. Benjamin Harkarvy was artistic director of the Juilliard School Dance Division from 1992 to 2002. He died two months before I graduated. He was the founder of Netherlands Dance Theater and a lifelong teacher. Upon Ben's death, decades of his notes, notebooks, teaching material, photographs, and clippings were published and made available to the public via the New York Public Library for the Performing Arts.

4. Artistic research, as I define it here, centers inquiry and innovation, while also emphasizing the necessity of collaboration. I agree with NYU Tisch, "Artists are natural adapters and translators in the work of interpretation and meaning-making," and love the way the language used by this source alludes to the intersection of scientific and linguistic processes involved in an artistic practice. See New York University Tisch School of the Arts, "What Is Creative Research?," accessed June 11, 2022, https://tisch.nyu.edu/research/what-is-creative-research-.

A course description for movement research that also resonates with me: "Movement is a language that captures the connections between the realm of the body and the world. The research process requires sensory awareness, improvising, building authentic movement vocabularies, aesthetic decision-making, and reflection. Our findings connect us to movement's power to teach, communicate, heal, express cultural identity, and understand our history." See Emory University, "Movement Research," accessed June 1, 2022, https://dance.emory.edu/academics/movement-research.html.

5. Marilyn Hunt, "Benjamin Harkarvy," *The Independent*, April 9, 2002, sec. Obituaries, https://www.independent.co.uk/news/obituaries/benjamin-harkarvy-9256858.html.

6. Rumpus Room Dance was nominated for *Dance Magazine*'s "25 to Watch" in 2010, just before we disbanded. See Martha Ullman West, "25 To Watch: Rumpus Room," *Dance Magazine*, December 2009, https://www.dancemagazine.com/25-to-watch-4/.

7. Banning Bouldin, New Dialect Founding Vision and Activities Statement, Nashville, TN, 2013.

Notes to pages 15–33

8. Justin Harvey, "abrasiveMedia," abrasiveMedia—Learn, Make, & Show Art in Nashville, n.d., accessed June 10, 2022, https://www.abrasivemedia.org.

9. Arts and Business Council of Greater Nashville, "Volunteer Lawyers and Professionals for the Arts (VLPA)," Arts and Business Council of Greater Nashville Cultivating Tennessee's Creative Community, accessed June 10, 2022, https://abcnashville.org/vlpa/.

10. The Arts and Business Council, with special thanks to Sarah Easley and Digigraph Design, "Starting a Nonprofit Arts Organization: Incorporation & the Tax Exempt Application Process," 2012.

11. OZ Arts Nashville, "Mission, History, Staff & Board of Trustees—OZ Arts Nashville," OZ Arts Nashville—Brave New Art, 2021, accessed June 10, 2022, https://www.ozartsnashville.org/mission-history-staff-board-of-trustees/.

12. 92NY Harkness Dance Center, "Artists in Residence (AIR)," accessed June 8, 2022, https://www.92y.org/dance/artists-in-residence.

13. New Dialect was named "Best New Dance Company" by the *Nashville Scene* thanks to our sold-out debut at OZ Arts Nashville in August 2014. See John Pitcher, "Best of Nashville 2014," *Nashville Scene*, October 2014, 264, https://www.newdialect.org/best-of-nashville-2014.

14. Kevin Bouldin first started working with New Dialect part-time, helping with administration and grant writing, in 2014/2015. We first paid him $500 a month—not pro bono, but close.

15. Asia Pyron is a dancer, choreographer, and director of PYDANCE. She attended New Dialect's Summer and Winter Intensives in 2020. Sensing an opportunity to grow both her company and the Nashville dance community, Asia relocated to Nashville immediately upon graduating from Boston Conservatory. See Asia Pyron, "About PYDANCE," PYDANCE, 2020, accessed June 1, 2022, https://www.pydance.online/about-basic.

16. Ryan P. Casey, "Could Moving Back to Your Hometown Be Your Best Career Move?," *Dance Magazine*, March 2019, dancemagazine.com/dance-career-hometown.

17. Lauren Kay, "Banning Bouldin Boosts Nashville Dance Community with New Dialect," *DanceTeacher*, July 2017, dance-teacher.com/banning-bouldin-in-nashville/.

18. South Arts, "Momentum: Dance Touring Initiative," South Arts, 2020, accessed April 18, 2022, https://www.southarts.org/programs/momentum/dance-touring-initiative.

19. The National Center for Choreography-Akron, "Creative Administration Research," accessed July 18, 2022, https://www.nccakron.org/creativeadminresearch.

8 & 1

1. Jeremy Stoller, "Reflections following a Residency," June 2022.

2. Cynthia I. Grossman and Anne L. Stangl, "Global Action to Reduce HIV Stigma and Discrimination," *Journal of the International AIDS Society* 16 (November 2013).

3. Stoller, "Reflections following a Residency."

DANCE AS A RADICAL ACT

1. Cornish College of the Arts is a Seattle arts conservatory perhaps best known as the alma mater of choreographer Merce Cunningham and the place where Cunningham met composer John Cage. Cornish alum Jacob (Jake) Robinson died in New York City (1981–2007).

2. Brendan Kiley, "What's Going to Happen to Oddfellows Hall?," *The Stranger*, October 25, 2007, https://www.thestranger.com/theater/2007/10/25/424509/whats-going-to-happen-to-oddfellows-hall.

3. On the Boards (OtB) is a nonprofit contemporary performance organization. It also launched a video streaming service of contemporary performance works, OntheBoards.tv. For more information, see OtB's website, https://www.ontheboards.org.

4. During Seattle Dance Forum, On the Boards' managing director was Diane Ragsdale, and its artistic director was Lane Czaplinski.

5. Brangien Davis, "Forum Sparks New Ideas for Dance Community," *Seattle Times*, February 17, 2004, http://community.seattletimes.nwsource.com/archive/?date=20040217&slug=dance17.

6. Seattle International Dance Festival, seattleidf.org.

7. Marcie Sillman, "Seattle's Tonya Lockyer Creates Community Through Dance," *KUOW*, July 9, 2013, http://archive.kuow.org/post/seattles-tonya-lockyer-creates-community-through-dance.

8. Sillman.

9. Michael Upchurch, "Tonya Lockyer: 'Powerhouse Personality' Turns Velocity Around," *Seattle Times*, July 7, 2013, https://www.seattletimes.com/entertainment/tonya-lockyer-lsquopowerhouse-personalityrsquo-turns-velocity-around/.

10. Edmund L Andrews, "Why Was the Last Recovery Slower Than Usual?," *Stanford Business*, April 3, 2019, https://stanford.io/2FSsKqB.

11. To learn more, see Kate Wallich's essay in this book, "How I Built This: Dance Church®." Dance Church benefited financially from Velocity's payment structure. Faculty kept the revenue from classes, after paying Velocity a small rental fee. I fought to keep this structure, with strong faculty support, so artists had a possibility of financial viability through teaching.

12. Brendon Kiley, "Tonya Lockyer, Champion for Local Dance, Departs Velocity Dance Center after Vertiginous Success," *Seattle Times*, June 20, 2018, https://www.seattletimes.com/entertainment/dance/tonya-lockyer-champion-for-local-dance-departs-velocity-dance-center-after-vertiginous-success/.

13. Upchurch, "Tonya Lockyer: 'Powerhouse'" (see n. 10 above).

14. Kiley, "Tonya Lockyer, Champion for Local Dance" (see n. 14 above).

15. Gemma Wilson, "2018 Exits and Entrances," Crosscut.com, December 28, 2018, https://crosscut.com/2018/12/2018-exits-and-entrances-seattle-regions-arts-scene.

16. Brendan Kiley, "A Dancer/Theater Person/Artist Rips Us a New One," *The Stranger*, May 5, 2010, https://www.thestranger.com/theater/2010/05/05/4001721/a-dancertheater-personartist-rips-us-a-new-one.

17. Brendan Kiley, "Another Way to Criticize the Critic," *The Stranger*, May 5, 2010, https://www.thestranger.com/theater/2010/05/20/4100737/another-way-to-criticize-the-critic.

18. *Stranger* Staff, "Stranger Genius Awards: The Short Lists," *The Stranger*, September 16, 2010, https://www.thestranger.com/pullout/2010/09/16/4885978/stranger-genius-awards-the-short-lists.

19. The title *So You Think It's Dance?* was also aimed, with a wink, at members of our dance community critical of the popular televised dance competition *So You Think You Can Dance?* I hoped to engage this group in interrogating who they considered welcome at Velocity.

20. *City Arts* thrived for twelve years as a magazine and online publication showcasing Seattle's "risk-taking" artists, arts organizations, and the issues they faced. Encore Media Group published *City Arts* from 2006 to 2018. It briefly returned as an all-digital platform in 2022. See Brangien Davis, "The Demise of Seattle's Monthly Arts Magazine," on Crosscut.com, November 9, 2018, https://crosscut.com/2018/11/demise-seattles-monthly-arts-magazine.

21. Ray Managh, "Disgusted 'Naked Dancing' Protestor Loses Court Action," *Irish Independent*, July 8, 2004, https://www.independent.ie/woman/celeb-news/disgusted-naked-dancing-protester-loses-court-action-25905364.html.

22. Kitty Holland, "Action against Dance Festival Fails," *Irish Times*, July 8, 2004, https://www.irishtimes.com/news/action-against-dance-festival-fails-1.1148139.

23. In a letter to the *Irish Times*, Bel wrote: "This is only theater. Everything is fake. The truth is outside the theater in the street, where some situations are really shocking. Who should I sue that allows people to live in the street?" See Jérôme Bel's website, RB Jérôme Bel, "Naked in the Presence of His Enemies," http://www.jeromebel.fr/index.php?p=5&lg=2&cid=209.

24. Mary Louise Schumacher, "Visual Arts Journalism: Newsroom Pressure and Generational Change," *Nieman Reports*, Spring 2019, https://nieman.harvard.edu/articles/visual-arts-journalism-newsroom-pressure-and-generational-change/.

25. Kiley later repeated his comment in *The Stranger* when Cherdonna and Lou disbanded, and included Maile Martinez's short film about Cherdonna and Lou screened during *So You Think It's Dance?* See Brendan Kiley, "Breaking Up Is Hard to Do (Even if You're Cherdonna and Lou)," *The Stranger*, July 10, 2013, https://www.thestranger.com/theater/2013/07/10/17212333/breaking-up-is-hard-to-do-even-if-youre-cherdonna-and-lou.

26. Jacqueline Louise Brock, "Dance: Insert Definition Here," SeattleDances.com, October 28, 2011, http://seattledances.com/2011/10/dance-insert-definition-here/.

27. Michael van Baker, "Three New Works Invite Repeated Viewing at Velocity's SCUBA 2013," *The Sunbreak*, February 15, 2013.

28. https://archive.velocitydancecenter.org/stance/category/speakeasy/.

29. Central District Forum for Arts and Ideas (CD Forum) is a Seattle nonprofit that "empowers Black artists and builds community through art." https://www.cdforum.org/.

30. Mattilda Bernstein Sycamore is an American activist and author of *The Freezer Door*, a *New York Times* Editors' Choice, one of *Oprah Magazine*'s Best LGBTQ Books of 2020, and a finalist for the PEN/Jean Stein Book Award. Sycamore's sixth anthology, *Between Certain Death and a Possible Future: Queer Writing on Growing Up with the AIDS Crisis*, is one of BookRiot's 100 Most Influential Queer Books of All Time.

31. Keith Hennessy is an award-winning choreographer and activist regarded as a pioneer of queer and AIDS-themed dance. Velocity's presentation of *Turbulence* was supported by New England Foundation for the Art's National Dance Project.

32. Tere O'Connor, "Artist's Notes," *BLEED: A Process Blog by Tere O'Connor and Jenn Joy*, December 2013, accessed August 15, 2022, http://bleedtereoconnor.org/artists-notes/.

33. Siobhan Burke, "All Born of a Chaos of Bodies," *New York Times*, December 19, 2014, https://www.nytimes.com/2014/12/20/arts/dance/tere-oconnors-bleed-at-danspace-project.html.

34. In 2014, Tere O'Connor was elected to the American Academy of Arts and Sciences. His biography on the amacad.org site reads: "Influential figure in the field of contemporary choreography.... Principal mentor of New York's avant-garde dance artists. Awards include three-time Bessie Award winner, the Doris Duke Fellow Performing Artist Award, a Guggenheim Fellowship, and a United States Artist Rockefeller Fellow." https://www.amacad.org/person/tere-r-oconnor. See also Melody Datz Hansen, "Clarity Is a Useful Fiction: An Interview with Choreographer Tere O'Connor," in *The Stranger*, November 19, 2014, https://www.thestranger.com/theater/2014/11/19/21064556/clarity-is-a-useful-fiction.

35. Claudia La Rocco, "Roundabout Way," *Artforum*, December 12, 2014, https://www.artforum.com/performance/claudia-la-rocco-on-tere-o-connor-at-on-the-boards-theater-49439.

36. Mariko Nagashima, "Velocity's BIG BANG Remix Party a True Blast," SeattleDances.com, September 26, 2011, http://seattledances.com/2011/09/velocitys-big-bang-remix-party-a-true-blast/.

37. Melody Datz Hansen, "Velocity's Big Bang Performance Party," *The Stranger*, September 17, 2013, https://www.thestranger.com/blogs/2013/09/27/17847972/velocitys-big-bang-performance-party.

38. On April 29, 1988, ACT UP New York staged a same-sex Kiss-In with a fact sheet to educate passersby about AIDS. Kiss-Ins became one of ACT UP's most successful tactics for overcoming homophobic responses to AIDS in the 1980s and '90s. During the time of the first Big Bang!, anti-LGBTQ hate crimes were rising in Velocity's neighborhood. In response, I invited couples who self-defined as LGBT to perform a durational Kiss-In for the Big Bang!. GenderTender organized others' participation. See Zach Stafford, "Violence in Capitol Hill: Is This the End of the Line for Seattle's Gay Neighborhood?" in *The Guardian*, February 23, 2016; and Emily Wooldridge, "As Capital Hill Deweirds, LGBTQ Hate Crime Takes Off," on Crosscut.com, August 26, 2014, https://crosscut.com/2014/08/capitol-hill-deweirds-lgbtq-hate-crime-takes.

39. Yellow Fish // Epic Durational Performance Festival was founded by Alice Gosti in 2013 and is now led by another Big Bang and Velocity Made in Seattle alum, Babette DeLafayette Pendleton. See https://www.yffestival.com/about.

40. Big Bang! Performance Party grew out of my art practice and scholarship, including my course Live Art and Choreographic Culture since 1960, developed for the University of Washington Center for Performance Studies, and the UW Program of Dance. Big Bang! was also inspired by public performance events I directed as *Textile Factory* where I invited thirty-plus artists to animate a city block with timed actions. The aim: not to plop art into life but to enhance, and bring attention to, the street life already happening around each action. The boundaries of performance became so osmotic that during one event an elderly man, unaware I was a part of the performance, came toward me, "The street is dreaming! The street is dreaming!" See Brendan Kiley, "Street People," in *The Stranger*, July 13, 2006.

41. Mariko Nagashima, "Velocity Kicks Off Season in Style," SeattleDances.com, September 26, 2012, http://seattledances.com/2012/09/velocity-kicks-off-season-in-style/.

42. Karen Nelson, "CI (Embodied) Interrogates Its Own History," *Contact Quarterly*, Winter/Spring 2018.

Notes to pages 44–56

43. Melody Datz Hansen, "Velocity's Big Bang Performance Party," *The Stranger*, September 27, 2013, https://www.thestranger.com/blogs/2013/09/27/17847972/velocitys-big-bang-performance-party.

44. velocitydancecenter.org.

45. The Made in Seattle artists named *Dance Magazine*'s "25 to Watch" 2014 were Kate Wallich, Andrew Bartee, and Danielle Agami. See Nicole Loeffler-Gladstone, Gigi Berardi, Victoria Looseleaf, "25 to Watch," *Dance Magazine*, December 31, 2014, https://www.dancemagazine.com/25_to_watch_/.

46. Victoria Looseleaf, "25 to Watch," *Dance Magazine*, December 31, 2014, https://www.dancemagazine.com/25_to_watch_/.

47. Kiley, "Tonya Lockyer, Champion for Local Dance" (see n. 12 above).

48. Janet Cardiff and George Bures Miller: https://cardiffmiller.com/walks/.

49. Ezra Dickinson and Tonya Lockyer, TEDx Talk, McCaw Hall, Seattle, 2014, https://youtu.be/TnNUbuArmHg.

50. For an additional perspective on Velocity during this period see Naomi M. Jackson's book *Dance and Ethics: Moving Towards a More Humane Dance Culture* (Intellect, 2022).

THE ARTIST IS THE EXPERT

1. Yanira Castro in collaboration with Makini (formerly known as jumatatu m. poe), Kaz Sherman, Sarah Lewitus (formerly Sarah Greenbaum), Brian Rogers, Tara Aisha Willis, Michael Sakamoto, Amy Smith, Emily Johnson, and Laura Colby, "Creating New Futures: Phase 1 Working Guidelines for Ethics & Equity in Presenting Dance & Performance," May 2020, https://drive.google.com/file/d/105YBk17paK7Zko-0d7vCU0JrKf72792a/view?usp=sharing.

2. "$125M Toward Artists' Futures," Creatives Rebuild New York, accessed January 6, 2024, https://www.creativesrebuildny.org/. CRNY is a three-year employment and guaranteed income project for 2,700 New York artists. See also "Leadership," Creatives Rebuild New York, accessed January 6, 2024, https://www.creativesrebuildny.org/leadership/. The intention of the Think Tank was to be a body that could codesign and guide CRNY's programs with technical expertise, strategic advice, and advocacy. For more on the Think Tank, see "Creatives Rebuild New York Announces Think Tank Members," *Creatives Rebuild New York* (blog), https://www.creativesrebuildny.org/2021/08/31/creatives-rebuild-new-york-announces-think-tank-members/ The Think Tank was made up of New York cultural workers—artists, culture bearers, administrators, organizers.

3. *Creating New Futures* (blog), https://creatingnewfutures.tumblr.com/. Creating New Futures' calls-to-action were shared publicly as Google Documents.

4. Yanira Castro, "Creating New Futures: Phase 2 Notes for Equitable Funding from Arts Workers," June 2021, https://drive.google.com/file/d/1_z_lYupVQpJwJ1hmGvrs_gxrTyyTZAlN/view?usp=sharing.

5. "Home," "Artist Employment Program," and "Guaranteed Income For Artists," Creatives Rebuild New York, accessed January 6, 2024, https://www.creativesrebuildny.org.

6. To read about the impact of CRNY's programs since its launch in 2022, see: https://www.creativesrebuildny.org/impact.

7. "About," Artplace America, accessed January 6, 2024, https://www.artplaceamerica.org/about/. Artplace America (aka Artplace) was a ten-year collaboration (2010–20) of a group of foundations, federal agencies, and financial institutions focusing on equitable community planning for the arts/culture sector. Maura Cuffie-Peterson served as senior program officer for Artplace America, from 2018 to 2020. She conceived and executed the Local Control, Local Field(s) initiative, an approach to participatory, trust-based philanthropy. accessed January 6, 2024.

8. "Discover EmcArts," Culture Source, accessed January 6, 2024, https://emcarts.culturesource.org/emcarts/ EmcArts LLC is a social enterprise focused on organizational change for arts leaders. See also Sherri Welch, "Detroit-Based CultureSource Moves into National Arts Group Consulting with EmcArts Acquisition," *Crain's Detroit Business*, July 20, 2022, https://www.crainsdetroit.com/nonprofit/culturesource-acquires-emcarts-moves-national-arts-group-consulting.

9. "Local Control, Local Fields," Artplace America, accessed January 6, 2024, https://www.artplaceamerica.org/areas-of-work/local-control-local-fields.(accessed January 6, 2024) The Local Control, Local Field(s) initiative convened and facilitated assemblies of practitioners in five geographies to determine the vision and strategies for a pool of funds for Creative Placemaking.

10. Each Think Tank member was paid $7,500 to participate in the Think Tank from September to December 2021 with bimonthly two-and-a-half-hour virtual meetings for subcommittees (AEP and GI) and monthly two-and-a-half-hour virtual meetings for the whole Think Tank.

11. "About the USFWC," United States Federation of Worker Cooperatives, accessed January 6, 2024, https://www.usworker.coop/. The United States Federation of Worker Cooperatives (USFWC) is a national grassroots membership organization for worker cooperatives.

12. "Partners," Creatives Rebuild New York, accessed January 6, 2024, https://www.creativesrebuildny.org/. CRNY is fiscally sponsored by Tides Center.

13. "Artist Employment Program," Creatives Rebuild New York, accessed January 6, 2024, https://www.creativesrebuildny.org/apply/artist-employment/. Quote: "By supporting artists working in collaboration with community-based organizations, AEP will offer a pathway to transforming relationships between artists and organizations. Equitable relationships encourage creative solutions, expansive thinking, and new methods of engagement while building capacity and stability for all involved."

14. "Artist Employment Program."

EMBODYING EQUITY-DRIVEN CHANGE

1. Work. Shouldn't. Suck., "Shared Leadership, Part 1 (EP.07)," accessed April 18, 2022, https://www.workshouldntsuck.co/podcast2/ep07.

2. This list is taken from the wisdom, teachings, and resources of the antiracism groups Courage of Care, and Stronghold. For more information visit https://courageofcare.org and https://www.wearestronghold.org.

3. Julian Carter, "Dancing around Race: Public Gatherings #1 and #3," *Dance Matters* (blog), April 4, 2019.

4. Jess Row, *White Flights: Race, Fiction, and the American Imagination* (Greywolf, 2019), 275.

5. Row, 275.

6. INCITE!, ed., *The Revolution Will Not Be Funded: Beyond the Non-profit Industrial Complex* (Duke University Press, 2017), 15.

7. Herrington J. Bryce, "Nonprofit Board Responsibilities: The Basics," *Nonprofit Quarterly*, August 21, 2017, https://nonprofitquarterly.org/nonprofit-board-governance-responsibilities-basic-guide/.

8. Kindful, "Board of Directors for Nonprofits," accessed June 4, 2022, https://kindful.com/nonprofit-glossary/board-of-directors/.

9. Audiences can listen to *Danzacuentos* interviews at danzacuentos.org.

10. Sidra Morgan-Montoya, "Nonprofit Industrial Complex 101: A Primer on How It Upholds Inequity and Flattens Resistance," *Community-Centric Fundraising*, August 10, 2020, https://communitycentricfundraising.org/2020/08/10/nonprofit-industrial-complex-101-a-primer-on-how-it-upholds-inequity-and-flattens-resistance/.

11. Candid, "Funders Have Not Embraced General Operating Support, Study Finds," *Philanthropy News Digest,* October 23, 2020, https://philanthropynewsdigest.org/news/funders-have-not-embraced-general-operating-support-study-finds.

12. Jhumpa Battahcharya and Annie Price, "BIPOC Nonprofit Leaders Deserve Better from Philanthropy," *Nonprofit Quarterly*, December 16, 2021, https://nonprofitquarterly.org/bipoc-nonprofit-leaders-deserve-better-from-philanthropy/.

13. BoardSource, "Leading with Intent: Reviewing the State of Diversity, Equity, and Inclusion on Nonprofit Boards," June 2021, https://leadingwithintent.org/wp-content/uploads/2021/06/2021-Leading-with-Intent-DEI-Report.pdf?utm_referrer=https%3A%2F%2Fleadingwithintent.org%2F.

14. Tema Okun and collaborators, "Characteristics," White Supremacy Culture, accessed April 17, 2022, https://www.whitesupremacyculture.info/characteristics.html.

15. Since writing this piece, some of the authors have transitioned into new roles at Bridge Live Arts. Hope Mohr has transitioned out of her codirector role and into an Affiliate Artist role for 2023. Karla Quintero has also transitioned out of her codirector role and is now B.L.A.'s marketing and development coordinator. Cherie Hill remains a codirector along with B.L.A.'s newest codirector, Rebecca Fitton.

CRAFTING RELATIONSHIPS AND MODES OF SUPPORT

1. I worked as Mark Morris's research assistant from 2011 to 2013, primarily preparing research dossiers to support in the creation of new works.

2. Hillary Kooistra was the general manager for A.I.M by Kyle Abraham from 2015–2022. "About the company," A.I.M, https://aimbykyleabraham.org/about. "Hillary Kooistra," LinkedIn, https://www.linkedin.com/in/hillary-kooistra-b022aa60/.

3. For the purposes of this essay I am using the phrase manager/producer as a conjunctive, which became common parlance in our conversations with LMCC over the last few years.

4. Arts administration academic training emerged in the USA in 1966, with postgraduate programs begun simultaneously that year at Yale University and Florida State University.

Notably, both of these programs were created immediately following the 1965 Rockefeller Foundation Report "The Performing Arts: Problems and Prospects," which stated in particular the need for professionally trained staff to field increasing institutionalization of the field, especially as related to bureaucratic processes such as grant processing, financial audits, and independent fundraising. There are now 93 postgraduate programs in the USA, according to the website of the Association of Arts Administration Educators (AAAE), "a membership organization representing the world's leading graduate and undergraduate arts administration programs—all training and equipping students earning an arts administration degree in arts leadership, management, entrepreneurship, cultural policy, and more." For further information about the development of arts administration programs in the USA consult Jonathan Paquette and Eleonora Redaelli, "Academic Beginnings: Arts Management Training and Cultural Policy Studies," in *Arts Management and Cultural Policy Research* (London: Palgrave Macmillan, 2015), https://doi.org/10.1057/9781137460929_3.

5. Dance/NYC is the dance-service organization for New York City. Their mission is "to promote the knowledge, appreciation, practice, and performance of dance in the metropolitan New York City area. It embeds values of justice, equity, and inclusion into all aspects of the organization." For further details visit their website: https://www.dance.nyc/. Dance/USA is the dance-service organization for the USA. Dance/USA describes their work as being "champions of an inclusive and equitable dance field by leading, convening, advocating, and supporting individuals and organizations. Dance/USA's core programs are focused in the areas of engagement, advocacy, research, and preservation." For further details visit their website: https://www.danceusa.org/.

6. Silas Riener, "question about project management this fall," email, 2013.

7. Building Up Infrastructures for Dance (BUILD), now defunct, was a program of the New York Foundation for the Arts (NYFA) that aimed to assist the development of the organizational environment so that time and resources would be available to create, conceive, and advance dance companies' artistic missions. Further information about the 2014 application cycle, referenced within the text, can be found here: "Building up infrastructure levels for dance (BUILD) Guidelines and Application 2014," Amazon Cloud Computing Services, https://s3.amazonaws.com/NYFA_WebAssets/Pictures/4dd3c5c1-4aad-4c84-b0ae-2ecb67db94b8.pdf.

8. Los Angeles Performance Practice, founded by Miranda Wright in 2010, is a nonprofit organization devoted to the production and presentation of contemporary performance by artists whose work advances and challenges multidisciplinary artistic practices. Their mission is "to support a unique and diverse constellation of artists and audiences through the active creation and presentation of groundbreaking experiences that use innovative approaches to collaboration, technology and social engagement." For more information visit their website: https://performancepractice.la/.

9. Pentacle began in 1974 when four choreographers and managing directors pooled administrative resources under a single nonprofit. In the nearly fifty years since then, the organization has grown and changed to support a wide roster of artists and offer services ranging from fiscal sponsorship, booking, financial management, and producing. For more information about their history and current programs visit their website: https://www.pentacle.org/. ArKtype, founded in 2005 by producer Thomas O. Kriegsmann, supports risk in live performance by creating dynamic support structures that temper infrastructure with creative growth. For more information about supported artists and activities visit their website: http://www.arktype.org/.

10. Alice Goldfarb Marquis, "The N.E.A. Plays to an Empty House," *New York Times*, February 24, 1996, https://www.nytimes.com/1996/02/24/opinion/the-nea-plays-to-an-empty-house.html.

11. Founded in 1999 after the National Endowment for the Arts (NEA) ended the majority of its grants for individual artists, Creative Capital described itself as "a nonprofit, grantmaking organization with the mission to fund artists in the creation of groundbreaking new work, to amplify the impact of their work, and to foster sustainable artistic careers." Their professional development programs for artists, offered both as workshops and as part of their grant packages to artists, center the belief that educational tools and skill sets are key to helping artists build sustainable practices. For more information see their website: https://creative-capital.org/. LMCC's Extended Life Dance Development Residency program, created by Sam Miller in 2014, is designed to sustain midcareer choreographers with essential financial, administrative, and presentation support. For more information see their website: https://lmcc.net/resources/artist-residencies/extended-life/.

12. Mariclare Hulbert, "National Center for Choreography-Akron Announces Open Application for Creative Administration Research Program," National Center for Choreography at The University of Akron, updated December 16, 2021, https://www.nccakron.org/_files/ugd/ad7034_b764cf3e1e6a4c11a310557450b317a1.pdf.

13. Producer Farm is a free, annual residency for professional, UK-based producers that aims to provide time and space to discuss their current work, network with other young professionals with five to ten years of experience, and develop future projects. For more information see their website: https://www.danceumbrella.co.uk/event/producer-farm/.

14. Next Generation: Producing Performing Arts is a program for emerging producers from Southeast Asia and Japan, organized by the Japan Foundation Asia Center every year since 2016. For more information about their most recent meet-up in 2020 see their website: https://asiawa.jpf.go.jp/en/culture/events/e-next-generation-2020/.

15. The Regional Producer's Career Development Program in Australia focuses on networking connections for administrators as part of the Local Giants initiative. For more information see their website: https://www.performinglines.org.au/2021/11/18/local-giants-program-invests-majorly-in-regional-arts-creative-capital/.

16. Founded in 1957, the Association for Performing Arts Professionals (APAP) is a service organization that works to strengthen the field and advance careers through professional development, grant support, advocacy, networking, and the annual APAP|NYC conference. For more information see their website: https://apap365.org/.

17. The Creative & Independent Producer Alliance (CIPA) describes themselves as "a US-based network of independent and creative producers who are dedicated to developing and supporting new live performance works across artistic disciplines. Our mission is to support and sustain the work of independent and creative producers and the artists and projects they produce by creating visibility and community, identifying and dispersing resources, and providing tools and advocacy for building new live works and sustainable practices across genres." For more information visit their website: https://www.cipausa.org/. Producer Hub, which often works in collaboration with CIPA, supports the professional development of independent and creative producers through networking, shared resources, and community advocacy. For more information visit their website: https://www.producerhub.org/.

18. Visit the *Creating New Futures* tumblr to read or listen to their public documents "Creating New Futures: Working Guidelines for Ethics & Equity in Presenting Dance & Performance and Notes for Equitable Funding from Arts Workers:" https://creatingnewfutures.tumblr.com/. See also Yanira Castro's writing within this publication for further detail.

BEG, BORROW, STEAL (BACK)

1. Edgar Villanueva, *Decolonizing Wealth: Indigenous Wisdom to Heal Divides and Restore Balance* (Berrett-Koehler, 2018).

2. Miguel Gutierrez, *Are You For Sale?*, Episode 6: "Beg, Borrow, Steal (Back)—How Dance Artists in the U.S. Fund Their Work," *Are You For Sale?*, September 30, 2021, https://www.areyouforsalepodcast.com/episodes/episode6.

3. Cynthia Oliver is a St. Croix, Virgin Island–reared dancemaker, performer, and scholar. Her work incorporates textures of Caribbean performance with African and American aesthetic sensibilities.

4. Rosie Herrera is a Cuban American dancer, choreographer, and artistic director of Rosie Herrera Dance Theater in Miami.

5. Antonio Ramos was born and raised in Puerto Rico, where he trained in jazz, salsa, and African dance. He is a Brooklyn-based choreographer and performer.

6. amara tabor-smith is a dancer, choreographer, and artistic director of Deep Waters Dance Theater. Tabor-Smith's work is described by the artist as "Afro Futurist Conjure Art."

7. Gordon Gano, "Add It Up," Track 4, Side 1 on *Violent Femmes* (Slash Records, 1983).

8. Gano.

9. Uta Hagen, Pennie Du Pont, and Karen Ludwig, *Uta Hagen's Acting Class* (Hal Leonard Corp. and Applause Theatre & Cinema Books, 2002).

10. Cardi B and Paul 4.0, "Cardi B/I'm glad you brung it up, cause I've been dying to talk about it," Paul 4.0, March 2, 2020, YouTube Video :05, https://youtu.be/xMVhZCosSoE.

11. Julius Wechter, "Spanish Flea," Track 4, Side 1 on *Herb Alpert and the Tijuana Brass* (A&M Records, 1966).

HOW I BUILT THIS

1. Gaga is a movement language developed in Israel by choreographer Ohad Naharin. Gaga classes direct participants (who need not necessarily be dancers) to pay close attention to their physical sensations to inform their improvisation. In the United States, Gaga gained popularity in the late 2000s. For more about Gaga, consult the website: https://www.gagapeople.com/en/about-gaga/.

2. Crystal Pite, a Canadian choreographer, worked with Ballet British Columbia and William Forsythe before making her own work. She founded her company Kidd Pivot in 2002. See Deborah Meyers and Linde Howe-beck, "Crystal Pite," in *The Canadian Encyclopedia*, 2012, https://www.thecanadianencyclopedia.ca/en/article/crystal-pite.

3. Fiscal sponsorship is an option to attract charitable funding without starting a nonprofit. The term *fiscal sponsorship* broadly refers to a number of contractual relationships that allow a person, group, or business to advance charitable or other exempt activities with the benefit

of the tax-exempt status of a sponsor organization. See Gene Takagi, "Fiscal Sponsorship: A Balanced Overview," *Nonprofit Quarterly,* January 28, 2020 (first posted online January 19, 2016), https://nonprofitquarterly.org/fiscal-sponsorship-a-balanced-overview/.

4. Marc Andreesen, "Product/Market Fit," *Stanford University, EE204: Business Management for Electrical Engineers and Computer Scientists* (blog), June 25, 2007, https://web.stanford.edu/class/ee204/ProductMarketFit.html.

5. Venture capital (VC) is a form of private equity and a type of financing that investors provide to start-up companies and small businesses that are believed to have long-term growth potential. Venture capital generally comes from investors, investment banks, and other financial institutions. See Adam Hayes, "What Is VC and How Does It Work?," *Investopedia,* updated July 15, 2023, https://www.investopedia.com/terms/v/venturecapital.asp.

6. Pioneer Square Labs is a startup studio and venture fund in Seattle, Washington; see https://www.psl.com/.

7. In business, the definition of "scale" is to increase revenue at a faster rate than costs. Businesses achieve this in several ways, from adopting new technologies to finding "gaps" in their operations that can be streamlined.

8. A proprietary event registration system is software that has been engineered and developed to meet the specific needs of the business for online event registration.

9. Total Addressable Market (TAM) is the overall revenue opportunity for a product or service. It is the most revenue you can generate if 100% of the market share is achieved. See Anna Tanerico, "Total Addressable Market (TAM)," Corporate Finance Institute, n.d., https://corporatefinanceinstitute.com/resources/knowledge/strategy/total-addressable-market-tam.

THE PRACTICE OF QUESTIONING AND GENERATING REVENUE

1. Deborah Hay, *Turn Your F^*king Head,* documentary distributed by The Routledge Performance Archive and Taylor and Francis, London, England, 2016.

2. *Reorganizing Ourselves,* performative lecture by Deborah Hay and Alva Noe, part of *Rewriting Dance,* a series of workshops, lectures, and performances produced by Hope Mohr Dance's Bridge Project, in association with Counterpulse, Joe Goode Annex, San Francisco, CA, November 7, 2015.

3. "Patronage," Wikimedia Foundation, last modified March 2, 2022, 03:47, https://en.wikipedia.org/wiki/Patronage.

4. *Moving Dance Forward,* Anne Gadwa Nicodemus, Rachel Engh, and Metris Arts Consulting commissioned by New England Foundation for the Arts, Boston, MA, October 2016.

5. This multitude of tax statuses is just that—a way of navigating US tax code, not clearly defined ways of operating.

6. At NCCAkron, our marketing manager, business manager, program manager, and graduate student assistants have written grants for our organization.

7. This idea first came up in a CAR Investigative Retreat with Jaamil Olawale Kosoko's team in January 2021.

8. "Virtual Festival: Performances," Jacob's Pillow, accessed August 6, 2022, https://www.jacobspillow.org/virtual-pillow/virtual-festival-performances/.

9. Pamela Tatge, email message to author, May 20, 2024.

10. "AMPLIFY Virtual Presentation Series," Dance Place, accessed August 6, 2022, https://www.danceplace.org/virtual-presentation-series/.

11. Christopher K. Morgan, email message to author, July 28, 2022.

12. "Chase and Facebook Announce 100 Small and Local Charities to Receive $25,000 Each From Chase Community Giving," JPMorgan Chase & Co. Press Release, December 16, 2009, https://jpmorganchaseco.gcs-web.com/static-files/333c33b3-f468-4faf-8135-929f5b75a489.

13. "Chase Community Giving Program Final Winners Announced," Philanthropy News Digest, January 29, 2010, https://philanthropynewsdigest.org/news/chase-community-giving-program-final-winners-announced.

14. "Chase and Facebook Announce Winning Charities in Final Round of Chase Community Giving," TMCNet.com, January 25, 2010, https://www.tmcnet.com/usubmit/2010/01/25/4588940.htm.

15. Stephanie Strom, "Charities Criticize Online Fund-Raising Contest by Chase," *New York Times*, December 19, 2009, https://www.nytimes.com/2009/12/19/us/19charity.html.

16. Michael M. Kaiser is the chairman of the University of Maryland's DeVos Institute of Arts Management. Kaiser was previously president of the John F. Kennedy Center for the Performing Arts (Washington, DC) as well as the executive director of the Royal Opera House (UK), American Ballet Theatre (NY), and Alvin Ailey American Dance Theater (NY). Brett Egan is president of the DeVos Institute, and was previously the executive director of Shen Wei Dance Arts (NY). Egan's clients have included the National Public Radio Foundation; The Apollo Theater; Sundance Institute; Motown Museum (MI); Outfest (CA); Center for Asian American Media (CA); and National Black Arts Festival (GA).

17. Michael M. Kaiser with Brett E. Egan, *The Cycle: A Practical Approach to Managing Arts Organizations* (Waltham, MA: Brandeis University Press, 2014).

CHOREOGRAPHY, PERFORMANCE, AND THE ABSOLUTE TRUTH ABOUT BEING AN ARTIST

1. This title was inspired by an article by Chris Martin, "Buddhism, Landscape, and the Absolute Truth about Abstract Painting," *Brooklyn Rail*, April 1, 2005, brooklynrail.org/2005/04/art/buddhism-landscape-and-the-absolute-trut.

2. This gathering of artists was a three-day convening in New York City of twenty choreographers with a collaborator from their administrative team. All were chosen to come together because of their contribution to the field of dance and performance, and because they were at a unique turning point in their career. We were asked not to disclose the name of the foundation that brought us together.

3. There is no evidence that can truly support these statements. The point of them is that I and many peers in the industry have shared these thoughts in private. As an artist I feel completely unaware of how funding decisions are made; the variables that make up the arts ecosystem, or

the rules that govern them. My innate drive and connection to being an artist is constantly under interrogation. Daring to say these things out loud is both a practice in saying what one feels needs to be said and letting go of that which I cannot control.

4. The idea of a VIP Pass is an idea I came up with to suggest that the more awards I receive the more presenters and funders will look at my work as merited. When you get a VIP Pass into a club, no one knows *why* you're important, just that someone else said you were. You skip the line. The merit of your work is therefore pre-decided versus the presenter or funder deciding based on their own experience of the work.

5. Andy Warhol, *America* (New York: Harper & Row, 1985).

6. "Professional Development—LMCC," *LMCC*, September 14, 2022, lmcc.net/resources/professional-development.

7. "The Bushwick Starr," The Bushwick Starr, accessed September 18, 2022, https://www.thebushwickstarr.org.

8. "Raja Feather Kelly," Princess Grace Foundation-USA, accessed September 18, 2022, https://pgfusa.org/award-winners-chronoorder/raja-kelly/.

9. "New York Live Arts," New York Live Arts, 2022, https://newyorklivearts.org.

10. "ImPulsTanz—Vienna International Dance Festival—6.7.–6.8.2023," ImPulsTanz—Vienna International Dance Festival, accessed September 18, 2022, https://www.impulstanz.com/en/.

11. "Collaborators," the feath3r theory, accessed September 18, 2022, http://thefeath3rtheory.com/collaborators.

12. "Black Queer Dancer Choreographer Director Pop Culture," the feath3r theory, accessed September 18, 2022, http://thefeath3rtheory.com/blue.

13. This is an adaptation of an original article I wrote for *Dance Magazine*. Raja Feather Kelly, "Has Anyone Asked Artists What They Need?," *Dance Magazine*, August 11, 2020, https://www.dancemagazine.com/raja-feather-kelly-3/.

14. "The Four Pillars of Sustainability," FutureLearn, 2017, https://www.futurelearn.com/info/courses/sustainable-business/0/steps/78337.

15. "Supporting Working Dance Artists | Akron, OH," NCCAkron, accessed September 18, 2022, https://www.nccakron.org.

SHARING RESOURCE STORIES

1. My parents, and by proxy my siblings and I, were leaders in the All-African People's Revolutionary Party.

2. Artist-activist and educator Sydnie L. Mosley shares her economic profile on her website: https://www.sydnielmosley.com/economicprofile.

3. Miguel Gutierrez's work is chronicled at https://www.miguelgutierrez.org/. His *Are You For Sale?* podcast can be found at https://www.areyouforsalepodcast.com/. You can also find a transcription of Episode Six in this book.

4. More information at https://angeledwardsart.com/.

5. More information at https://gonzalezinfo.com/.

6. More information at https://www.dakotacamacho.com/.

7. More information at http://amyelainesmith.com/.

8. IBR, Income-Based Repayment, is one of the federal government's income-driven repayment programs for federal student loan recipients. The program caps maximum monthly payments on loans at a percentage of the borrower's monthly income, as opposed to an objective amount derived from calculating a repayment period of ten years. See https://studentaid.gov/manage-loans/repayment/plans/income-driven.

9. More information at https://makinimakes.com/projects/.

10. For more information on how US philanthropy relates to the United States' historical involvement with kidnapping and enslavement of African people, and the various legacies emboldened in the wake of those human crimes, you can see Julia Travers, "Making Amends: How Funders Can Address Slavery's Legacy," *Inside Philanthropy*, December 19, 2019, https://www.insidephilanthropy.com/home/2019/9/19/making-amends-how-funders-can-address-slaverys-legacy. Also see Edgar Villanueva and Chuck Collins, "Opinion: It's Time for Wealthy Donors to Embrace Reparations, Not More Charity," Outside the Box, *MarketWatch*, September 29, 2020, https://www.marketwatch.com/story/its-time-for-wealthy-donors-to-embrace-reparations-not-more-charity-11601384684.

11. Edgar Villanueva gets into some of these histories in his book *Decolonizing Wealth: Indigenous Wisdom to Heal Divides and Restore Balance* (Oakland, CA: Berrett-Koehler, 2019).

12. An LLC (limited liability company) allows a business owner to be considered separate from the business that they own for tax purposes. Classifying an LLC as an S Corp allows the business owner to pay themself as an employee of the business, as opposed to paying themself based on an owner's draw system.

13. Please see *Creating New Futures: Working Guidelines for Ethics & Equity in Presenting Dance & Performance,* "Phase 1 Document," at https://creatingnewfutures.tumblr.com/.

14. See *Creating New Futures*, 13–17.

15. More information at https://www.artistsu.org/.

16. More information at https://creative-capital.org/.

17. For the "Valuing Your Time" worksheet and other resources Amy Smith has developed for artists, see https://amyelainesmith.com/resources/.

18. Visit https://makinimakes.com/feesworksheet/ for a digital and editable copy of the spreadsheet.

19. For more information on gentrification in my family's Cedar Park neighborhood of West Philadelphia: Jake Blugmart, "The Changing Streets of Cedar Park," *City Life, Philadelphia Magazine*, March 11, 2017, https://www.phillymag.com/news/2017/03/11/cedar-park-gentrification-west-philadelphia/.

20. Intrauterine insemination.

21. In vitro fertilization.

THE FRUITS OF DISSATISFACTION

1. Grace Sato and Lawrence T. McGill, "Mapping the Dance Landscape in Chicagoland," Chicago, IL: Candid, Sustain Arts, See Chicago Dance, and Fractured Atlas, June 2019, doi.org/gfvcs8.

2. For more details on this and other Khecari policies and practices visit khecari.org/values.

3. Paul Arnsberger et al., "A History of the Tax-Exempt Sector: An SOI Perspective," *Statistics of Income Bulletin* (Washington, DC: Internal Revenue Service, Winter 2008), irs.gov/pub/irs-soi/tehistory.pdf.

4. Giacomo D'Alisa, Federico Demaria, and Giorgos Kallis, eds., *Degrowth: A Vocabulary for a New Era* (Routledge, 2014), doi.org/10.4324/9780203796146.

5. *Degrowth*.

6. This is based on the work of British anthropologist Robin Dunbar, and the numerical limit of those we can know personally is often referred to as "Dunbar's number." The ideas have been widely disseminated recently but are cogently expressed in Geoffrey West's book *Scale: The Universal Laws of Life, Growth, and Death in Organisms, Cities, and Companies* (Penguin Random House, 2018).

ADMINISTRATIVE POINTS OF VIEW FROM CREATIVE LIVING

1. Dava Sobel, *Longitude: The True Story of a Lone Genius Who Solved the Greatest Scientific Problem of His Time* (Walker, 1995). The determination of longitude was figured out by John Harrison by 1761 using a very accurate clock to measure "Greenwich Mean Time," which he invented, as different from local time, as told by the sun's position in the sky over the boat. It took him fifty years to build the clock, and it is a fascinating story about triangulation and *time* as the cornerstones of navigation of space. In order to figure out where you are you have to use time to figure out space. Which is what dance is.

2. "Investing in Creativity: A Study of the Support Structure for U.S. Artists," Urban Institute, 2003, https://www.urban.org/sites/default/files/publication/50806/411311-Investing-in-Creativity.PDF. Midcareer artists, especially in dance, have access to fewer funding opportunities, need more space, stretch thin their personal networks. See Miguel Gutierrez's podcast *Are You For Sale?* for a brief but comprehensive survey of the history of arts funding in the country currently known as the United States. (A transcript of Episode Six can be found in this book. Also see the article "Art is Work: A Dancer's Reflection" by Megan Wright in *New Labor Forum* (November 17, 2021) for a personal but in-depth look at how these funding structures impact dancers in real world circumstances: https://newlaborforum.cuny.edu/2021/11/17/art-is-work-a-dancers-reflection/.

3. Robert Moor, *On Trails: An Exploration* (Simon & Schuster, 2017) is a good source for thoughts on trails, trail words, and trails of thoughts, written by the author as he traveled around the globe.

4. https://www.rashaunsilasdance.com

5. While not the point of origin for our naming of this body of work, Robert Moor's "Tracing (and Erasing) New York's Lines of Desire," *New Yorker,* February 20, 2017, provides an overview of the wider use of this phrase: https://www.newyorker.com/tech/annals-of-technology/tracing-and-erasing-new-yorks-lines-of-desire.

6. adrienne maree brown, *Emergent Strategy: Shaping Change, Changing Worlds* (AK Press, 2017).

7. Careening, not to be confused with careering. Careening is exposing your underbelly, the keel of your ship. Careening rocks side to side until you flip-turn upside down. Careering shares its Latin root with running, with the road. Interesting that the word we use to describe a life at work is also the word which means moving while completely out of control. https://aceseditors.org/news/2020/are-you-careening-or-careering, and https://www.grammarphobia.com/blog/2019/06/career-careen.html.

8. Victoria Brooks's context essay in the program for *Tesseract,* a dance and film project choreographed by Rashaun and Silas with Charles Atlas that premiered in 2017, can be found here: https://empac.rpi.edu/events/tesseract. From Brooks's essay: "Robert A. Heinlein's 1941 novella *And He Built a Crooked House* describes a California architect who designs a house based on a four-dimensional cube, a tesseract, comprised of eight cubed rooms. Unbeknownst to him or his clients, however, an earthquake has caused the invisible fourth dimension to shift prior to their first tour through the building. The tesseract house then takes its new inhabitants on a disorienting journey through multiple rooms, perspectives, and timescales that ends with another earthquake-induced slip of space/time as they are dropped with a jolt into the desert landscape of Joshua Tree National Park." See Robert Heinlein, *And He Built a Crooked House.* (Street and Smith, 1940).

9. A P&L is a Profit and Loss report, generated in this case through the accounts management website www.quickbooks.com. P&Ls show income and expenses, and any discrepancies. P&Ls are fundamental for navigating the making of dance inside a capitalist economy, as any grant application budget or tax return will ask that you show greater revenues than expenses. In making dances in my experience there are almost always more costs.

10. In vying for reelection, Abraham Lincoln used this phrase in a speech June 9, 1864, to encourage voters to stick with him and not to disrupt governance in a time of volatility. It seems to have deeper roots in a joke about an Irishman falling off one of two horses while crossing a channel and being coached by those on land to choose the stronger swimmer of the two.

11. The Roches, "Quitting Time," Track 9 on *The Roches,* Warner Bros. Records Inc. WB 56 683, originally released 1979, vinyl. Lyrics by Margret A. Roche.

12. Five main factors have contributed to this trend: retirement, relocation, reconsideration, reshuffling, and reluctance. See Joseph Fuller and William Kerr, "The Great Resignation Didn't Start with the Pandemic," *Harvard Business Review,* March 23, 2022.

13. If you look for this word in the dictionary you will discover I made it up. I combined "product-oriented" and "productive" to define an approach to work and life that relies on both.

14. Purifoy was an early example of artist-as-administrator. He was the founding director of the Watts Towers Art Center, Los Angeles. In the late 1980s, after eleven years of public policy work for the California Arts Council, where he initiated programs such as Artists in Social

Institutions, which brought art into the state prison system, Purifoy moved his practice out to the Mojave Desert. I came upon Purifoy's Outdoor Museum while on a residency at Joshua Tree. The sculptures extend the life of objects most would consider garbage. See "Noah Purifoy," About Noah Purifoy, http://www.noahpurifoy.com/about-noah.

15. Wendy Perron makes a case for this in *The Grand Union: Accidental Anarchists of Downtown Dance 1970–1976* (Wesleyan University Press, 2020), portraying the infamous improvisation group as the pinnacle of a lineage from John Cage and Anna Halprin that sought to blur the line between art and life.

16. The Roches, "Quitting Time."

Contributors

Nora Alami is a Moroccan American dance artist and creative consultant living in Brooklyn, New York. Her choreography has been presented at New York Live Arts, La MaMa Moves!, Danspace Project, Triskelion Arts, Center for Performance Research, and Movement Research at Judson Church. She has performed at the New York Arab Festival, Edinburgh Fringe Festival, River to River Festival, and toured to the Focus on Mediterranean Choreography platform. As a creative consultant, Alami has worked with The Africa Center, Alliance of Artist Communities, FAILSPACE, Lower Manhattan Cultural Council, Peoplmovr, Gibney, American Realness, Los Angeles Performance Practice, and independent artists. Presently, Nora collaborates with Jasmine Hearn as a creative producer.

Julia Antonick and **Jonathan Meyer** have been working together since 2007 and have codirected Khecari since 2010. Through Khecari they have created over thirty projects, crafting worlds to entice audiences into a willing confrontation with rewarding discomfort. Through the years, Antonick and Meyer have utilized collaboration, choreographic process, radical care, and critical problem-solving in the office as well as the studio, investigating hetarchy, equity, community, and personal agency on both sides of the proscenium. They live in West Rogers Park, Chicago, with their child Corbie. Khecari.org

Christy Bolingbroke is founding executive/artistic director for the National Center for Choreography-Akron (NCCAkron). As such, she is responsible for setting the curatorial vision and business model to foster research and development opportunities in dance. Previously, she served as the deputy director for advancement at ODC in San Francisco, overseeing curation, performance programming, marketing, and development organization-wide. Prior to ODC, she was the director of marketing at the Mark Morris Dance Group in Brooklyn, New York. She earned a BA in dance from the University of California, Los Angeles, and an MA in performance curation from Wesleyan University.

Banning Bouldin is a dance artist and community organizer based in Nashville, Tennessee. She received a BFA from the Juilliard School and has worked internationally with Aszure Barton, Cullberg Ballet, Lar Lubovitch, Jacquelyn Buglisi, and Wen Wei Wang. She is a two-time United States Artist Fellowship nominee. Her works have been commissioned by Visceral Dance Chicago, Springboard Danse Montréal, Northwest Dance Project, Whim W'Him, SALT, Groundworks Dance Theater, and Gibney Dance Company. Banning is the founder and director of New Dialect, a southern destination and resource for contemporary dance artists to collaborate and contribute to the larger international dance ecology.

Yanira Castro's work is rooted in communal construction as a rehearsal for radical democracy. She is an interdisciplinary artist born in Borikén (Puerto Rico), living in Lenapehoking (Brooklyn), and working at the intersection of communal practices, performance, installation, and interactive technology. Yanira forms iterative, multimodal projects that center the complexity of land, citizenship, and governance in works activated and performed by the public. She is the recipient of two New York Dance and Performance ("Bessie") Awards for Outstanding Production, and various commissions, residencies, and national grant awards. Since 2009, she's collaborated with a team of artists as *a canary torsi*. www.acanarytorsi.org

Maura Cuffie-Peterson serves as the director of strategic initiatives for the Guaranteed Income for Artists program at Creatives Rebuild New York, one of the largest basic income pilots in the nation, moving over $43 million directly to artists across New York State. Previously she was the senior program officer for ArtPlace America, where she conceived and executed the Local Control, Local Field(s) initiative, a novel approach to participatory and trust-based philanthropy. This initiative placed over $12.5 million directly under the control of practitioners across the country. She has held a variety of positions in arts, culture, justice, and organizational change.

Katy Dammers is the deputy director and chief curator, performing arts at REDCAT, CalArts' center for the visual and performing arts in Los Angeles. Her curatorial practice presents, organizes, and contextualizes contemporary art in performance commissions, exhibitions, festivals, site-specific installations, and publications. She has held past leadership positions at The Kitchen, FringeArts, and Jacob's Pillow. Dammers has also worked as a creative administrator, and was the general manager for choreographers Rashaun + Silas from 2014–2022, in addition to organizing projects with Jennifer Monson, Donna Uchizono, and Tere O'Connor.

Michelle Fletcher is a live performance maker, director, educator, artist manager, and psychodynamic therapist based in Lenapehoking, colonially known as New York. Fletcher earned her BFA from North Carolina School of the Arts, MFA from Florida State University, and MSW from NYU. Fletcher was a Fulbright Scholar at The Jerusalem Academy of Music and Dance, teaching contemporary technique and dance technology. Her dances have been presented at ODC Theater, CounterPulse, Triskelion, and CPR. Fletcher's film *Dan's House* headlined the Dance for Camera Festival at Lincoln Center and San Francisco. She currently serves as manager to Beth Gill and Miguel Gutierrez.

Raja Feather Kelly is a choreographer and director, and the artistic director of the dance-theater-media company the feath3r theory, for which Kelly has created eighteen premieres, most recently *UGLY Part 3: BLUE* and the forthcoming *The Absolute Future*. Kelly's most recent works outside of TF3T are *White Girl in Danger* (Second Stage), *Bunny Bunny* (UC San Diego), and *Scenes for an Ending* for Ririe-Woodbury Dance Company. He choreographed the Broadway musical *A Strange Loop* (Lyceum Theatre) and is the winner of two Tony Awards, including Best Musical. Accolades include a Princeton Arts Fellowship, three Princess Grace Awards, an Obie Award, an Outer Critics Circle honor, and many others.

Contributors

Chelsea Goding-Doty is the senior program officer, Leadership Initiatives at New York Foundation for the Arts. Previously, she worked with Kaneza Schaal as managing director, producing and touring works of opera and theater. She has served as managing director at Gallim, studio director at SFactor New York, and director of education at New York City Center. In 2010, she cofounded Harlem Arts Festival, a multidisciplinary performing and visual arts festival presented annually in Harlem, New York. Chelsea holds a BS in arts administration from Butler University. She is a co-active coach, a Nonprofit Lifecycles Institute Capacity Consultant, and a member of the Creative & Independent Producer Alliance.

Miguel Gutierrez is a multidisciplinary artist based in Lenapehoking/Brooklyn, New York, and Tovaangar/Los Angeles. He creates empathetic and irreverent spaces for himself and other QTPOC folx to dream. His work has been presented nationally and internationally in venues such as Festival d'Automne/Paris, the Walker Art Center, and the 2014 Whitney Biennial. He is a recipient of a Guggenheim Fellowship, United States Artists Fellowship, Foundation for Contemporary Arts Award, four New York Dance and Performance "Bessie" Awards, and a 2016 Doris Duke Artist Award. He is an associate professor of choreography at UCLA in the department of World Arts and Cultures/Dance. www.miguelgutierrez.org

Cherie Hill is a choreographer, educator, and administrator whose art explores human expression through the body in collaboration with nature, music, and visual imagery. She has published in *Gender Forum*, *The Sacred Dance Journal*, *Dance Education in Practice*, and *In Dance*. She has presented at multiple conferences, including Dance/USA, WAA, NDEO, and IABD. Her artist residencies include Milk Bar, the David Brower Center, and CounterPulse. As a performer, she has worked with BARD, Makomba West African Drum & Dance, David Dorfman Dance, Kiandanda Dance, & Helander DT. Cherie is a codirector at Bridge Live Arts, an assistant professor at CSUSM, and the founder of IrieDance.

Rosie Herrera is a Cuban American dancer, choreographer, and artistic director of Rosie Herrera Dance Theater in Miami. She is a graduate from New

World School with a BFA in dance performance. Her work has been commissioned and presented nationally. Rosie is also a classically trained lyric coloratura soprano and performs with the Performers Music Institute Opera Ensemble as well as working as an independent director and creative consultant throughout Miami. With over a decade of experience in both dance and cabaret, she has collaborated on interdisciplinary productions across Miami and created original short films and music videos.

Delphine Lai is a writer, arts advocate, and arts administrator with twenty-five years of nonprofit experience. In 2009, she founded Del Arts Consulting to support the creation of new work, to make the arts more accessible to all, and to further art as a means for social change. Previously, she oversaw the SFMOMA Director's Circle and Artist's Circle individual giving programs. At Stanford University, Delphine studied the creative process, earning a BS in product design engineering and a BA in English with a creative writing emphasis. She is also NCCAkron's organizational dramaturg.

Tonya Lockyer is a socially-engaged artist, somatic researcher, and cultural strategist. Named a "key cultural changemaker" (*Seattle Times*), Lockyer has choreographed and produced projects, mentored artists, designed programs, cofounded festivals, and directed organizations that continue to have a profound impact on the US dance ecology. A native Newfoundlander, Lockyer has collaborated with some of the most groundbreaking experimentalists of our times and enjoyed a critically acclaimed inter/national performance career. She has taught at universities and festivals in the United States, Canada, Europe, and Asia and continues to work with artists and organizations to help create a more sustainable future.

Aaron Mattocks is a Pennsylvania native, Sarah Lawrence College alumnus, and two-time New York Dance and Performance ("Bessie") Award nominee for Outstanding Performer (2013, 2016). He was the director of programming at The Joyce Theater from 2018 to 2022. Previously, he was executive director of Big Dance Theater, producing director for Pam Tanowitz, general manager for the Mark Morris Dance Group, and producer for Faye Driscoll and Beth Gill. He is a creative strategist for movement-based artists at critical stages of growth, transition, and opportunity. He is currently the chief operating officer for the Fisher Center at Bard.

Contributors

Rashaun Mitchell is a Guggenheim Fellow and recipient of the New York Dance and Performance ("Bessie") Award for "Outstanding Emerging Choreographer." He received three Princess Grace Awards, a Foundation for Contemporary Art Grant, and a "Bessie" for "Sustained achievement in the work of Merce Cunningham 2004–2012." Mitchell's choreographic work with collaborator Silas Riener involves the building of collaborative worlds through improvisational techniques, digital technologies, and material construction. Since 2010, Mitchell and Riener have created over twenty-five multidisciplinary works including site-responsive installations, gallery performances, dances for film, and concert dances in venues such as Brooklyn Academy of Music, Barbican Centre, and the Walker Arts Center.

Hope Mohr (she/her) is an artist and advocate working across dance, visual art, and writing through practices that collide improvisation and set forms. As an attorney, she works at the intersection of the arts and the solidarity economy. She founded Hope Mohr Dance in 2007 and in 2019 began co-stewarding the organization's transition to a model of distributed leadership and a new name, Bridge Live Arts. She transitioned out of coleadership at B.L.A. in 2023. Her book *Shifting Cultural Power* (2021) was published in the NCCAkron Series in Dance by The University of Akron Press. www.hopemohr.org

Dominic Moore-Dunson is an award-winning dancer, producer, teaching artist, and speaker and the founder of MooreDunson Co., an arts, media, and entertainment company committed to producing "Urban Midwest Storytelling." As an artist, Dominic is featured in *Dance Magazine*'s 2023 "25 to Watch" and is a 2021 Top 40 finalist for the National Dance Project Grant, a 2019 Jacob's Pillow Choreography Fellow, and a 2019 Cleveland Arts Prize winner. Moore-Dunson cofounded the Akron Black Artist Guild, an organization committed to building a network of Black artists in Akron, Ohio. He is a graduate of National Arts Strategies' Executive Program for Arts & Culture Strategies at the University of Pennsylvania.

Cynthia Oliver is a New York Dance and Performance ("Bessie") Award–winning choreographer, a 2022 Guggenheim Fellow, a 2021 United States Artist and Doris Duke Artist, whose work incorporates Caribbean performance elements with African and American aesthetic sensibilities. She has toured the globe with David Gordon Pick Up Co., Ronald K. Brown/Evidence, Bebe

Miller Company, and Tere O'Connor Dance and as an actor in works by Laurie Carlos, Greg Tate, Ione, Ntozake Shange, and Deke Weaver. She earned a PhD in performance studies from New York University and is a professor in dance at the University of Illinois, Urbana-Champaign.

Makini is an artist, performer, educator, voyager, fabulist. Makini's work expands dreaming space within conversations among and about Black queer and trans folx, and designs performance environments that recognize History as only one option for the contextualization of the present. Collaboratively, Makini imagines options for artists to understand themselves as part of a larger community of workers who are envisioning pathways toward economic ecosystems that prioritize care, interdependence, and delight. Makini's dance work is influenced by various sources, including early family dance parties, technical training in contemporary Africanist and other dance forms, and sociological and anatomical movement study.

Karla Quintero is a Latin American artist whose work explores intimacy, consumption, and bicultural existence. Her current practices include a solo practice rooted in cross-genre improvisation, and a partnering practice with collaborator Belinda He, rooted in listening. She is deeply curious about ways of working in dance that support longevity and solidarity. In addition to her work as a performing artist, she currently works as Bridge Live Arts marketing and development coordinator and as a therapeutic Pilates practitioner with the Movement Care Collective. Quintero graduated with a BA in urban studies from Barnard and a BFA from SUNY Purchase Conservatory of Dance.

Antonio Ramos, born and raised in Puerto Rico, received a BFA in dance from SUNY Purchase. Antonio began his career performing with Ballet Theatre of Puerto Rico, Ballet Hispánico of New York, Ballet Concierto and Ballet Municipal (Puerto Rico). Antonio has performed with choreographers such as Mark Dendy, Neil Greenberg, Stephen Petronio, Merián Soto, and Donna Uchizono, among others. He was a 2011–12 National Association of Latino Arts and Cultures Award recipient. Antonio is also a Licensed Massage Therapist, Zero Balancing Practitioner, Watsu Practitioner, and a professional teacher of Awareness Through Movement® and Functional Integration® from The Feldenkrais Method®.

Contributors

Silas Riener is a dance artist. He is a New York Dance and Performance ("Bessie") Award and Creative Capital Award winner, and a graduate of Princeton University and NYU's Tisch School of the Arts. He was a member of the Merce Cunningham Dance Company from 2007 to 2012. His physical practice synthesizes improvisation, formal dance training, athletic sports, and building and construction. He has an ongoing choreographic collaboration with his partner Rashaun Mitchell.

amara tabor-smith (she/they) is an Oakland, California–based dance and performance maker, and the artistic director of Deep Waters Dance Theater. She describes her work as Conjure Art. Her interdisciplinary site-responsive and community-specific performance-making practice utilizes Yoruba Lukumí spiritual technologies to address issues of social and environmental justice, race, gender identity, and belonging. Her work is rooted in Black, queer, feminist principles that insist on liberation, joy, home fullness, and well-being. She is a 2021 Rainin Fellow, a 2019 Dance/USA Fellow, a 2018 United States Artist Fellow, and a 2017 Urban Bush Women Choreographic Center Fellow. Amara is currently a teaching artist in residence at Stanford University.

Kate Wallich is a multifaceted artist who lives by her artistic manifesto to bring dance and dancers to the forefront of culture. Named one of *Dance Magazine*'s "25 to Watch," she has made a profound impact in the dance field through numerous commissions, presentations, and residencies at renowned institutions. In 2010, Kate founded Dance Church®, an all-levels movement class that has garnered a devoted following of over 200,000 people taking classes. Dance Church® reached a global audience after expanding online, leading to the launch of an online platform and expansion into new cities. She currently lives and works in Los Angeles.

Marýa Wethers (she/her), based in Lenapehoking (New York City) since 1997, is a creative producer working with Edisa Weeks/DELIRIOUS Dances, OzuzuDances, and Rosy Simas Danse and is the director of the GPS/Global Practice Sharing program at Movement Research. As a curator she conceived the three-week performance series "Gathering Place: Black Queer Land(ing)" at Gibney Dance (2018) and curated for Mount Tremper Arts Watershed Lab Residency (2019, 2018), the Queer NY International Arts Festival (2016, 2015) and Out of

Space @ BRIC Studio for Danspace Project (2003–7). As a contemporary dancer, Marýa received a 2017 New York Dance and Performance ("Bessie") Award for Outstanding Performance with the Skeleton Architecture collective.

Pioneer Winter is a Miami-based choreographer and director of Pioneer Winter Collective, an intergenerational and physically integrated dance-theater company rooted in social practice and community, queer excellence, and beauty beyond the mainstream. Recognized by *Dance Magazine*'s "25 to Watch," Pioneer's work democratizes performance in public spaces, museums, galleries, stage, and film. Their work has developed through the support of NCCAkron, NEFA, Knight Foundation, Mellon Foundation, Creative Capital, and Miami-Dade County Cultural Affairs. As an extension of their creative practice, Pioneer curates ScreenDance Miami Festival presented by Miami Light Project. Pioneer is assistant teaching professor in the Honors College and College of Communication, Architecture + The Arts at Florida International University.

Miranda Wright is the executive director at the Center for the Arts at Kayenta, located in the Southwest Desert of Utah. Previously, she founded Los Angeles Performance Practice in 2010 and the LAX Festival in 2013. Miranda works primarily with artists in contemporary dance and theater, developing and advancing new works. Miranda was an organizing member of the Creative & Independent Producer Alliance (CIPA) and is a member of the International Presenting Commons. She has worked closely with artists Milka Djordjevich, Lars Jan, Andrew Schneider, Netta Yerushalmy, and others, on projects that have toured nationally and internationally.

Index of Names and Organizations

Abraham, Kyle, xviii, 91
abrasiveMedia, 15–16
Agami, Danielle, 45
Ailey, Alvin, 77
Akron School for the Arts, 5
Alami, Nora, 97
Antonick, Julia, xix
Arc of Engagement model, 203–04
Are You For Sale? (podcast), xviii, 107, 170
ArKtype, 97
Artists U, 175
ArtPlace America, 55, 212, 225
Assaf, Roy, 19
Association of Performing Arts Professionals (APAP), 103, 215
Ate9, 45

Bartee, Andrew, 45
Bartenieff, Irmgard, 124
Barton, Aszure, 13, 225
Battle, Robert, 12
Beacham, Jermone Donte, 172
Bel, Jérôme, 39, 209
Bell, Sidra, 20, 125
Belmont University, 19
Bhattacharya, Jhumpa, 84–85
Big Bang! Remix Party, 42–44, 210
Black Card Project, 5–6, 7
Black Lives Matter movement, xvi
BLEED Project, 41–42
Bolingbroke, Christy, xviii
Boston Conservatory, 20
Bouldin, Banning, xvii
Bouldin, Kevin, 20
Bridge Live Arts, 70–88, 227, 229, 230
Bristol Old Vic, 102
Brooklyn Council on the Arts, 118
brown, adrienne maree, xv
Bryan, Barbara, 89, 94
Bushwick Starr, The, 161

Calderon, Sarah, 55, 59
Calvert, Snowflake, 84
Camacho, Dakota, 170
Campisano, Frank, 30
Cardiff, Janet, 47
Carter, Julian, 76
Castro, Yanira, xvi–xvii
CD Forum (Central District Forum for Arts and Ideas), 40
Centennial Performing Arts Studios, 18
Center for Effective Philanthropy, 84
Chase Community Giving, 142–43
Cheekwood Botanical Gardens, 19
Cherdonna Shinatra, 38, 45, 209
Chopra, Lili, 89
City Arts, 38–39, 209
Community Engagement Residency (CER) program, 86–87
Coriolis, 43
Cornish College of the Arts, 33, 124–25, 207
Courville, Mike, 70
COVID-19 pandemic, xvi–xvii, 6, 16, 20, 48, 53, 55, 103, 132–33, 140, 162–65, 174
Creating New Futures, xvii, 53–54, 103, 211
Creative Administration Research initiative, xi, xiv, 20, 102, 145–48, 165, 201
Creative Connections initiative, 29–30
Creative & Independent Producer Alliance (CIPA), 103, 215, 227, 232
Creatives Rebuild New York (CRNY), xvii, 53–67, 211, 225
Cronus Land, The 184, 185
Crush Ventures, 133
Cuffie-Peterson, Maura, xvii
Cunningham, Merce, xiii, 229, 231
Czaplinski, Lane, 41, 125

d9 Dance Collective, 33
Dammers, Katy, xviii–xx, 194
Dance Church®, xviii, 36, 45, 125–34, 208, 231
Dance Magazine, 20, 45, 229, 231, 232
Dance Place, 141
Dance Teacher Magazine, 20
Dance Umbrella (UK), 102
DanceNet, 35
Dance/NYC, 94, 214, 227, 231
Dance/USA, 94, 214, 227, 231
Danspace Project, 90, 94, 101, 224, 232
De La Cruz, Aeon, 30
Desire Lines, xix, 191–92
Dickinson, Ezra, 45, 46–48
Dream, Yalini, 86
Duchamp, Marcel, xiii
Dunbar, Robin, 221

Edwards, Angel, 170
Egan, Brett, 144–46
Ekundayo, Ashara, 121
EmcArts, 58
Equal Pay Policy, xix, 182–85
Escobedo, Dulce, 84
Escobedo, Marianna, 84
Espinoza, Mario Ismael, 83

Fagan, Garth, 3
feath3r theory, the, xviii, 160
Floyd, George, xvi, 6
Fractured Atlas, 127
Frist Art Museum, 19
Frye Art Museum, 133

Gaga movement language, 124, 216
GenderTender, 43
Gibney Dance Center, 133
Gill, Beth, 95–96, 226, 228
Gillis, Margie, 12
Gilmore, Ruth Wilson, 77
GoFundMe, 143
González, Jonathan, 170
Goodyear Black Network, 5
Gosti, Alice, 43, 45
Graham, Martha, 77
Graham & Walker, 133
Grass Stains program, 27–29

Guaranteed Income for Artists. *See* Creatives Rebuild New York
Guggenheim Fellowship, 117, 227, 229
Gutierrez, Miguel, xviii, 170, 226

Haim, Mark, 45
Hankins, Allie, 125
Hanson, Dayna, 39
Harkarvy, Benjamin, 12, 206
Harkness Dance Center, 17–18
Hartmann, Tristan Ching, 82–83
Hay, Deborah, 43, 136, 144
Hearn, Jasmine, 97, 224
Hennessey, Keith, 41
Herrera, David, 83
Herrera, Rosie, 19
Hill, Cherie, xvii
HIV/AIDS, 24–25, 210
Hope Mohr Dance (HMD), 70, 72, 74–75, 79–81, 229
Human-Centered Design Thinking (HCDT), xvii, 5
Hurley, Wes, 42

ICA Boston, 126
ImPulsTanz Vienna International Dance Festival, 162
In Between Time, 102
inCOPnegro, 7–9
Insight Center, 84–85

Jacob's Pillow, 20, 45, 92, 140–41, 226, 229
Japan Foundation, 102
Jiroh, Safi, 72, 80, 82
Jobaris, Jessica, 38
Johnson, Tammy, 86
Juilliard School, 11–13, 225

Kaiser, Michael, 144–46
Kang, Emil, 55
Karlin, Stefanie, 36
Kelly, Raja Feather, xviii–xix
Kendzior, Megan, 94
Khecari, 181–88
Kickstarter, 125, 143
KID Venture Capital, 133
Kiley, Brendan, 39
King, Alonzo, 77

Index of Names and Organizations

Kitchen, The, 226
Knight Foundation, 6, 232
Koplowitz, Stephan, 28
Kuehner, Jody. *See* Cherdonna Shinatra

Laage, Joan, 43
LA Dance Project, 134
Lai, Delphine, xviii
Laks, Stephan, 13
Lambda Living, 26
La Rocco, Claudia, 41
Leaders of Equality through Arts and Performance (LEAP), 26
LeaderSpring, 72, 85. *See also* Jiroh, Safi
Lincoln University, 170, 176
Lockyer, Tonya, 124–25
Los Angeles Performance Practice, 93, 96, 214, 224, 232
Love the Everglades Movement, 26
Lowe, Rick, xiii
Lower Manhattan Cultural Council (LMCC), 89, 92, 101, 102, 103, 224
Lucaciu, Ana, 18

MaC Venture Capital, 133
Made in Seattle program, 44–48. *See also* Velocity
Makini, xvii, xix
MAP Fund, 116
Marquez, Niurca, 30
Martinez, Maile, 38
MASS MoCA, 126
Mattocks, Aaron, 95
Mellon, Andrew W., Foundation, 20, 55, 232
Metro Parks Dance Division (Nashville), 17–18, 19
Meulener, Barbara, 30
Meyer, Jonathan, xix
Miller, George Bures, 47
Miller, Michele, 34
Miller South School for the Visual and Performing Arts, 5
Mitchell, Rashaun, xix, 90, 94, 98–101
Mohr, Hope, xvii
Monson, Jennifer, 90, 216
Moon, Waxie, 39
Moore-Dunson, Dominic, xvii

Moore Theater (Seattle), 37, 45
Morgan, Christopher K., 141
Morgan-Montoya, Sidra, 84
Morris, Mark, 77, 90, 133, 225, 228
Mosley, Sydnie L., 170
Mother for you I made this, 46–48
Museum of Modern Art (MoMA), 92

Nagashima, Mariko, 41
Naharin, Ohad, 12, 216
Nashville Arts and Business Council, 16
Nashville Ballet, 13
National Association of Latino Arts & Culture, 116, 230
National Center for Choreography-Akron (NCCAkron), 20, 102, 139, 144–48
National Dance Project (NDP), 45, 48, 95–96, 116, 138, 229
National Endowment for the Arts (NEA), xii, xix, 19, 102, 117, 215
Navarro, Cinthia Pérez, 84
New Dialect, 14–21
New England Foundation for the Arts (NEFA), 138, 140. *See also* National Dance Project
New York Foundation for the Arts, 94, 117, 214, 227
New York Live Arts (NYLA), 95, 162, 224
New York State Council for the Arts (NYSCA), 118
New York Times, 162
Niehoff, KT, 34, 38

O'Connor, Tere, 41–42, 90, 210, 226, 230
Oddfellows Hall (Seattle), 34, 35
O'More School of Design, 19
On the Boards (OtB), 34–35, 41–42, 48, 126
O'Neal, Amy, 39, 44, 45
OZ Arts Nashville, 17–19

Patreon, 9
Pendleton, Babette DeLafayette, 45
Pentacle, 97, 214
Performing Arts Connections Australia, 103
Pew Fellowship in the Arts, 176
Pioneer Square Labs, 133

Pioneer Winter Collective (PWC), 23–30
Pite, Crystal, 124, 216
Post-Election Community Response Forum, 40
Price, Annie, 84–85
Princess Grace Awards, 226, 229
Project Row Houses, xiii
PSL Ventures, 133
Purifoy, Noah, 196, 222–23
Pyron, Asia, 207

Quijada, Victor, 125
Quintero, Karla, xvii

Rashaun + Silas, 90, 94, 98–101, 226
RED Studio Collective, 34, 124, 125
Reeber, Amelia, 43
Regensburger, Karl, 162
Reimagine New York Commission, 55
Rice, Tamir, 5
Riding, Douglas, 38
Riener, Silas, xix, 90, 94, 98–101
Rizzo, Christian, 38
Robert Rauschenberg Foundation, 125
Robinson, Jacob, 207
Rumpus Room Dance, 13

Sagisi, Suzette, 82
Sanchez-Colberg, Ana, 28
Schaal, Kaneza, 99
Seattle Art Fair, 37
Seattle Dance Forum, 34
Seattle Festival of Alternative Dance and Improvisation (SFADI), 33
Seattle International Dance Festival, 35
Sides, Molly, 43
Simonson, Lynn, 124
Skinner, Joan, 124
Smith, Amy, 170, 175
Snelling, Lauren, 18
So You Think It's Dance?, 38–40
Speakeasy Series, 40–42
Spike Ventures, 133
St. Mark's Cathedral (Seattle), 37, 45
Stoller, Jeremy, 23, 26
Stranger, The, 38–39, 44, 45
Studio Kate Wallich (SKW), 123–31
SUNY Purchase, 20, 230
Swarthmore College, 171–72, 173, 174–75
Sycamore, Mattilda Bernstein, 41, 209

Táíwò, Olúfẹ́mi, 179
Temple University, 172
Tennessee Performing Arts Center, 19
Tess, Rachel, 13
Tharp, Twyla, 102
Tinney Contemporary, 19
TPAM (Performing Arts Meeting—Yokohama), 102
Trump, Donald, xvi, 40

Uchizono, Donna, 90, 230
Ugly (Part I, Part II, Part III), 162
Umanoff, Nancy, 90–91
United States Artists Fellowship, 118, 227
Uprichard, Laurie, 94

Vago, Lavinia, 125
Vanderbilt Children's Hospital, 19
Vanderbilt University, 19
Velocity, 34–46, 48, 125, 126, 128
Verdecia, Lyvan, 84
Villanueva, Edgar, 107
Vissers, Rosa, 36
Volunteer Lawyers and Professionals for the Arts (VLPA), 16

Walker Art Center, 126, 227, 229
Walker, Jayland, 8, 206
Wang, Sophia, 83
Warhol, Andy, 157–58
Waxie Moon, 39
Wilkening, Kathryn, 17
Wilkins, Helanius, 3
Winter, Pioneer, xvii
World Health Organization, 132
Wright, Megan, 83
Wright, Miranda, 214

YC, The, 43, 126–30
YC2, 128–29
Yellow Fish Epic Durational Performance Festival, 43

Zeitgeist Gallery, 19
Zhurbin, Lev LJOVA, 18
zoe|juniper, xviii